Walking London
2nd Edition

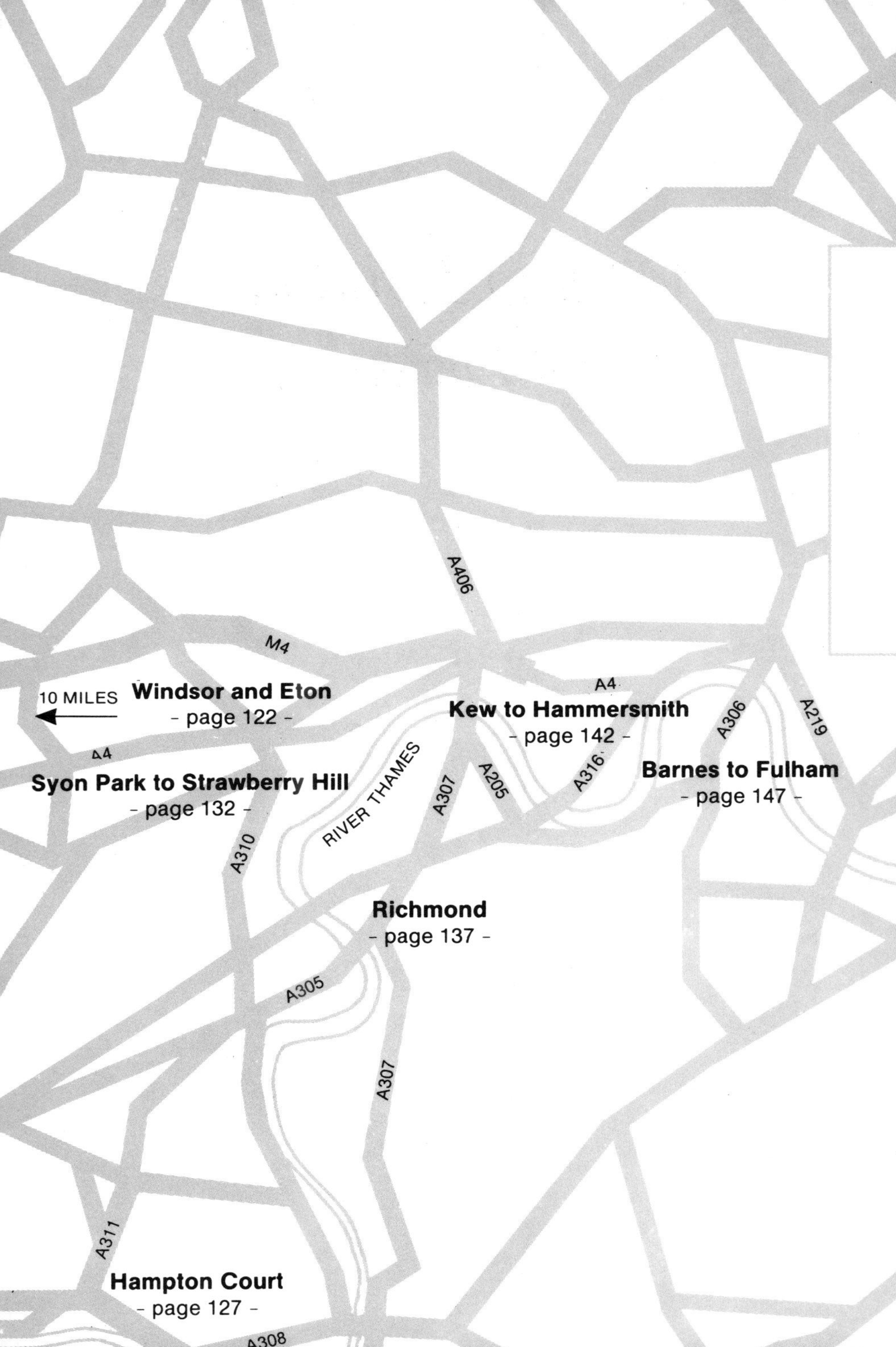
M4
A406
A4
10 MILES
Windsor and Eton
- page 122 -
Kew to Hammersmith
- page 142 -
A306
A219
A4
Syon Park to Strawberry Hill
- page 132 -
RIVER THAMES
A307
A205
A316
Barnes to Fulham
- page 147 -
A310
Richmond
- page 137 -
A305
A307
A311
Hampton Court
- page 127 -
A308

Walking London
2nd Edition

Walking London
2nd Edition

ANDREW DUNCAN

THIRTY ORIGINAL WALKS
IN AND AROUND LONDON

PASSPORT BOOKS
NTC/Contemporary Publishing Group

This edition first published in 1999
by Passport Books, a division of
NTC/Contemporary Publishing Group, Inc.
4255 West Touhy Avenue
Lincolnwood (Chicago), Illinois 60646-1975
U.S.A.

ISBN 0-8442-0144-8

Library of Congress Catalog Card Number: 98-67237
Published in conjunction with New Holland Publishers (UK) Ltd

Commissioning Editor: Sydney Francis
Editors: Jo Finnis, Tracey Williams
Designer: Paul Wood
Cover design: Paul Wood

Phototypeset by AKM Associates (UK) Ltd
Printed and bound in Singapore by
Kyodo Printing Co (Singapore) Pte Ltd

Photographic Acknowledgements
Andrew Lawson: Plates 1, 3, 4, 5, 8, 9, 11, 12, 13, 16, 24, 28, 30; Michael Freeman: Plates 14, 15, 17, 19, 23, 25, 27; Anthony Lambert: Plate 2; Derek Forss: Plates 18, 21, 22, 29; Sydney Francis: Plates 6, 7, 10; Andrew Duncan: Plate 26; Bob Turner: Plate 20; Fergus Noone: Plate 31.

Front cover: Pickering Place, St James's (Timothy Woodcock Photolibrary)

Contents

Preface

As a relative newcomer to London, I set out to write this book with a pretty average knowledge of the city: in other words, I knew where different districts were relative to each other, and I could navigate my way around the various places where I had lived and worked without using an A-Z Street Atlas.

By the time the book was finished, I had got to know large areas of London quite intimately, and I realized that in the process my attitude to the city had been quietly but radically transformed.

Although never a sufferer from the rootlessness and alienation which blights the lives of so many city dwellers, it suddenly dawned on me that I had actually begun to feel at home here. So much at home, in fact, that I no longer dreamt of returning to the dales and moors of my native Yorkshire. As my outlook changed, so London became a much friendlier place and life in general that much better.

No doubt New Holland never realized the book would have quite such an effect when they commissioned me to write it, but I owe them my thanks nonetheless.

I am also indebted to Jo Finnis, my editor at New Holland, for her efficiency and support, to all the friends and friends of friends, too numerous to name, who checked the routes and made sure all my directions and comments were accurate; to Sydney Francis for originally commissioning the book and for walking three of the routes; to Frank Atkins for information about the history of Hampton; to the staff of Kensington Library, the best public library around; and, last but not least, to all the anonymous voices at the end of the telephone line who patiently answered my questions about opening times, access and many other matters now forgotten.

Andrew Duncan
Kensal Green

Introduction

London's streets, squares, alleys and lanes; its parks, heaths, gardens and open spaces; its palaces, villages, docks, canals and rivers - all offer an amazing variety of terrain for the dedicated urban explorer. One minute you can find yourself breezing down some grand thoroughfare or strolling nonchalantly round an elegant square as though you owned it. The next you could be treading cautiously down narrow lanes and dark alleys, peering into cobbled courtyards, squeezing through gates and wickets, tramping through woods or puffing up hill and down dale startling deer and other creatures rare even in the countryside.

Walking London contains nearly 100 miles of walks through this endlessly surprising landscape, more than enough to keep even the most hardened city walker on his or her feet for a good while to come.

There are 30 walks altogether: 29 in London and 1 - mainly for the benefit of foreign visitors - in Windsor. All the walks are original, invented by me over a winter and a summer and then individually checked by a small army of pedestrian friends.

Each walk acts as a guide to a different part of London. In general, these are the most historic and attractive parts of the capital, the two usually going together. Like conventional guidebooks, the walks take you to most of the well-known places, but they also steer you off the beaten track into forgotten corners of London where few tourists stray and in some cases where few people go at all.

Wherever the walk happens to be, the emphasis is always on the visually attractive and stimulating, not on trying to cover every single place of interest that a guidebook would mention. As you will discover in this book, views take priority over venues.

History plays a strong part in the book - you cannot get away from it in London - but anything interesting, unusual or simply puzzling, whether old or new, gets a mention. My overall aim has been to try to anticipate any questions you may have about anything you can actually see *en route* and, subject to limitations of space, to provide satisfying answers.

How to choose a walk

(1) If you do not know London at all, read the summaries at the start of each walk to get the flavour of the different districts.

(2) If you want a special kind of walk or a walk including a visit to a market, museum, garden or other attraction, go to the 'Categories' listing beginning on page 13. If you cannot find what you are looking for there, try the index beginning on page 175.

(3) If you want to see what places are open to the public and when on any partic ular walk, skim through the 'opening times' listing (beginning on page 166) under the walk's title, or look at the map of the walk. The Ⓗ symbol indicates historic buildings, churches and other attractions open to the public; the Ⓜ symbol, art galleries, displays and exhibitions. See this page for further details on the maps and the use of symbols, and page 17 for the full key to the maps.

When to do the walks

Apart from the Inns of Court walk, which has to be done on a weekday because the Inns are closed at weekends, any walk can be done on any day of the week and at any time of day, subject to a few restrictions listed in the 'route notes' at the start of certain walks.

Remember that at weekends the inner city areas are likely to be quieter than on weekdays - the City in particular is virtually deserted - and that the quieter parts of town - parks and gardens mainly - are likely to be more crowded.

Distance and duration

The walks range in length from 2 miles to 6 miles (3.2 to 9.6 kilometres) with over half between 2½ and 3½ miles (4 and 5.6 kilometres) - the average is actually 3¼ miles (5.2 kilometres). A list of walks in order of length is given on page 16. The approximate duration is given at the beginning of each walk. Bear in mind that timings are based on my pace, which is quite quick, and do *not* allow for stops.

Transport

All the walks start and finish at either Underground stations or at railway stations (usually overground) in places not covered by the Underground network. Riverboat and riverbus services are also listed to provide maximum transport flexibility for the car-less. (I have left buses out because experience shows that bus information changes too often to be reliable in a guidebook of this kind.) If you do have a car, try leaving it at home and use public transport instead. You will be doing your bit for the environment, and, take it from me, planning your journey will increase the sense of adventure in your outing.

Refreshments

City walking is not like country walking. Tarmac is a lot harder on the feet than turf, and the less than pure air tends to enervate rather than exhilarate. Traffic noise and the endless bustle of people are also tiring.

My advice therefore is to take things very easy. Do not try to do the walks in a rush, and stop or rest whenever you feel the need. If fuel is required, try the places recommended at the beginning of each walk under 'refreshments'.

Maps and symbols

A detailed, but easy to follow map accompanies each walk. The route is clearly marked in green. Places of interest along it are labelled, those open to the public being also marked with an Ⓗ (historic buildings and other attractions) or Ⓜ (museums, art galleries, displays and exhibitions). Churches are indicated by a cross and labelled. An accompanying Ⓗ means that it is open to the public at times in addition to normal service times. Other symbols used are Ⓟ for public parks, gardens and open spaces, and Ⓣ for toilets. The same symbols have also been included in the text to alert you in case you missed them on the map. All opening times are listed walk by walk beginning on page 166. For full details of symbols and abbreviations, see the key to the maps on page 17.

Plaques and waymarks

On many of the walks you will see coloured wall-plaques commemorating people, places and events. The most common are the circular blue plaques put up by the old Greater London Council. Other plaque-providing organizations include local councils and history societies. A surprising amount can be learnt from these plaques, most of which are pointed out on the walks.

In the City and West End you will also see waymarks for three official walks: the **London Wall Walk**, the **Heritage Walk** and the **London Silver Jubilee Walkway**. The first two are in the City and the third, a ten-mile marathon created to mark the Queen's Silver Jubilee in 1977, covers both the City and the West End. The London Wall Walk follows the course of the old city wall of the City of London and is marked by wall plaques with pictures and text. The routes of the other two are marked by metal discs set in the ground. Mapguides for all three walks are available from bookshops and tourist information centres.

Historical background

Throughout the book certain key people and seminal events in London's past crop up again and again. To save explaining who and what they were each time, I have brought them all conveniently together here.

The development of modern London

First, something about the City and the history of London. The City is the financial district of modern London and the oldest part of the capital. It actually means the City of London, the ancient Roman city founded 2000 years ago and, although not physically demarcated in any way, still very much an entity in its own right as well as being entirely self-governing with its own Lord Mayor and police force. The City of Westminster, the other 'city' within modern London, was founded 1000 years later. It grew up around Westminster Abbey and the royal palace which Edward the Confessor built alongside (now the Houses of Parliament). This was in the 11th century, shortly before the invasion of the Normans from northern France in 1066. In subsequent centuries the land between the cities of London and Westminster was gradually built up (the modern Strand and Fleet Street), and streets and houses were built east, west and north. As late as 1800, however, London was still a comparatively small city, bounded on the west by Hyde Park, on the north by Marylebone Road and Euston Road, and on the east by poor working class settlements beyond the Tower of London and the City. In the south there was a fringe of building along the river bank, nearly matching in breadth the developed area in the north, but not nearly so deep. The population was about 1.1 million.

In the 19th century London positively exploded, thanks to the railways. Its land area increased by about seven times and its population shot up to 6.6 million despite a phenomenally high death rate caused by overcrowding, disease and insanitary living conditions. Hundreds of farms, cottages, country houses and villages were swallowed up in this remorseless expansion, hence the frequent references in the walks to such and such a place having been a quiet country village until engulfed by the tide of new building in the 1800s. London's population reached its maximum of 8.6 million in 1939. Today it is about 7 million.

The dissolution of the monasteries

Henry VIII initiated the dissolution of the monasteries in 1536 as part of his religious policy of a break with Catholic Rome, but he was also motivated by a desire to grab the enormous wealth of the religious houses. Inmates were either executed or pensioned off, depending on whether or not they accepted the king instead of the pope as head of the church. The actual buildings, of which there were many in medieval London, became royal property. Most of them were subsequently sold off and knocked down and their sites re-developed.

The Great Fire of London

The Great Fire broke out on the night of 2 September 1666 in Pudding Lane in the east of the City. During the next three days, fanned by strong easterly winds, it spread west as far as Fleet Street. The extent of destruction was very great. Two-thirds of the medieval City was destroyed, including 13,200 houses, 44 livery halls and 87 out of more than 100 churches, old St Paul's Cathedral among them. Only 9 people were killed, however. The City was subsequently rebuilt, but on the old medieval street plan.

Burial grounds

By the 17th century the graveyards of London's parish churches were full to bursting, so detached burial grounds were opened. By the 1850s these too had become disgustingly overcrowded, so large cemeteries in the suburbs were created. These are still in use. Many of the old central London burial grounds and churchyards have been converted into public gardens. Several feature in these walks.

The Blitz

The Blitz or heavy bombing of London began in August 1940 and lasted until May the following year. Once again the City was very badly hit, nearly a third of its built-up area being razed by bombs and fires. In June 1944 the VI and then the V2 rockets began to descend on London, affecting the suburbs particularly. Overall, air raids in World War II killed over 15,000 people and damaged or destroyed over 3.5 million houses.

Sir Christopher Wren (1632-1723)

The most famous architect in the history of London. A scientist to start with, he became professor of astronomy at Oxford while still in his 20s. In the early 1660s he turned increasingly to architecture. While the ashes of the Great Fire were still warm he produced a plan for the rebuilding of the City. Although it was not adopted, Wren was still commissioned to design 52 of the new City churches and the new St Paul's Cathedral, his masterpiece. As Surveyor General of the King's Works from 1669 he designed Kensington Palace, vast new wings at Hampton Court, the Royal Naval College at Greenwich and the Royal Hospital at Chelsea.

Samuel Pepys (1633-1703)

Civil servant and diarist. Born in London, the son of a City tailor, Pepys rose to become the most senior civil servant in the Admiralty and an important figure in the history of British naval administration. But it is his intimate and acutely observed diary which has made him such a well-known and popular historical figure. The diary covers the years 1660 to 1669 and is a mine of information on the London of the period. It is particularly important for its vivid eye-witness accounts of two cataclysmic events in London's history: the Great Plague of 1665, which killed nearly

100,000 people, perhaps one seventh of the city's population, and the Great Fire of 1666. Pepys himself watched the City burn from an alehouse on Bankside.

The Adam brothers (18th century)
Architects and interior designers. William Adam, a leading Edinburgh architect and laird of Blair Adam, had four sons, three of whom he trained as architects. His second son Robert (1728-92) was by far the most talented and, after he had opened an office in London in 1758, became the leading neoclassical architect and interior designer of his day, ably assisted by his brothers James and William. The Adam brothers were responsible for the Adelphi, Apsley House, Home House in Portland Square, Portland Place and Chandos House.

Dr Samuel Johnson (1709-84)
Writer, scholar and brilliant talker. Johnson was born in Lichfield but lived in London from his late 20s onwards. With his bulky figure and rasping Midlands voice he was familiar to all who frequented the taverns and coffee houses of Fleet Street and the drawing rooms of fashionable London society. In 1763 he met James Boswell (1740-95), dissolute son of a Scottish judge and himself a lawyer. Boswell recorded much of Johnson's pungent and witty conversation and later used it as the basis of his marvellous biography of the great man. It included Johnson's often-quoted remark: 'When a man is tired of London he is tired of life; for there is in London all that life can afford.'

John Nash (1752-1835)
Architect. The son of a Lambeth engineer and millwright, Nash's early career was chequered; in 1783 he was even declared bankrupt. But re-established and with the patronage of George III's eldest son, the Prince Regent, Nash became the architectural king of Regency London, responsible for Regent's Park and its terraces, Regent Street, Buckingham Palace, Marble Arch and the Haymarket Theatre.

Charles Dickens (1812-70)
Novelist and social campaigner. Born in Portsmouth, Dickens was brought to London by his parents when he was 10. Not long afterwards his father was imprisoned for debt in the notorious Marshalsea debtors' prison and Dickens found himself put to work in a blacking warehouse, though still only 12 years old. Later he got himself more congenial employment as a reporter and then, while still in his 20s, became a popular and very successful novelist. He had an obsession with London and all its horrors and degradations, and regularly tramped the streets going into the dingiest and most dangerous districts in search of scenes and characters for his stories. Today, Victorian or rather Dickensian London, lives on in his still popular novels.

Kings and queens
Events and places are often dated by reference to kings and queens. For those of you who are rusty on your royals, here is a quick reminder of their regnal dates - from William the Conqueror to our own Elizabeth II.

William the Conqueror
1066-87
William II
1087-1100
Henry I
1100-35
Stephen
1135-54
Henry II
1154-89
Richard I
1189-99
John
1199-1216
Henry III
1216-72
Edward I
1272-1307
Edward II
1307-27
Edward III
1327-77
Richard II
1377-99
Henry IV
1399-1413
Henry V
1413-22
Henry VI
1422-61
Edward IV
1461-83
Edward V
1483
Richard III
1483-85
Henry VII
1485-1509
Henry VIII
1509-47
Edward VI
1547-53
Mary
1553-58
Elizabeth I
1558-1603
James I
1603-25
Charles I
1625-49
Commonwealth
1649-53
Protectorate
1653-60
Charles II
1660-85
James II
1685-89
William and Mary
1689-1702
Anne
1702-14
George I
1714-27
George II
1727-60
George III
1760-1820
George IV
1820–30
William IV
1830-37
Victoria
1837-1901
Edward VII
1901-10
George V
1910-36
Edward VIII
1936
George VI
1936-52
Elizabeth II
1952-

Categories of walks

PANORAMA WALKS

Dulwich:
North over south London as far as the City

Greenwich:
North over the Isle of Dogs and the City

Highgate to Hampstead:
South over the City, north London and the West End

Regent's Park:
South over the West End

Richmond:
West to Windsor Castle and east to St Paul's Cathedral

WATERSIDE WALKS

River Thames (East to West):
Greenwich
Wapping to Limehouse
Bankside and Southwark
Lambeth and the South Bank

Barnes to Fulham
Kew to Hammersmith
Syon Park to Strawberry Hill
Richmond
Hampton Court
Windsor and Eton

Canal:
Regent's Canal

Boating Lakes:
Central Parks (Serpentine in Hyde Park)
Regent's Park
Dulwich

SHOPPING AND MARKET WALKS

Bayswater to Belgravia:
Bayswater Road art market, Harrods and Knightsbridge

Clerkenwell:
Exmouth Market

Covent Garden:
Covent Garden, Jubilee Market,

Inns of Court:
Old Curiosity Shop, London Silver Vaults

Islington:
Camden Passage antiques market

Kensington:
Kensington High Street

Marylebone:
St Christopher's Place and Oxford Street

Mayfair:
Piccadilly market, Bond Street, Burlington and Royal Arcades

Notting Hill:
Portobello Road market

Regent's Canal:
Camden Lock market, Camden Passage antiques market, Chapel Street market

Soho to Trafalgar Square:
Berwick Street market

PARKS AND GARDENS WALKS

Barnes to Fulham: Barn Elms Park, Bishop's Park including gardens of Bishop's Palace

Bayswater to Belgravia: Kensington Gardens

Central Parks:
St James's Park, Green Park, Hyde Park, Kensington Gardens

Chelsea:
Ranelagh Gardens, Chelsea Physic Garden

Dulwich:
Dulwich Park and Sydenham Hill Nature Reserve

Hampton Court:
Palace Gardens, Bushy Deer Park and Waterhouse Garden in Bushy Park

Kew to Hammersmith:
Kew Gardens, grounds of Chiswick House

Greenwich:
Greenwich Park

Highgate to Hampstead: Waterlow Park, Hampstead Heath
and grounds of Kenwood House

Kensington:
Holland Park

Syon Park to Strawberry Hill:
Syon Park, Marble Hill Park

Regent's Park:
Regent's Park

Richmond:
Richmond Park, grounds of Ham House, Petersham meadows

Westminster and St James's:
St James's Park, Green Park

COUNTRY HOUSE WALKS

Highgate to Hampstead:
Kenwood House, Fenton House

Kew to Hammersmith:
Chiswick House

Richmond:
Ham House

Syon Park to Strawberry Hill:
Syon House, Marble Hill House, Strawberry Hill

ROYALTY WALKS

Bayswater to Belgravia:
Kensington Palace

Central Parks:
Kensington Palace

The City (East):
Tower of London

Hampton Court:
Hampton Court Palace

Westminster and St James's:
St James's Palace, Clarence House, Buckingham Palace

Windsor and Eton:
Windsor Castle

VILLAGE WALKS

Barnes to Fulham:
Barnes

Dulwich:
Dulwich Village

Greenwich:
Greenwich

Hampton Court:
Hampton

Highgate to Hampstead:
Highgate and Hampstead

Kew to Hammersmith: Kew and the riverside communities of Strand-on-the-Green, Chiswick Mall and Hammersmith Upper Mall

Richmond:
Petersham and Ham

Syon Park to Strawberry Hill:
Isleworth and Twickenham

CIRCULAR WALKS

Kensington
Chelsea
Mayfair
Westminster and St James's
Bloomsbury
Covent Garden
Inns of Court
Fleet Street and St Paul's (The City West)
The City (East)
Windsor and Eton
Richmond
Greenwich

CONNECTING WALKS

Central Parks - Kensington
Regent's Canal - Islington
Regent's Canal - Clerkenwell
Westminster and St James's - Central Parks
Lambeth and the South Bank - Inns of Court
Bankside and Southwark - City (East)
Bankside and Southwark - Wapping to Limehouse
City (East) - Wapping to Limehouse

NEARLY CONNECTING WALKS

(One stop on the Underground line unless otherwise stated)

Notting Hill - Kensington
Notting Hill - Bayswater to Belgravia
Mayfair - Covent Garden
Bloomsbury - Covent Garden
Soho to Trafalgar Square - Mayfair
Soho to Trafalgar Square - Covent Garden
Lambeth and the South Bank - Bankside and Southwark
Inns of Court - Bankside and Southwark
Clerkenwell - Fleet Street and St Paul's (short walk down Aldersgate Street and St Martin's Le Grand)
Wapping to Limehouse - Greenwich (six stops on the Docklands Light Rail)
Richmond - Kew to Hammersmith

WALKS IN ORDER OF LENGTH (MILES/KILOMETRES)

2/3.2	Covent Garden
2/3.2	Inns of Court
2/3.2	Clerkenwell
2/3.2	Fleet Street and St Paul's (The City West)
2½/4	Marylebone
2½/4	Lambeth and the South Bank
2½/4	Bloomsbury
2½/4	Soho to Trafalgar Square
2½/4	Bankside and Southwark
2½/4	The City (East)
2¾/4.4	Kensington
3/4.8	Mayfair
3/4.8	Westminster and St James's
3/4.8	Islington
3¼/5.2	Wapping to Limehouse
3½/5.6	Notting Hill
3½/5.6	Regent's Park
3½/5.6	Hampton Court
3½/5.6	Barnes to Fulham
3½/5.6	Greenwich
3½/5.6	Dulwich
3¾/6	Chelsea
3¾/6	Central Parks
3¾/6	Windsor and Eton
4/6.4	Bayswater to Belgravia
4½/7.2	Syon Park to Strawberry Hill
4½/7.2	Richmond
4½/7.2	Kew to Hammersmith
4¾/7.6	Regent's Canal
6/9.6	Highgate to Hampstead

Key to maps

Route of walk

= = = Path

Railway line

Underground station

Railway station

Docklands Light Rail station

Church

Ⓗ Historic building or other attraction open to the public; churches open to the public at times in addition to normal service times - see pages 166-173 for opening times

Ⓜ Museums, art galleries, displays and exhibitions open to the public - see pages 166-173 for opening times

Ⓟ Public parks, gardens and open spaces open every day throughout the year

Ⓣ Public toilets

Abbreviations

RD.	Road
ST.	Street
LA.	Lane
AV.	Avenue
PL.	Place
SQ.	Square
TER.	Terrace
WLK.	Walk
GDNS.	Gardens
CRES.	Crescent
GRO.	Grove
YD.	Yard
CT.	Court
M.	Mews
GA.	Gate
MKT.	Market
GRN.	Green
DRI.	Drive
VS.	Villas
PAS.	Passage
BRI.	Bridge
BLDGS.	Buildings
APP.	Approach
ST.	Saint
GT.	Great
PK.	Park
W.	West
E.	East
S.	South
UP.	Upper
LWR.	Lower
LIT.	Little

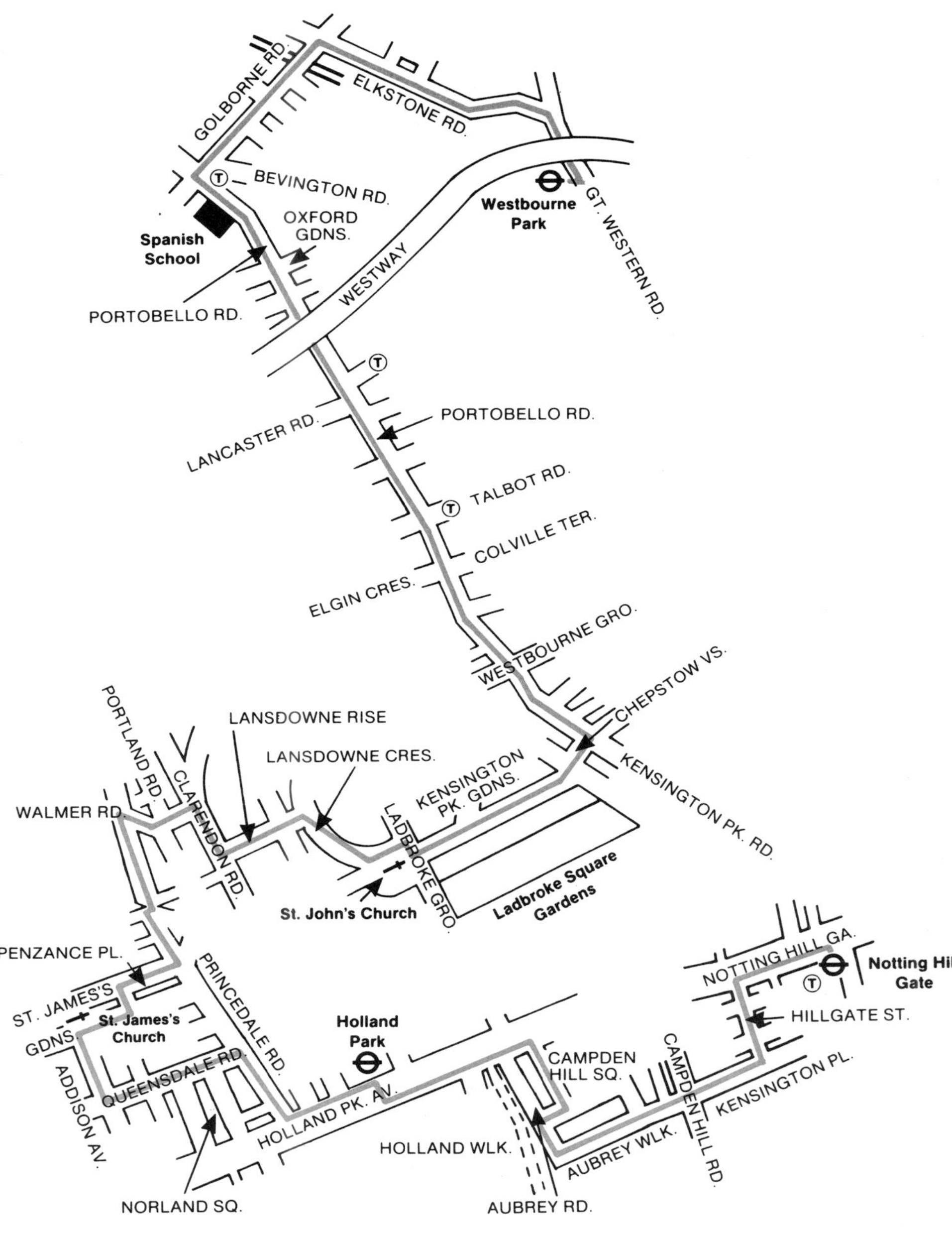
GOLBORNE RD.
ELKSTONE RD.
BEVINGTON RD.
Westbourne Park
GT. WESTERN RD.
Spanish School
OXFORD GDNS.
PORTOBELLO RD.
WESTWAY
PORTOBELLO RD.
LANCASTER RD.
TALBOT RD.
COLVILLE TER.
ELGIN CRES.
WESTBOURNE GRO.
WESTBOURNE
CHEPSTOW VS.
PORTLAND RD.
LANSDOWNE RISE
LANSDOWNE CRES.
KENSINGTON PK. GDNS.
KENSINGTON PK. RD.
WALMER RD.
CLARENDON RD.
LADBROKE GRO.
St. John's Church
Ladbroke Square Gardens
PENZANCE PL.
PRINCEDALE RD.
NOTTING HILL GA.
Notting Hill Gate
ST. JAMES'S GDNS.
St. James's Church
Holland Park
HILLGATE ST.
ADDISON AV.
QUEENSDALE RD.
CAMPDEN HILL SQ.
CAMPDEN HILL RD.
KENSINGTON PL.
HOLLAND PK. AV.
HOLLAND WLK.
AUBREY WLK.
NORLAND SQ.
AUBREY RD.

Notting Hill

Summary: Located north of Kensington in west London, Notting Hill is the scene of the Notting Hill Carnival and the world-famous Portobello Road antiques market. The walk starts at the northern end of the district, runs the whole length of the Golborne Road and Portobello Road markets, and then explores steep Notting Hill itself, the site of London's finest Victorian housing development. The final part of the walk climbs leafy Holland Park and crosses Campden Hill Square to the top of Campden Hill before returning to Notting Hill Gate.

***Start:* Westbourne Park Station (Hammersmith & City Underground line; trains from Paddington).**
***Finish:* Notting Hill Gate Station (District, Circle and Central Underground lines).**
***Length:* 3½ miles (5.6 kilometres).**
***Time:* 2½ hours.**
***Refreshments:* Pubs and a few cafés throughout the route, especially in the early stages and at the end of the walk on Notting Hill Gate, where you will also find the usual high street fast-food restaurants. Look out for the Lisboa café on Golborne Road, the Café Grove (first-floor terrace) on Portobello Road about a third of the way into the walk, and the Windsor Castle (excellent beer garden) on Campden Hill near the finish (all mentioned in the text).**
***Route note:* Best walked early on a Saturday when the Portobello Road antiques market is open but not too busy.**

Come out of Westbourne Park Station and turn left into the Great Western Road. Go under the Westway overhead motorway and take the first turning on the left into Elkstone Road just beyond the Big Table furniture co-operative. Follow this road for some distance, between commercial buildings on the left and Meanwhile Gardens on the right; then railway tracks on the left (the main line to the West Country) and the 30-storey Trellick Tower on the right. Turn left, crossing over the bridge into Golborne Road. The Saturday market here trades in old clothes and every conceivable kind of junk, and is really an extension of the main Portobello Road market which begins further along the route.

Portobello Road market

Walk along Golborne Road (past the Lisboa on the left) and just beyond the entrance to Bevington Road Ⓣ on the left, turn left into Portobello Road - the less affluent end of both the market and the Notting Hill district. This part of Notting Hill was not developed until the 1860s and the market started (unofficially) around the same time. Portobello Road was originally a farm track leading from the village of Notting Hill Gate to Portobello Farm, which stood about where you are now. The farm was named in the 18th century in honour of the 1739 naval battle when the British defeated the Spanish off Puerto Bello in the Gulf of Mexico.

Continue along Portobello Road past the bilingual Spanish school (built as a Franciscan convent in 1862) on your right. Cross Oxford Gardens and walk down to Portobello Green under the Westway, opened in 1970. At this point the quality of the merchandise in the market begins to improve. There are also some bric-à-brac stalls, a foretaste of the antiques to come. From the Westway here (Ⓣ on left in Tavistock Road) to the junction with Colville Terrace and Elgin Crescent, Portobello Road is an ordinary shopping centre and thriving food market, though it has an unusual collection of shops - mostly fairly smart street fashion plus the occasional art gallery and a tattoo studio at No. 201. Café Grove is on your right at the junction with Lancaster Road (Ⓣ toilets at the junction with Talbot Road).

At the end of August each year over a million revellers pack into Portobello Road and the surrounding streets to enjoy the carnival procession. The Notting Hill Carnival started as a school pageant in 1966 and then developed, not always happily, into today's massive Caribbean jamboree with decorated floats, steel bands and masqueraders in extravagant costumes. Many people from former British colonies in the West Indies settled in this area during the 1950s.

The proper antiques market starts at the Colville Terrace/Elgin Crescent junction and continues all the way up the hill across Westbourne Grove to Chepstow Villas. In several places it has bled into adjoining streets, in particular Westbourne Grove. Antiques, the main attraction of today's Portobello Road market, were not a feature until 1948 when dealers moved here after the closure of the Caledonian Antique Market in Islington. Virtually anything can be bought here and prices are not outrageous.

Victorian housing boom

At the end of the market turn right into Chepstow Villas. On the left No. 39 has a plaque to Louis Kossuth, the Hungarian nationalist who sought refuge in England following the failure of Hungary's 1848-9 revolution against her Austrian masters. The house must have been very newly built then because work on the street did not start until the late 1840s. At the junction go straight across into Kensington Park Gardens. On the left No. 7 has a plaque to Sir William Crookes, the scientist who, among other things, discovered the metal thallium in 1861. Half way along on both sides of the street there are gates leading into large communal gardens (access for residents only). Notting Hill has 13 of these large communal gardens and Ladbroke Square Gardens (on the left) is the largest in London. They were included in the original Victorian landscaping scheme in order to entice prospective purchasers out of the West End.

At the end of Kensington Park Gardens, cross Ladbroke Grove and walk to the right of St John's Church (1845) into Lansdowne Crescent. In pious Victorian

England a church was as important a part of the infrastructure of a new and untried residential area as drains and street lighting, and many churches - like St John's - were built before the houses. St John's immediate predecessor on this marvellous hilltop site was a racecourse grandstand. Having built a few houses which had not proved the financial success he had hoped, the landlord of the area, James Weller Ladbroke, let some land to a local man who had the bright idea of laying out a racecourse round Notting Hill, using the hill itself as a natural grandstand. The racecourse opened in 1837, but was forced to close four years later when jockeys refused to ride on it, claiming the heavy going made it too dangerous.

Follow Lansdowne Crescent round to the right. Then turn left into Lansdowne Rise which plunges down the western slope of Notting Hill. At the bottom, turn right into Clarendon Road and then first left into Portland Road. Keep going straight ahead to Walmer Road at the bottom, passing on the way Hippodrome Mews, named after the racecourse. Turn left on Walmer Road.

A few yards further along on the left an old pottery kiln stands by the roadside. As its plaque indicates, it is a relic of the potteries and brickfields which covered this low-lying clay-land before it was developed. Pig-keepers also lived here, their animals helping to make the Potteries and the Piggeries one of the most notorious slums in the whole of Victorian England. Avondale Park behind you, opened in 1892, was then a vast pit of stinking slurry known as the Ocean. Somehow all this squalor existed until the 1870s side by side with the middle-class suburb on the slopes of the hill above.

Walk to the right of the bar-restaurant (straight ahead) into Princedale Road and then turn right into Penzance Place. At St James's Gardens, turn left and then right to St James's Church. The plaque on the church railings mentions that while most of the square was built in the four years after 1847, it was not actually finished until 15 years later because of shortage of funds, a good indication of how costly and risky these huge middle-class Victorian developments were. Shortage of money also meant that the church was not given the spire that its architect, Lewis Vulliamy, had designed for it.

Leafy Campden Hill

At the church turn left into Addison Avenue, the most stylish street in this development, and then left again into Queensdale Road which leads into Norland Square. Norland House which once stood here was a small country house with a 50-acre estate owned by the royal clockmaker, Benjamin Vulliamy, father of the architect Lewis Vulliamy.

When you reach the Prince of Wales pub turn right into Princedale Road (where *Oz* magazine was based at the time of the police raid following its famous 'Schoolkids' issue) and then left into Holland Park Avenue (Lidgate's, the leading organic butchers, is on the left). At Holland Park Station go over the crossing and continue up Holland Park Avenue past the statue of St Volodymyr which was put up by London's Ukrainian community in 1988. Cross the entrances to Holland Walk (leads to Kensington High Street) and Aubrey Road and turn right into steep Campden Hill Square, begun in 1826. Turner painted sunsets from the garden in the middle, and John McDouall Stuart, his health broken by hardships suffered in the first official crossing of the Australian continent, died at No. 9 in 1866.

Views from the hill

At the top of the square turn right and then left into Aubrey Road. On the right Aubrey House, set in its own two-acre (0.8-hectare) walled garden, is the last of several country houses which once existed on Campden Hill. Lady Mary Coke, eccentric authoress of entertaining diaries, lived here from 1767 to 1788. One entry relates how her cow - called Miss Pelham - escaped from the grounds one day 'and went very near as far as London before I heard of her. I believe she thinks my place too retired, for she was found among a great herd of cattle.' Aubrey House is still privately owned and in the mid 1990s changed hands for £20m.

At the house turn left along Aubrey Walk which will take you to Campden Hill Road. Cross the road (Windsor Castle pub to the right) into Kensington Place. Far ahead you can see the BT Tower rising above the West End, exactly three miles from where you are standing. Half way down Kensington Place at the Fox Primary School turn left into Hillgate Street. This leads through Hillgate Village, a grid of narrow streets and small, but elegant mid 19th-century houses, to Notting Hill Gate. This is the main street of the Notting Hill area, its name a reminder of the old toll gate which stood here until the 1860s to raise money for road maintenance. On the Gate, turn right and walk along to Notting Hill Gate Station Ⓣ where the walk ends.

Kensington

Summary: Kensington is an historic village suburb in west London, close to Kensington Palace and Kensington Gardens. It is spread out on the south-facing slope of Campden Hill and bisected by its fashionable High Street. While Kensington Palace was in use gentry and nobility dominated the area but when the court moved out, artists and writers settled here. This circular walk starts and finishes in Kensington High Street and includes the parish church, Kensington's two historic squares (one now 300 years old), Holland House and Park, the Melbury Road artists' colony centred on the Leighton House Museum and Art Gallery, and many attractive streets and houses in a rich variety of architectural styles.

***Start and finish:* High Street Kensington Station (Circle and District Underground lines).**
***Length:* 2¾ miles (4.4 kilometres).**
***Time:* 2 hours.**
***Refreshments:* High street restaurants in Kensington High Street and pubs *en route*. Look out for the Scarsdale pub in Edwardes Square, about half-way through the walk, the café in Holland Park after about two-thirds of the walk, and the Elephant and Castle pub near the end.**

Come out of Kensington High Street Station, turn right onto the High Street and walk along past Marks and Spencer and BHS. Take the first turning on the right into Derry Street. No. 99 towards the end on the right is the entrance to the famous roof gardens Ⓗ built over the Derry and Toms department store in the 1930s. Derry Street leads on into the north-west corner of Kensington Square - one of the oldest and prettiest squares in London. By the mid 1600s wealthy people were moving to the then country village of Kensington in search of a healthier lifestyle. This square was developed in the 1660s to meet the growing demand. When Kensington Palace was built years later the square and surrounding houses were naturally taken over by courtiers and Kensington itself became known as the Old Court Suburb.

Continue walking along the right hand (western) side of the square. Many well known people have lived here over the years. No. 33 on the right, for example, was once the home of the actress Mrs Patrick Campbell, who dominated the London stage in the 1880s and 1890s. Turn left at the bottom of the square. The utilitarian philosopher John Stuart Mill lived in No. 18 in 1837-51 and it was here that his maid inadvertently used the manuscript of the historian Thomas Carlyle's first major book to light the fire. Nothing daunted, Carlyle wrote it again and the book, *The History of the French Revolution*, came out in 1837.

Kensington New Town

Nos. 11 and 12 are the only original 17th-century houses in the square to have survived (note the names of former occupants painted on the carved porch of No. 11). Beyond these houses take the first right into Ansdell Street. At the end of the street turn left into St Alban's Grove, passing on the left Prue Leith's School of Food and Wine. Cross Stanford Road and Victoria Road and continue into Victoria Grove, turning right into Launceston Place. These streets form a self-contained development known as Kensington New Town, which was built over market gardens in the 1840s by John Inderwick, a wealthy tobacconist and pipe-maker. He owned a clay mine in the Crimea and introduced meerschaum pipes into England. You will still find an Inderwick's tobacconist's in Carnaby Street in the West End of London. The small but elegant houses on his development have always been popular and demand will no doubt remain high so long as the New Town continues to be an official conservation area.

Before Launceston Place reaches Cornwall Gardens turn right through an archway into Kynance Mews, still paved with cobblestones from the days of horse and carriage. Opposite No. 24 turn right up some steps into Victoria Road, and then turn left by Christ Church into Eldon Road, named after a large house called Eldon Lodge which once stood near here. At the end of the road take a left turn into Stanford Road and go through the passageway at the end of the cul-de-sac into Cornwall Gardens.

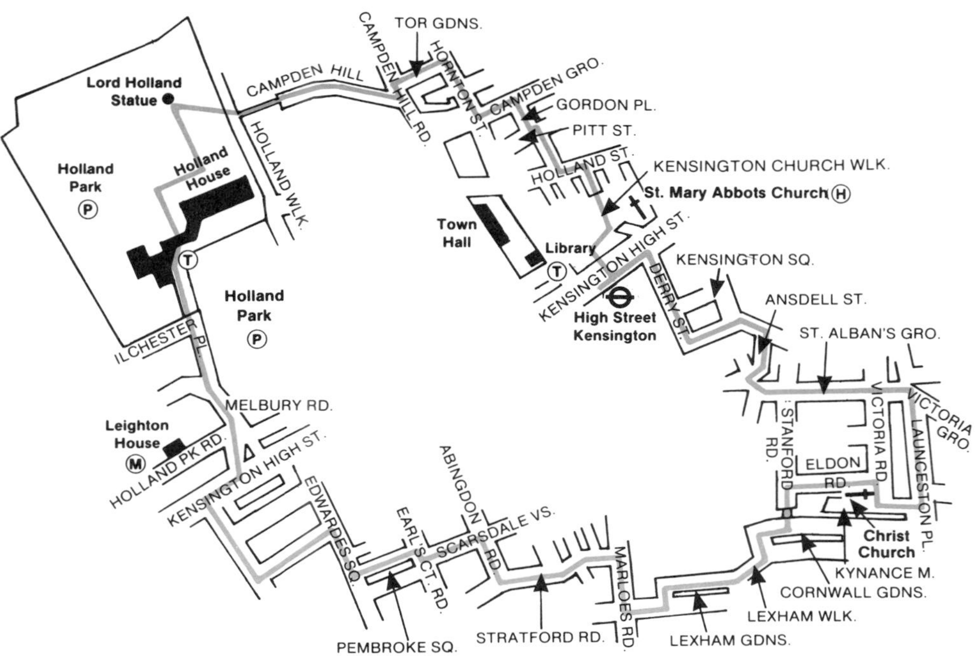

Fashionable flats

The whole character of the area changes here as the pretty, countrified, houses of Kensington New Town give way to the heavy stuccoed terraces and sombre apartment blocks of High Victorian South Kensington. These blocks were built mainly in the later 19th century when living in flats became the fashionable thing to do among London's ever-expanding middle classes. From the property developer's point of view they also meant that more people could be accommodated on a given amount of land, thus generating more profit.

Turn right when you come to Cornwall Gardens and then turn left. On the left the novelist Ivy Compton-Burnett lived in the corner house from 1934 until her death in 1969. Ahead to the left is a house (No. 52) with a plaque in memory of Joaquim Nabuco, Brazilian ambassador to Britain at the turn of the century (he was here only until 1902, not 1905 as the plaque says). Nabuco, although a conservative, had been mainly responsible for the abolition of slavery in Brazil in 1888. Some years before that he had spent time as a newspaper correspondent in Britain.

Before you reach Nabuco's house turn right down the slope of Lexham Walk, cross Cornwall Gardens Walk and enter Lexham Gardens. Keep to the right round Lexham Gardens. Take the first right turn and then turn right again into Marloes Road. Opposite the entrance to Kensington Green, a housing development covering the site of St Mary Abbots Hospital and the former Kensington workhouse, turn left into Stratford Road and follow the road as it winds left and right. When you get to the junction with Abingdon Road turn right and then first left into Scarsdale Villas. At the end, cross Earl's Court Road into Pembroke Square walking to the right of Rassell's nursery. Turn right out of Pembroke Square into Edwardes Square (Scarsdale pub on the right) and take a left turn, walking along the south side of the square past the Temple (the gardener's lodge).

French connection

Edwardes Square is the second of Kensington's historic squares, although it is a century younger than Kensington Square. It was built on land belonging to William Edwardes, second Lord Kensington, between 1811 and 1819 when the Napoleonic Wars were raging. The developer was French by birth and had kept his French name - Louis Léon Changeur. As building progressed, Changeur's ancestry helped to generate the rumour that he was a Napoleonic agent and that the square was being built, not for the harmless representatives of the professional middle classes, but for the officers of Napoleon's army. The feared French invasion failed to materialize so Changeur's loyalty to his adopted country – and the absurd rumour regarding it - was never put to the test.

Continue along the south side of the square and then turn right along the west side. When you reach the main road (Kensington High Street) turn right and walk along Earl's Terrace (the earliest part of Edwardes Square) and cross the road at the first set of traffic lights. Continue along the High Street in the same direction, turning left when you reach Melbury Road.

Once part of the Holland House estate, this area was developed in the 19th century and quickly became an artists' colony. Its most famous resident was the painter,

Lord Leighton, whose large house with the rear conservatory can be seen through the trees as you cross Holland Park Road on the left. It is now the Leighton House Museum and Art Gallery Ⓜ.

Continue along Melbury Road as far as the junction with Ilchester Place. The house on the corner here is the former home of the Victorian and Edwardian painter Sir Luke Fildes, whose most famous painting, *The Doctor* (1881), hangs in the Tate Gallery. The Tower House next door to Fildes's house was once the home of the Gothic Revival architect and designer, William Burges. He designed the house and its medieval interiors himself, intending it to be 'a model residence of the 15th century'. In 1969 the actor Richard Harris bought it and completed the interior according to Burges's original designs.

The Holland Estate

Leave Melbury Road here and walk up Ilchester Place into Holland Park Ⓟ. This was once the park and grounds of Holland House, the large Jacobean manor house of Kensington, the remains of which can be seen ahead. In the 18th century the house was bought by Henry Fox, the first Lord Holland and the father of the great Whig (liberal) politician, Charles James Fox. While in the possession of the third Lord Holland (1773-1840), the house was a meeting place for Whig politicians, writers and intellectuals; the names of Byron, Macaulay, Sir Walter Scott, Melbourne, Disraeli and Dickens were all recorded in Lady Holland's still-surviving dinner books. In World War II the house was virtually destroyed by bombs. The one remaining wing is now a youth hostel, the Garden Ballroom a restaurant and the Orangery an exhibition centre Ⓣ.

When you reach the buildings, look left through the archway where there is a superb set of murals depicting a garden party at Holland House in the 1870s. Go straight on through the colonnade (café to right) and branch right through the walled garden to the terrace on the north side of the house. Here turn right towards the house, left across the North Lawn, and then walk along Rose Walk to the statue of the third Lord Holland, a good likeness by G. F. Watts and Joseph Boehm, done in 1872. Turn sharp right here, follow the path round to the right and then turn left out of the park by crossing Holland Walk (connecting Notting Hill with Kensington) into a passageway with high walls on either side. This leads through Holland Park Comprehensive School into Campden Hill.

The school was built in the 1950s following the demolition of Argyll and Moray Lodges, two of a chain of seven country lodges built along the ridge of Campden Hill between Holland House and Campden House, of which more in a minute. Beyond the school, the gate lodge of Moray Lodge and the coach house of Holly Lodge (where the historian Lord Macaulay died in 1859) still survive, dwarfed by buildings of King's College, London, on the right.

At the end of Campden Hill cross Campden Hill Road into Tor Gardens. The second house on the right on the far side of Campden Hill Road bears a plaque in memory of Ford Madox Ford, grandson of the Pre-Raphaelite painter, Ford Madox Brown. Ford wrote over 80 books and edited some notable literary periodicals, yet only three people attended his funeral at Deauville in France in 1939. Belated recognition, however, now seems to be coming his way. The apartment block at the eastern end of Tor Gardens is Campden House Court. It stands on the site of another of Kensington's Jacobean mansions, Campden House. The house was named after its builder, Viscount Campden, whose country home was in the Gloucestershire market town of Chipping Campden.

At the end of Tor Gardens turn right into Hornton Street. At the bottom of the hill you can see the red brick and glass of Kensington's new town hall Ⓣ. Take the second turning on the left into Campden Grove and the first right turn into Gordon Place, crossing Pitt Street half way down. When Kensington was a country village Gordon Place was an avenue running from Campden House at the top of the hill, down to the High Street at the bottom. Now Gordon Place ends in a pedestrian-only cul-de-sac of small houses with luxuriant front gardens.

At the Elephant and Castle pub turn left and walk along Holland Street, a pretty street with several antique shops and 18th-century houses. Originally it was a coach road along the south side of Campden Hill connecting Holland House with Kensington Palace ahead. Just beyond No. 21 on the right turn right into Kensington Church Walk. This leads past a group of shops to a small courtyard with half a dozen secluded houses. Go on into the churchyard gardens at the west end of St Mary Abbots Ⓗ, the parish church of Kensington, built in 1872. An earlier church had been built on this site in the 1100s by the Abbot of Abingdon. The land was granted to the abbey by the lord of the manor, hence the 'abbot' part of the name. Ahead is the local church school with 18th century figures of a boy and girl decorating its rear wall: they originally adorned the front of the first school building which stood on Kensington High Street. Follow the path round to the right and then left past the churchyard garden until you reach Kensington High Street. The walk ends back at High Street Kensington Station on the other side of the road.

Chelsea

Summary: Chelsea is a village suburb on the Thames close to central London. Modern Chelsea is neatly bisected by the King's Road but historic Chelsea, including the 17th century Royal Hospital, Physic Garden, Old Church, Henry VIII's manor house, Sir Thomas More's house and the Chelsea Porcelain Works, lay between the King's Road and the Thames. This circular walk includes these historic features, plus St Luke's church, the Chelsea Farmer's Market, and the former homes of some of the writers and artists who lived in this once-bohemian district: George Eliot, James Whistler, Thomas Carlyle, Tobias Smollett and Hilaire Belloc, to name only a few.

Start and finish: **Sloane Square Station (District and Circle Underground lines).**
Length: **3¾ miles (6 kilometres).**
Time: **3 hours.**
Refreshments: **All manner of places to eat and drink on the King's Road, and a few pubs along the route including one at the half-way point where Milman's Street meets the King's Road. Also, various restaurants in Chelsea Farmer's Market about three-quarters of the way through the walk.**
Route note: **Chelsea Hospital grounds are open daily 10 am to 4 pm but closed during the Chelsea Flower Show held at the end of May.**

On leaving Sloane Square Station you will find yourself in Sloane Square, named after Sir Hans Sloane, lord of the manor of Chelsea in the 18th century and one of the key figures in its history. To your right is the Royal Court Theatre where many new writers have had their plays first performed, including John Osborne with *Look Back in Anger* in 1956. Go over the zebra crossings and walk along the left hand side of the square Ⓣ into the King's Road, the high street of modern Chelsea. During the 1960s the King's Road became the playground of 'swinging London' and since then has been the most fashionable shopping area outside the West End.

The Chelsea Pensioners

Continue along the King's Road, passing on the left the Duke of York's barracks, now the headquarters of Britain's volunteer army. Cross Tenham Terrace and Walpole Street and take the next turning on the left into Royal Avenue. Far ahead you can see the entrance to the Royal Hospital, the home for old soldiers founded by Charles II in 1682 and designed by Christopher Wren. The Hospital inmates are known as Chelsea Pensioners and are recognized by their old-fashioned blue or red uniforms. At the end of Royal Avenue turn left into Leonard's Terrace and then right along Franklin's Row. To your right is Burton's Court, a sports ground used by soldiers from local barracks. Cross the main road (Royal Hospital Road) to enter the Royal Hospital grounds Ⓗ.

At the second gate, turn right into Light Horse Court and go straight ahead through the arch leading into the colonnade. Half way along there is a doorway on the right leading into the Hospital's dining hall and chapel. On leaving the hall, continue straight ahead into the middle of the central court (Figure Court), which is flanked by wings left and right. About 400 pensioners live here in small curtained cubicles ranged along the middle of great open dormitories known as Long Wards.

The bronze statue in the centre of the court by Grinling Gibbons depicts Charles II in the dress of a Roman emperor. Above the colonnade in the central range of the building a Latin inscription announces that the Hospital is for the support and relief of maimed and superannuated soldiers and that it was founded by Charles II, enlarged by James II and completed by William III in 1692. In the opposite direc-

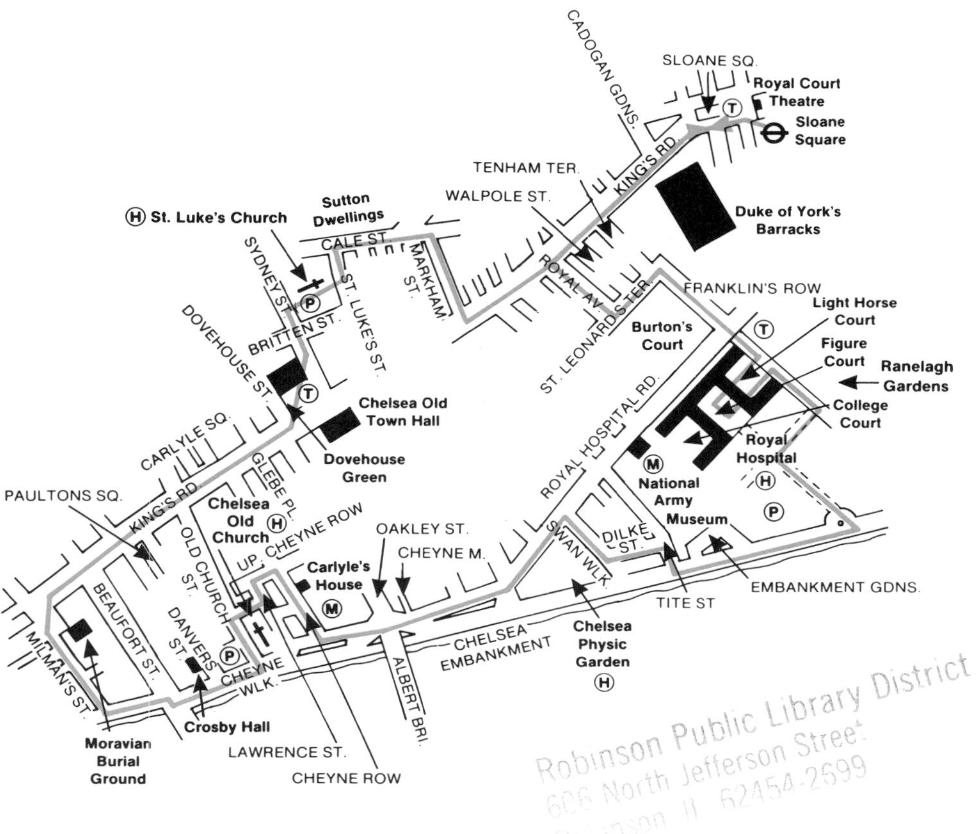

tion there is a good view across the Hospital grounds to the former Battersea Power Station on the south side of the River Thames.

In front of the flagpole turn left along the terrace and pass through another arch into Light Horse Court. Turn right out of the Court and go through the gate ahead. Another gate immediately on your left leads into Ranelagh Gardens, the site of the most famous of all the pleasure gardens opened in London during the 1700s. The centrepiece of Ranelagh Gardens was a huge rotunda where visitors promenaded or drank tea and wine accompanied by an orchestra playing from a bandstand. Mozart once performed here. There is a picture of the Rotunda, which was demolished in 1805, in the little summer house in the centre of the gardens.

Walk on past the entrance to Ranelagh Gardens and turn right in front of the Hospital into the public park area Ⓟ. (The Chelsea Flower Show is held here in May each year. At this time you will have to retrace your steps to the Hospital entrance, turn left into Royal Hospital Road and walk past the National Army Museum Ⓜ to pick up the route at Swan Walk.) Turn left down the central walk past the 1849 Chilianwallah memorial commemorating the hardest action ever fought during the subjugation of India. Nearly a quarter of the 12,000 British troops involved were killed or wounded. Go straight on out of the park and turn right onto Chelsea Embankment.

Pagodas and power stations

Looking out over the river now you can see, from left to right, the old power station, Chelsea Bridge leading to Wandsworth and Battersea, and Battersea Park, with its Bhuddist Peace Pagoda, built in 1985 by Nipponzan Myohoji Bhuddists, on the riverside. Continue to the right along the embankment, past Embankment Gardens, and then turn right into Tite Street. Oscar Wilde and the painters James McNeill Whistler, John Singer Sargent and Augustus John all lived or worked here around the turn of the century. Almost immediately turn left into Dilke Street. On the left, No. 7 with the lantern above the front door is the London Sketch Club, an artists' club founded in 1898 by *Punch* cartoonist Phil May.

At the end of Dilke Street turn right into Swan Walk. This one-sided street runs along the east side of Chelsea Physic Garden Ⓗ, which you can glimpse through the gate on the left. This botanical garden was started over 300 years ago by the City Apothecaries' Company and is still active in botanical research. Some of the first cotton seed planted in America was exported from here in 1732.

Carry on to the end of Swan Walk (where there is a plaque on the left about the Physic Garden) and turn left into Royal Hospital Road. At the end of the road turn right just before the strip of garden into Cheyne Walk, a long terrace running right along the Chelsea waterfront. Before the embankment was built in 1874 the river came right up to the side of the Walk. Over the centuries many famous people have lived here, a large proportion of them writers and artists. No. 4 was the last home of the novelist George Eliot; Lloyd George (World War I Prime Minister) lived at No. 10; Vaughan Williams (composer) once lived on the site of Nos. 12-14; and Rosetti (painter), Swinburne (poet), and George Meredith (writer) were all former residents of No. 16 (plus pet wombat!).

Cheyne Walk converges with Chelsea Embankment just before Albert Bridge. A narrow lane leads off to the right, underneath No. 24 Cheyne Walk. A plaque on the right hand wall of the lane explains that Chelsea Manor House, built by King Henry VIII in 1536 once stood here. It was later the home of Sir Hans Sloane. After Sloane's death in 1753 the old house was demolished, although part of the garden (along with mulberry trees said to have been planted by Queen Elizabeth I) still survives beyond the wall at the end of the mews.

Go past the mews, cross Oakley Street and take the first turning on the right into Cheyne Row. You are now in the centre of the old riverside village of Chelsea. On the right No. 10 has a plaque to Margaret Damer Dawson, founder of the women's police force of which she was first chief officer (she died in 1920 aged 45). Further along on the right, No. 24 was home for nearly half a century to the humbly born historian and social critic, Thomas Carlyle, one of the most influential intellectual figures of the 19th century. Carlyle's house is now a National Trust museum Ⓜ. At the end of Cheyne Row turn left into Upper Cheyne Row and then left again into Lawrence Street.

On the right a plaque mentions the famous Chelsea Porcelain Works, which produced porcelain here for almost 40 years until the factory was moved to Derby in 1784. Nearby was a large house where the novelist Tobias Smollett lived for 12 years, keeping open house to all his friends despite his own chronic shortage of money. Further along on the left, two old houses, Duke's House and Monmouth House, share a common porch, probably a relic of a large residence known as Monmouth House which stood at the northern end of Lawrence Street. In the 17th century the mansion belonged to Charles II's illegitimate son, the Duke of Monmouth, who was beheaded in 1685 after leading an unsuccessful rebellion against his uncle, James II.

Chelsea residents

At this point turn right into Justice Walk and then left into Old Church Street. This was Chelsea's main street until 1830 when the King's Road became a public thoroughfare (until then it had been a private road used only by the royal family *en route* to various country retreats). Chelsea Old Church Ⓗ (rebuilt after being bombed in World War II) is at the southern end of the street. Henry VIII married Jane Seymour here in 1536 and Sir Hans Sloane was buried here in 1753 - his grave is marked by an urn beneath a stone canopy at the east end of the churchyard. The modern statue in front of the church facing the river is of Sir Thomas More, a Chelsea resident and Lord Chancellor under Henry VIII, who was beheaded in 1535 for refusing to accept the king's religious reforms. Parts of More's 16th century chapel and many other fascinating old monuments survive in the church.

At the church turn right along Cheyne Walk and go past Roper's Garden Ⓟ, created out of a bombsite on land once given by Sir Thomas More to his son-in-law Will Roper. Cross Danvers Street. On your right is Crosby Hall, part of a medieval wool merchant's house which was brought here from the City earlier this century when it was threatened with demolition. The present site of the hall was once Sir Thomas More's garden, an appropriate location for it since Crosby Hall was More's London home before he built his country house at Chelsea.

Cross Beaufort Street (the actual site of More's house - demolished in 1740) and continue along Cheyne Walk. Ahead you can see the tower and other modern residential developments covering the former wharves and railway sidings at Lots Road. On the right No. 93 Cheyne Walk has a plaque to the novelist Mrs Gaskell, best known for her book *Cranford* (1853). No. 98 was built in 1674 for Lord Lindsey, Charles II's Lord Chamberlain; in 1774 it was split up into seven separate houses. In 1752 it was occupied by Count Zinzendorf and other members of the Moravian Protestant Church who came to England to escape persecution in their native Germany. Whistler was a later resident and it was here that he painted the famous picture of his mother. Further along, on the corner of Milman's Street, No. 104 has two plaques, one to the writer Hilaire Belloc and the other to the Chelsea-born artist Walter Greaves who died in 1930 leaving numerous pictures of his birthplace.

Turn right here into Milman's Street. Just beyond the pub on the right at the northern end of the street a large pair of gates marks the entrance to the Moravian burial ground Ⓗ, once part of the grounds of Lindsey House. Go past the gates and onto the King's Road again. Cross over and turn right. Continue walking past Paultons Square (1830s) and Old Church Street on the right and on the left Carlyle Square, built as Oakley Square around 1830 and later renamed in honour of Thomas Carlyle. On the right beyond the entrance to Glebe Place are the oldest houses on the King's Road, built in 1720. There are plaques here to the actress Ellen Terry and to film director Carol Reed of *The Third Man* fame, but not to Lady Sybil Colefax, a famous society hostess who lived at No. 211 in the 1930s.

When you get to Dovehouse Green, an old burial ground on the far side of Dovehouse Street, cut diagonally across to the far left corner and go through Chelsea Farmers Market (or along the path by the fence if the market is closed) into Sydney Street Ⓣ. Facing up the street to the right is Chelsea's old town hall. The old borough is now part of the Royal Borough of Kensington and Chelsea and is governed from Kensington.

Cross Sydney Street and turn left, crossing over Britten Street. Then turn right into the gardens Ⓟ beside St Luke's Church Ⓗ. This fine 2500-seat church, opened in 1824 to accommodate Chelsea's expanding population, was one of the first Gothic revival buildings of the 19th century. The open space all round sets it off magnificently. Charles Dickens was married here in 1836.

Cut across the gardens to the east end of the church and turn right out of the gates. Go under the arch into St Luke's Street and then turn left towards the council homes in Sutton Dwellings. Turn right onto Cale Street and follow the road to the little green surrounded by shops and restaurants. When you reach Markham Street turn right and then, at the end of the street, turn left back onto the King's Road. When you get to Cadogan Gardens just before Peter Jones, notice on No. 31 across the road to your right the plaque to the composer and folk-song collector Percy Grainger (famous for his *English Country Gardens* melody) who came to London from Australia in 1901. The walk ends back at Sloane Square Station straight ahead.

Bayswater to Belgravia

Summary: A fairly long walk through Kensington Gardens, the museums area of South Kensington and the exclusive residential districts of Knightsbridge and Belgravia. Places of interest include Kensington Palace, the Albert Memorial, the Albert Hall, the Victoria and Albert and other museums, the Brompton Oratory, Harrods and Belgrave Square. The walk finishes at Knightsbridge Station but directions are given for continuing on to Speaker's Corner in Hyde Park.

Start: **Queensway Station (Central Underground line).**
Finish: **Knightsbridge Station (Piccadilly Underground line). Speaker's Corner is close to Marble Arch Station (Central Underground line).**
Length: **4 miles (6.4 kilometres).**
Time: **2½ hours.**
Refreshments: **Plenty of places in Queensway at the start of the walk, but then not very many until you reach Knightsbridge about half-way along the route. There are some nice pubs in the Belgravia mews near the end of the walk, particularly the Grenadier in Wilton Row and the two pubs in Kinnerton Street.**
Route note: **Do this walk on a Sunday if you want to see the Bayswater Road art market and Speaker's Corner in action.**

Leave Queensway Station and turn right. Cross the main road (Bayswater Road) at the traffic lights Ⓣ and turn right. On Sunday mornings artists and art dealers display their wares along the pavement hanging their paintings on the park railings. At the next set of traffic lights turn left through the gates into the Broad Walk of Kensington Gardens Ⓟ. Far to the right you can see the mansions (most of which are embassies) in Kensington Palace Gardens. The first building you come to on your right is the Orangery of Kensington Palace. Opposite the Round Pond the palace Ⓗ itself comes into view beyond the sunken gardens (see the Central Parks walk, page 42, for more information about the palace). Beyond the palace and the second of the two covered seats on the left, take the second turning on the left and then immediately fork right, keeping to the right of the bandstand. Walk straight across the next path you come to, following the sign to the Flower Walk Ⓣ. Go straight across the next path as well and then sharp left through the gates along the Flower Walk.

Patrons of the arts

At the first cross-roads turn right towards the Albert Memorial. This commemorates Queen Victoria's husband, Prince Albert, who died in 1861. The Prince is shown

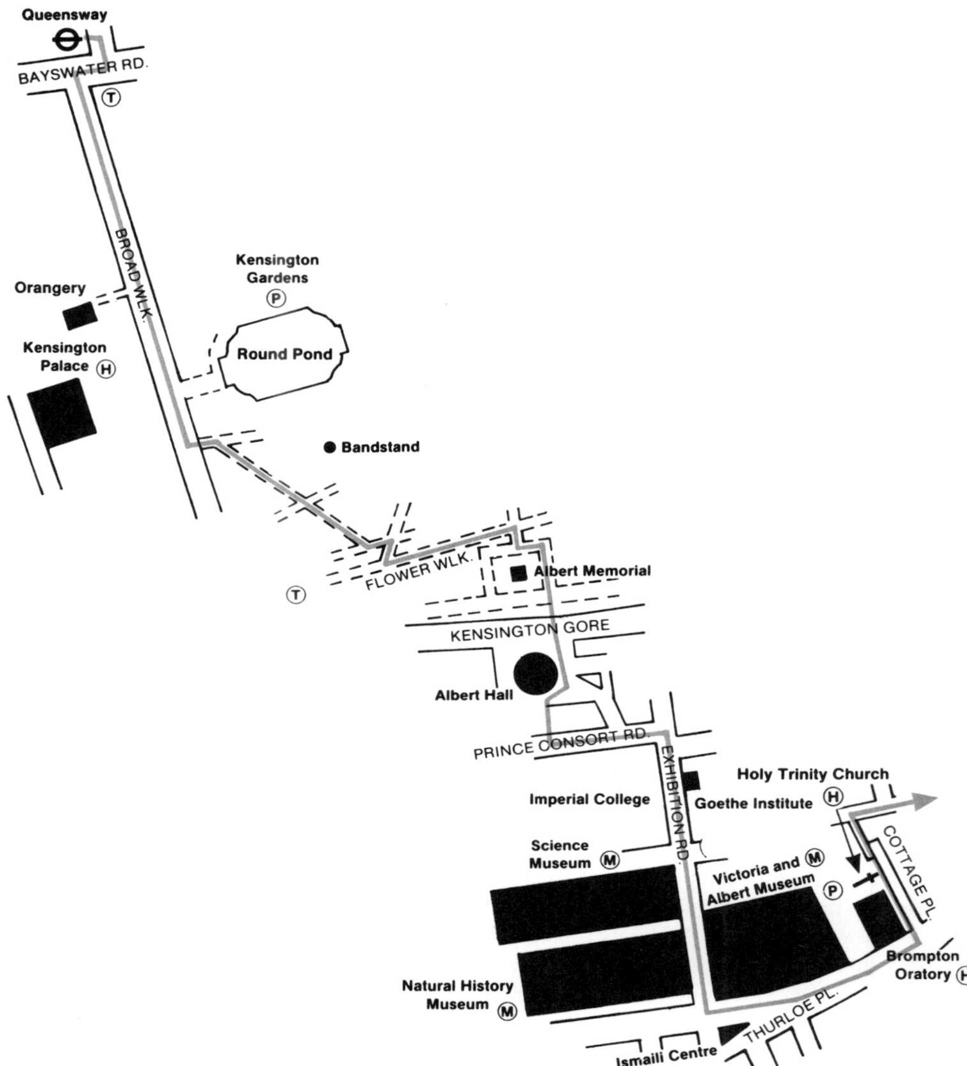

seated beneath an inlaid and enamelled Gothic canopy, holding a catalogue of the Great Exhibition of 1851. Around the base of the memorial is a white marble frieze depicting in life-size 169 painters, architects, poets, musicians and sculptors, a tribute to the Prince's patronage of the arts. Walk down the steps in front of the memorial and cross the road (Kensington Gore) to the Albert Hall, opened in 1870 as another tribute to the Prince and a major venue for a wide variety of concerts and performances including the annual Promenade concerts of classical music.

Go left round the Hall and then left again at the back down the steps. Cross Prince Consort Road to the Royal College of Music and turn left, passing the Royal School of Mines, now part of Imperial College of Science, Technology and Medicine, itself a college of London University.

When you reach Exhibition Road, cross at the traffic lights and turn right down the hill. On your left is the Goethe Institute, a German cultural and information centre. On the right, after the entrance to Imperial College, there is a whole series of museums, beginning with the Science Museum Ⓜ. Round the corner to the right on Cromwell Road, is the Natural History Museum Ⓜ. Meanwhile on your left you pass the Henry Cole Wing of the Victoria and Albert Museum Ⓜ, Britain's national museum of art and design, and then the main block of the museum.

This part of South Kensington, stretching from the Albert Hall down to the V & A (Victoria and Albert) is generally called the museums area and is a direct

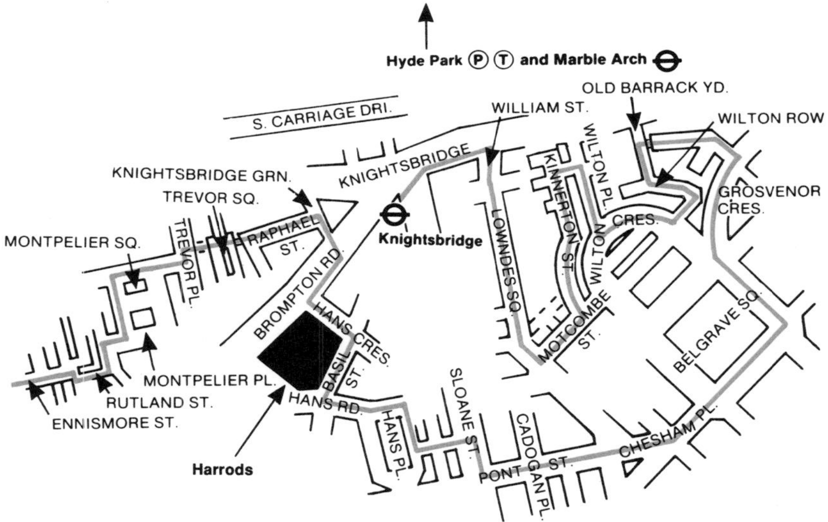

product of the 1851 Great Exhibition which Prince Albert helped to organize. Thousands of objects from all over the world were sent to the Exhibition, which was held in an enormous glass hall in Hyde Park and visited by six million people in six months. The profits generated by the Exhibition were used to buy land and build museums, colleges, schools, and a hall of arts and sciences (the Albert Hall) to further the educational aims of the Exhibition and also to extend, in the words of the organizers, 'the influence of science and art upon productive industry'.

At the traffic lights turn left into Cromwell Gardens (leading into Thurloe Place), passing along the main front of the V & A. On the right now is the Ismaili Centre, dedicated to the religion and culture of Islam. Beyond the V & A on the left you pass first a statue of a wizened Cardinal Newman, the 19th-century Church of England clergyman whose conversion in 1845 to Catholicism, fully recognized in Britain only 16 years before, caused a national uproar. Next on the left you pass Oratory House and then Brompton Oratory Ⓗ, which was the main centre of Roman Catholic worship in London before Westminster Cathedral was built in 1903.

The Ennismore heritage

Beyond the Oratory (just before Cottage Place) turn left between some white posts and walk along a path leading to Holy Trinity Church Ⓗ. The red-tiled building on the right is the former Brompton Road underground station, opened on the Piccadilly Line in 1906 and closed in 1934. The walled-off platforms still survive deep below ground level. Follow the path around the east end of the church, past the old churchyard (now a secluded and peaceful garden Ⓟ) into a cobbled mews of brightly painted houses called Ennismore Gardens Mews. All the Ennismore street names in this area refer to the Earls of Listowel, also Viscounts Ennismore, who owned all the here when it was developed in the 19th century.

Turn right along the mews and continue straight on under the arch into Ennismore Street. Walk past the Ennismore Arms, then the Clock House set back from the road in its own little courtyard, and then on the right, the entrance to Rutland Mews South. Keep going into Rutland Mews East. Near the end turn right through the gate in the boundary wall of the Rutland Estate and then left into Rutland Street. You are now in Knightsbridge. At Montpelier Walk turn left, then right into Montpelier Place and take the first left turn into Sterling Street. This brings you into Montpelier Square, with the tower of the Knightsbridge Barracks of the Household Cavalry rising up behind. This square was built in the 1830s at a time when the French resort of Montpelier was particularly popular with English tourists.

Walk up the left side of the square and then turn right along the top. When you get to Trevor Place, turn left and then right by the pillar box along a path leading into Trevor Square. As you cross the bottom of Trevor Street you can see Knightsbridge Barracks at the far end, modern home of the Household Cavalry. When the square was built most of the houses were apparently occupied by the mistresses of the cavalry officers. 'Trevor' was Sir John Trevor, a high-ranking 17th-century lawyer who had a small country house nearby.

Walk through the passage on the other side of the square into Raphael Street. Go past the office block on the left, under the arch and turn right onto Knightsbridge Green. Once part of the old village of Knightsbridge, the green is now just a triangle of tarmac with a tree in the centre. Knightsbridge was so called because of the bridge which used to carry the road from London to Kensington over the River Westbourne. The river is still running but is piped underground for most of its course.

Harrods' secret

On the main road (Brompton Road) turn right towards Harrods. Cross over at the first set of traffic lights and walk along Hans Crescent between Harrods and the entrance to Knightsbridge Station. Harrods now covers a whole block and is one of the largest stores in London. Its origins lie in a Knightsbridge grocer's shop which a City tea merchant called Henry Harrod bought in 1849. In 1861 his son Charles bought the shop from his father and developed it into today's world-famous emporium. His secret was impeccable service. When the store was completely destroyed by fire just before Christmas in 1883, the firm still made all its deliveries in time for Christmas Day.

Turn right round the back of the store along Basil Street and left at the end down Hans Road. Keep to the left round Hans Place, taking the second left along Hans Street into Sloane Street. This connects Sloane Square with Knightsbridge. The names 'Hans' and 'Sloane' came from Sir Hans Sloane, an 18th century physician, landowner (he was lord of the manor of Chelsea) and President of the Royal Society, whose collections formed the nucleus of the British Museum.

Turn right on Sloane Street and then left at the traffic lights along Pont Street, with the gardens of Cadogan Place on either side. The third house on the right along the terrace bears a blue plaque to Mrs Jordan, a famous 18th-century comedy actress, known for her wit both on and off stage. When her royal lover, the Duke of Clarence, later King William IV, proposed reducing her allowance she sent him a saucy reply in the form of the bottom part of a play advert which read: 'No money returned after the rising of the curtain'!

Pont Street leads into Chesham Place and also into Belgravia, an aristocratic quarter centred on Belgrave and Eaton Squares, developed between the 1820s and 1850s on land belonging to the Dukes of Westminster. The same family still owns much of Belgravia, and Mayfair too. Eaton Hall in Cheshire is the duke's country house and Belgrave is a small village near Leicester where the Westminsters once had an estate. The family name is Grosvenor.

Maze of mews

Follow Chesham Place round into Belgrave Square and continue along the south side of the square. Although Belgravia as a whole is still largely residential, most of the houses in Belgrave Square are either embassies or the headquarters of various organizations This side of the square is occupied by the Norwegian embassy, the Saudi Arabian Cultural Bureau, the Spiritualist Association and the Royal Agricultural Society of England. At the end of the south side, turn to the left and walk along the east side of the square.

At the top right corner of the square walk over the zebra crossing and turn right along Grosvenor Crescent. Take the first left into Grosvenor Crescent Mews (the wheatsheaf over the arch is the Grosvenor family crest). This leads into a whole maze of mews once crowded with horses and carriages belonging to the big houses in the square and adjoining streets. Walk straight on to the end of the mews and go through the gate in the wall into Old Barrack Yard, relic of an 18th-century foot guards' barracks. Turn left under the arch and walk down the pretty cobbled street. Go through the gate and down the steps at the end by the Grenadier pub and then left along Wilton Row. When you reach Wilton Crescent (an Earl of Wilton was father-in-law to one of the Westminsters) turn right and then right again into Wilton Place. The house by the tree on the far side has a blue plaque to George Bentham, nephew of 'utilitarian' Jeremy Bentham. George was a shy but incredibly diligent botanist who spent every day from 10 am to 4 pm at the Royal Botanic Gardens at Kew. There he compiled enormous catalogues of all the newly-discovered plants and flowers which an army of collectors was then sending in from all over the world.

About half way along Wilton Place turn left into Kinnerton Street and then left again, still in the same street. This is an attractive little backwater with two good pubs, a shop selling old newspapers, and attractive little courtyards leading off to the right. The cow-keepers, grocers, saddlers and other tradesmen who serviced the big houses in the area lived here and the then-uncovered Westbourne river flowed at the ends of the little courts.

Follow Kinnerton Street to the end and turn right into Motcomb Street. The Halkin Arcade, paved with enormous stone flags, leads off left and right. On the right also is the entrance front to the Pantechnicon (the name is carved high up on the façade). Built in 1830 as a fireproof complex of warehouses, stables and coach houses, it was, ironically, almost totally destroyed by fire in 1874. Part of the Wallace Collection of paintings which was stored there at the time also went up in the flames.

At the end of Motcomb Street turn right into Lowndes Square, built in the 1840s. Carry on into William Street and walk up to Knightsbridge. The walk ends at Knightsbridge Station, a hundred yards to the left. If you want to continue on into Hyde Park (perhaps to hear the speakers at Speaker's Corner if it is a Sunday), carry straight on over Knightsbridge and South Carriage Drive into the park Ⓟ, through the Dell and up the bank to the Serpentine Road Ⓣ. Ahead there should be five tarmac paths fanning out across the northern part of the park. The middle and widest path leads directly to Speaker's Corner and Marble Arch, and to Marble Arch Station.

Central Parks

Summary: A central London walk from Westminster to Kensington through a green swathe made up of four royal parks: St James's Park, Green Park, Hyde Park and Kensington Gardens. Places of interest along the route include the Houses of Parliament, the Treasury and Foreign Office, the Cabinet War Rooms, Buckingham Palace, St James's Palace, Clarence House, Apsley House (the Wellington Museum) at Hyde Park Corner, the Serpentine, the Peter Pan statue and Speke memorial in Kensington Gardens, and Kensington Palace.

***Start:* Westminster Station (District, Circle and Jubilee Underground lines).**
***Finish:* High Street Kensington Station (District and Circle Underground lines).**
***Length:* 3¾ miles (6 kilometres).**
***Time:* 2½ hours.**
***Refreshments:* Cafés in St James's Park (off the walk to the right of the bridge over the lake), Hyde Park and Kensington Gardens (Orangery of Kensington Palace). Then a wide selection of pubs and restaurants at the end of the walk in Kensington.**

Leave Westminster Station (Big Ben and the Houses of Parliament will be opposite, and turn right. Cross the road at the traffic lights Ⓣ and turn right into Parliament Street. Take the first left turn under the arch into King Charles Street (the Treasury is on the left and the Foreign Office is on the right) and go down the steps at the end of the street, passing the statue of Lord Clive, founder of the British Empire in India in the 18th-century. To your left is the entrance to the subterranean Cabinet War Rooms Ⓗ used by Churchill and his government during World War II.

Wine-bibbing elephant

Cross Horse Guards Road and enter St James's Park Ⓟ the oldest, most intimate and garden-like of the royal parks in London. In 1660 Charles II opened the park to the public, converting it into a popular resort where people strolled and talked, played games and fed the ducks. James I, grandfather to Charles II, once kept a zoo in the park: this included an elephant which drank a gallon of wine every day, as well as three pelicans given to James I (or was it his grandson Charles II? – authorities differ) by the Russian ambassador. There are still pelicans in the park, along with over 30 other species of birds, including ducks, geese, gulls and swans.

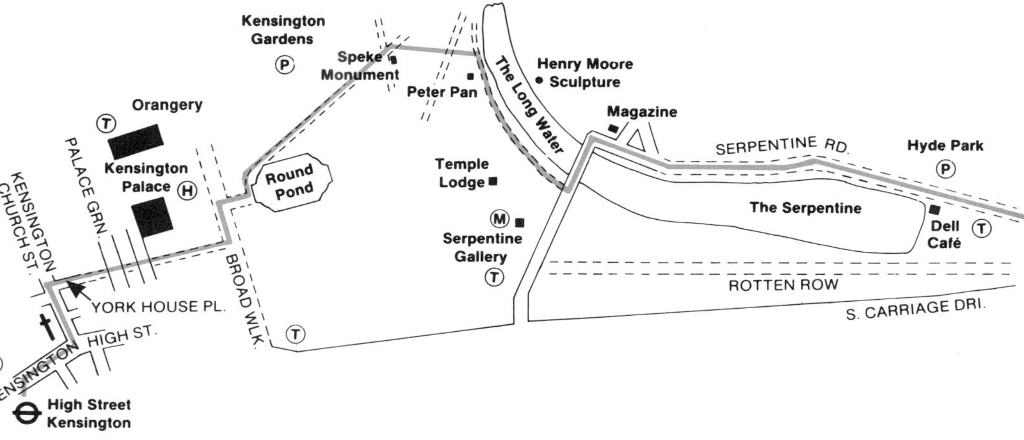

Follow the lakeside path, with the lake on your right, until you come to a bridge. As you cross over the bridge you will see to your left the gilded memorial to Queen Victoria and the public front of Buckingham Palace, and to your right the domes and pinnacles of Horse Guards, the Old Admiralty and other government offices in Whitehall. The copper-green pitched roofs belong to the Ministry of Defence.

Once over the bridge (café to the right), carry on to the gates at the top of the bank Ⓣ. Cross the Mall at the traffic lights and turn left. Behind the wall on your right is the garden front of St James's Palace, originally built in the 1500s by Henry VIII. The large house next to the palace with the stuccoed façade is Clarence House, built for the royal Duke of Clarence by John Nash in 1828 and now the London home of the Queen Mother. Beyond Clarence House is Lancaster House, a government conference centre where the Lancaster House Agreement on Zimbabwe was negotiated in 1979. Until the early part of this century this was the palatial town house of the Dukes of Sutherland.

Military heroes

Just beyond Lancaster House turn right into Queen's Walk and then go through the opening to your left into Green Park Ⓟ. Continue along this wide path, crossing the park's Broad Walk, a grassy avenue with double lines of trees on either side. This links Piccadilly at the top with Buckingham Palace at the bottom. Green Park is the plainest of the central parks, with no lake or fountains and very few flowers. The trees are mainly limes, planes and hawthorns.

When you get to the crossroads with the lamp in the middle, continue straight on (by taking the third path from the left) and when this path meets the path along the perimeter of the park, bear left towards the park's apex at Hyde Park Corner. Here, turn right out of the park, using the Green Park subway to reach the central reservation on the far side of the road. Hyde Park Corner is dominated by the Duke of Wellington, the English military hero who defeated Napoleon at Waterloo in

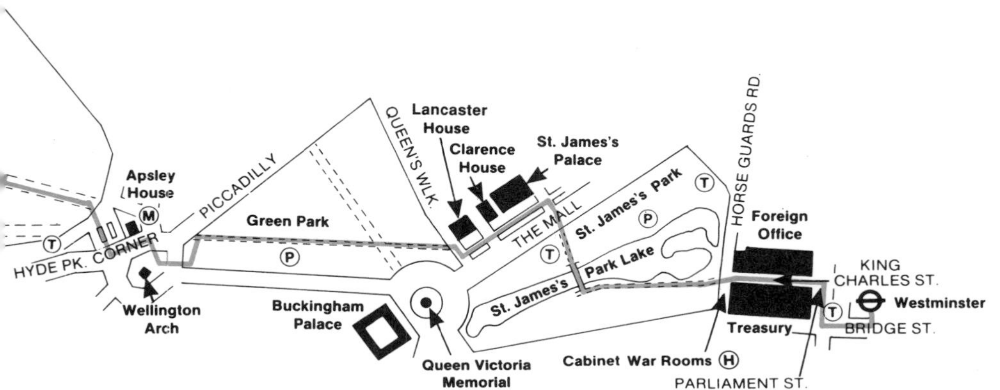

1815. Facing you is Apsley House, the Duke's former London home, now the Wellington Museum Ⓜ. Opposite the house is a mounted statue of the Duke wearing a tricorn hat. To your left there is a huge triumphal arch called the Wellington (or Constitution) Arch (housing London's second smallest police station). The other sculptures on the green here commemorate the World War I dead from the Machine Gun Corps (the nude figure of David, to your right) and the Royal Regiment of Artillery (the huge stone howitzer over on the far side).

Along the Serpentine

Walk towards Apsley House and leave Hyde Park Corner by the Park Lane subway, following the signs to Hyde Park and the Wellington Museum. Turn right at the top of the steps. Go around the front of Apsley House and then turn right through the gates, crossing South Carriage Drive into Hyde Park Ⓟ. To the right is yet another tribute to Wellington (and also his men) - a statue of the legendary hero Achilles, cast from captured cannon. Wellington was often referred to by grateful contemporaries as the 'Achilles of England'.

There are two main paths to the left leading through Hyde Park. The one on the left with a sanded track for riding is Rotten Row, the name thought to be a corruption of *Route du Roi*, the royal road built by King William III in the 1690s, leading from Westminster to his new palace at Kensington. The walk, however, takes you along Serpentine Road, the path on the right.

Walk along the road past the cavalry memorial and bandstand Ⓣ. Soon you come to the Dell Café and the Serpentine lake, created in 1730 by damming the River Westbourne. Activities on the lake include swimming from the end of May to mid September and boating, and sometimes skating in winter. In 1826 a businessman won a bet of one hundred guineas by driving his van and four horses over the frozen lake. To the left you can see the tower of Knightsbridge horseguards barracks. Over to the right the large boulder was placed here by Norwegian seamen in 1978 as a token of gratitude for hospitality and support received during the Second World

War. Further away to the right, behind the hedge and thick screen of trees, there are four acres of greenhouses where all the bedding plants for the royal parks are grown.

Just before the bridge, take the right fork, along the left-hand side of the car park, onto the road dividing Hyde Park from Kensington Gardens. Turn left opposite the Magazine (a gunpowder and ammunition store built in 1805 and now used by park maintenance staff) and cross the bridge. Half-way across there is a fine view of the Houses of Parliament. On the far side of the bridge, turn right off the road through Temple Gate into Kensington Gardens Ⓟ.

Sculptures and statues

On your left now is the Serpentine Gallery Ⓜ, built in the 1930s as a tea house and now an Arts Council-sponsored gallery for modern art exhibitions. Take the path on the right leading down to the lake, here called the Long Water. To the left above the bank you can see the Temple, built in the 18th century for Queen Caroline, the wife of George II. Queen Caroline also ordered the digging of the Serpentine, and of the Round Pond which you come to shortly. On the opposite bank of the Long Water is Henry Moore's sculpture, The Arch. Further along, the path enters a small piece of riverside woodland and garden with an extraordinary statue of Peter Pan in the centre. J M Barrie was living near Kensington Gardens when he wrote the Peter Pan story and he reputedly had the statue erected overnight so that when children came for their daily walk they would think the fairies had brought it.

Immediately beyond the woodland turn left across the grass towards the obelisk memorial to John Speke (in summer only the base is visible through the trees). Speke was the first explorer to trace the source of the Nile to Lake Victoria in 1864. Looking left from the obelisk, the east front of Kensington Palace and the graceful spire of Kensington parish church (St Mary Abbots) can be seen at the end of the broad avenue to the left. Walk up the avenue (or use the tarmac path in the trees to the right if you prefer) until you come to the Round Pond.

Walk to the right of the pond, aiming for the white statue of Queen Victoria (by her daughter, Princess Louise) in front of the palace Ⓗ. (The Orangery café Ⓣ is to the right.) Turn left along the Broad Walk and then take the first right turn along the south front of the palace, passing the immaculate gardens, often with rabbits playing on the lawn. The statue in the middle of the gravel walk leading up to the palace is of a wigged and hatted King William III who, in the 1690s, commissioned Wren to convert Nottingham House into Kensington Palace because he hated stuffy old Whitehall Palace down by the Thames in Westminster. Queen Victoria was born at Kensington Palace and lived there until she inherited the throne in 1837 at the age of 18. Diana, Princess of Wales, lived here until her death in Paris in 1997.

Walk straight ahead through the gates out of the park onto Palace Green. Cross the road and walk along the opposite footpath (York House Place) which brings you to Kensington Church Street. Turn left down to the junction with Kensington High Street (St Mary Abbots church Ⓗ is on your right). Go across Kensington High Street and turn right towards High Street Kensington Station where the walk ends.

Regent's Canal

Summary: The Regent's Canal runs from Little Venice in west London to the Thames at Limehouse in east London. This long but quite straightforward walk follows the canal along the first and most interesting section, between Little Venice and Islington. The walk passes through Regent's Park and Camden Lock Market *en route* and ends near Camden Passage antiques market. The canal environment is changing rapidly as the old warehouses and factories are converted or demolished to make way for waterside homes and offices. It is still possible, however, to capture something of the atmosphere of the canal as a major commercial highway, and the towpath walk will always provide an uncommon view of London.

Start: **Warwick Avenue Station (Bakerloo Underground line).**
Finish: **Angel Station (Northern Underground line).**
Length: **4¾ miles (7.6 kilometres).**
Time: **2½ hours.**
Refreshments: **The Warwick Castle pub in Warwick Place and the floating café in Little Venice at the start of the walk. A variety of shops, pubs, stalls etc in and around Camden Lock market at the half-way stage and at Islington at the end of the walk.**
Route notes: **Camden Lock Market is open on Saturdays and Sundays. Camden Passage Market in Islington is open on Wednesdays and Saturdays. The canalside walk opens at 7.30 am on weekdays and 9 am on Sundays and public holidays and closes at dusk in winter.**

Take the 'Clifton Villas' exit from Warwick Avenue Station and walk up the right hand side of Warwick Avenue with the church behind you. Turn right into Warwick Place, left into Blomfield Road and then walk onto the bridge ahead. This area is known as Little Venice. The story of Little Venice starts with the Grand Union Canal, which enters the Thames at Brentford in west London. This was built at the end of the 18th century to link the Thames with the new industrial areas in and around Birmingham. Later an extension to Paddington was built to bring the canal closer to London's expanding West End. This is the canal entering the basin under the bridge. It continues in the far right corner to its original terminating basin at Paddington. Then in 1812 work began on another extension to take the canal from Paddington round north London to London's new docks downstream of the City. This new extension was called the Regent's Canal. The basin here at Little Venice was built as the junction between Regent's Canal and the Paddington branch of the Grand Union.

Horse-drawn barges

Return to Blomfield Road. Follow the road to the right along the side of the basin, keeping to the pavement since the towpath walk is blocked off ahead. Cross Warwick Avenue Ⓣ at the traffic lights and carry on alongside the houseboats, whose residents have exclusive use of this part of the towpath. At the end of this tree-lined stretch the canal funnels into the Maida Hill tunnel (272 yards/250 metres long) and the towpath disappears. In the days of horse-drawn barges the horses were released from the towropes and led over the top of the tunnel while the bargemen 'legged' the barges through the tunnel by lying on their backs and 'walking' along the tunnel roof.

When you come to Edgware Road, go over the zebra crossing to the right and

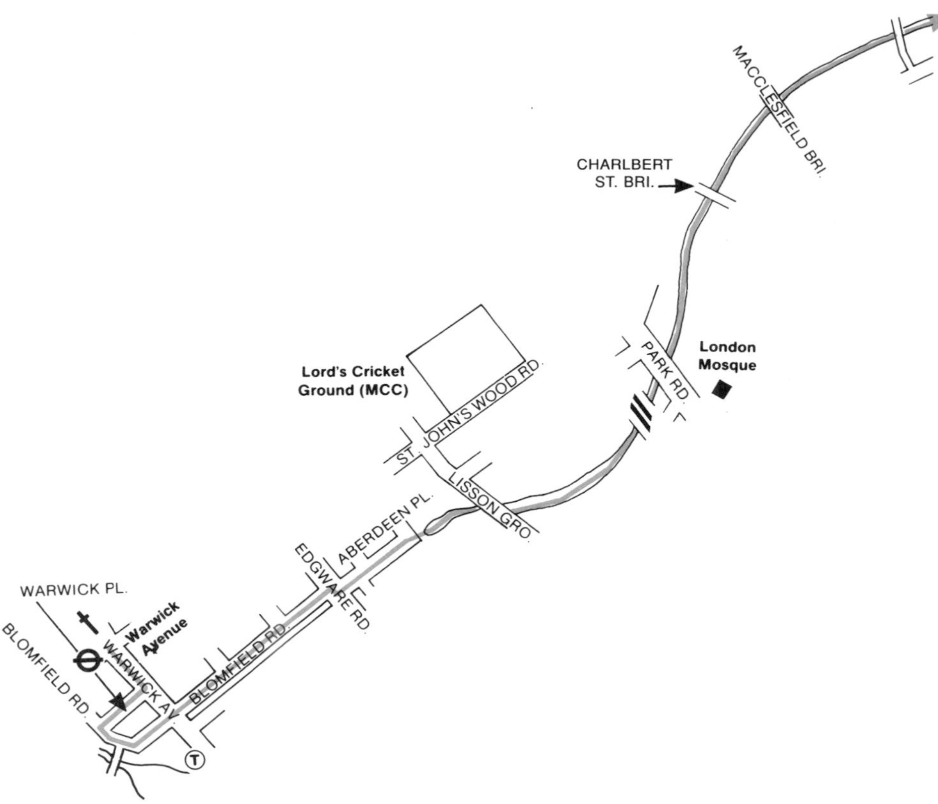

walk up Aberdeen Place. Go through the passage at the end of the road, on the far side of the electricity sub-station. At the end of the passage, descend the steps to the canal where it emerges from the tunnel. The walk now follows the towpath until the tunnel near the end of the walk at Islington.

Beyond the next bridge (Lisson Grove) the canal broadens. On the right bank here, there was once a wharf where boats loaded and unloaded at the freight yards

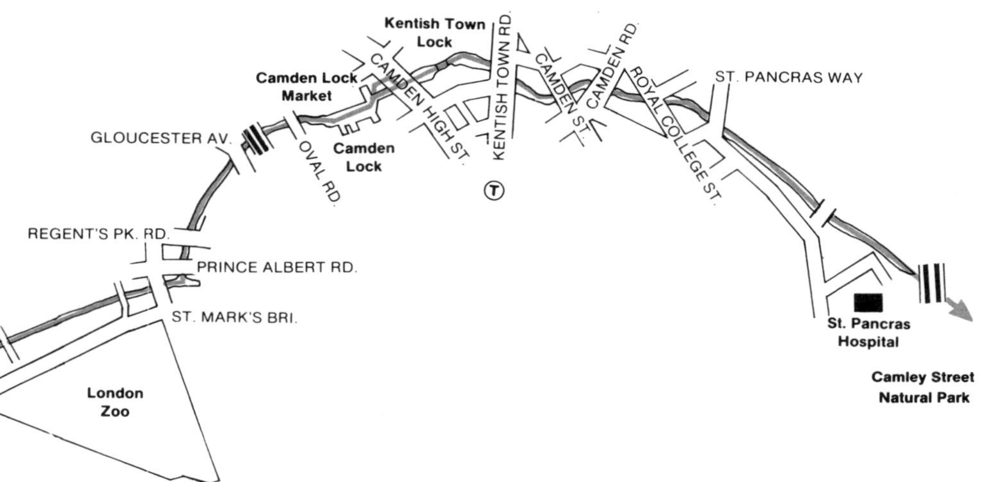

of the Marylebone railway. The canal then runs under the bridge which carries trains into Marylebone Station. The next bridge carries the Metropolitan underground line and a further bridge carries Park Road, which borders the western side of Regent's Park. Lord's cricket ground is just a short distance to the left of the canal at this point.

The canal now swings to the left and enters a cutting as it follows the northern perimeter of Regent's Park. The canal was originally intended to pass through the park, but the route was changed when it was realised that commercial traffic would lower the tone of the exclusive residential development. To the left above the terraced gardens is Grove House, built in 1823 for George Bellas Greenhough, a natural scientist and the first president of the Geological Society. To the right through the trees the dome and minaret of the London Islamic mosque are just visible. Then come three new villas built in historic styles.

Blow-up bridge

The first bridge in Regent's Park carries the River Tyburn, one of London's many hidden rivers, over the canal. The Tyburn eventually flows into the Thames near Vauxhall Bridge. The next bridge, Macclesfield Bridge, is popularly known as Blow-up Bridge after a barge, laden with gunpowder, exploded directly underneath it in October 1874. When the bridge was rebuilt, the iron columns were turned round, which explains why the deep grooves caused by the constant rubbing of taut towropes are on the landward rather than the water side. Similar grooves can be seen in many other places along the canal.

After the next bridge the canal enters London Zoo: to the left is the aviary and to the right are the animal pens (the building in the centre with the raised roof is for the giraffes). Beyond the zoo lies the Cumberland basin, the truncated arm of the canal which once served a large market near Euston Station. Earlier this century the market was closed and after World War II this branch of the canal was filled

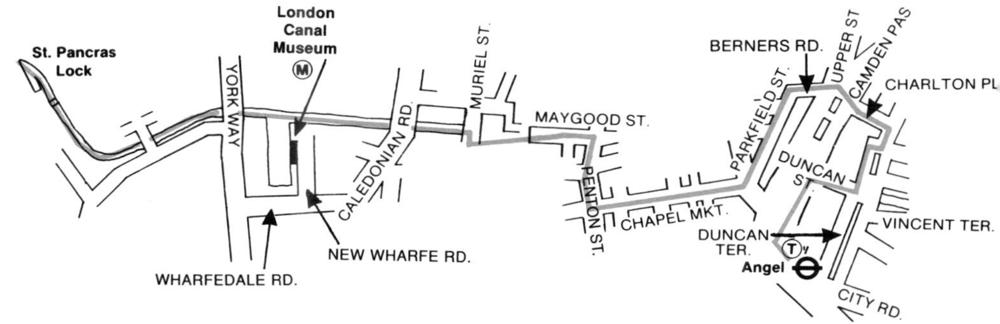

in with rubble from London's bomb sites. (The site of the market is preserved in the street named Cumberland Market - just east of Regent's Park - and the market basin is now covered in allotments.) The canal now turns sharply to the left, another consequence of the decision to change the original route. The next short section demonstrates the charm of the canal when houses and gardens come down to the water's edge. Half-way along this section on the towpath side the bank is cut away and an underwater ramp descends to the bed of the canal. A plaque on the wall explains how this, and similar ramps elsewhere on the canal, were used to rescue barge horses when the noise made by new-fangled steam engines heading in and out of Euston caused them to bolt and fall in the water.

Ahead, the modern bridge built in the style of a medieval castle is known as Pirate Castle. On the right-hand side is a youth club called the Pirate Club and on the lefthand side is a pumping station for the electricity network. Electricity cables have been laid under the towpath to bring power to central London from generating stations on the Thames estuary and pumping stations like this one circulate water round the cables to keep them cool.

An old wharf market

Beyond Pirate Castle and the bridge carrying trains into Euston Station, the towpath climbs over the entrance to a subterranean basin in a former Gilbey's Gin warehouse. The towpath then crosses the canal over an iron bridge, deeply grooved by towropes. Just before the bridge, a doorway in the wall leads into Camden Lock Market, an old wharf converted into an arts and crafts centre and weekend antiques market.

Cross the bridge and go past the old lock-keeper's cottage on the right. This lock is the first of twelve which lower the canal down to the level of the Thames at Limehouse. At that point it is about 90 feet (27 metres) lower than it is now. Go through the gate onto Camden High Street, turn left over the road bridge and then left again down the slope. This will bring you back down to the towpath. Turn left under the road bridge and continue along past Hawley Lock and, on the opposite side of the canal, a former brewery converted into television studios in the 1980s. Beyond the next lock (Kentish Town) and bridge (Kentish Town Road) there are new flats and a supermarket on the right-hand bank.

Stations and freight yards

The canal now flows under three more bridges in quick succession. The first bridge is Camden Street; the second Camden Road; and the third Royal College Street. By looking up at the last bridge you can see that the original narrow brick bridge has been made much wider to carry more traffic. As the canal approaches the next bridge (St Pancras Way) it turns south towards King's Cross and St Pancras railway stations.

After quite a while you come to Camley Street bridge and a bridge carrying railway lines from the Midlands into St Pancras Station. The station concourse is raised about 20 feet (6 metres) above ground level in order to be level with the railway tracks after they have crossed the canal at this point. The basin beyond on the right, now used as a mooring by the St Pancras Cruising Club, once had sidings overhead from which cinders from steam locomotives were tipped into barges waiting underneath. Walking on a little further, you come to St Pancras Lock and then to the Camley Street Natural Park, opened on a former coal depot site in 1985 by Camden Council and the London Wildlife Trust. Behind the park is a clutch of 19th-century gas holders and beyond them, the spire of St Pancras Station.

Now the canal makes a sharp turn to the left, around the stables of one of the old railway companies, and steers its course towards Islington. Here the canal becomes narrower but then, at the petrol station to the right, it becomes even wider than its normal width. Two tunnels run beneath the canal here, bored in 1852 to carry the Great Northern Railway (GNR) into King's Cross. If you climb the bank on the left you will be able to see both King's Cross and St Pancras Stations (the latter's roof single-span only). The Midland Railway also used King's Cross until its own station, St Pancras, was opened in 1868. On the left the 19th century freight yards and warehouses built by the GNR still await redevelopment.

Beyond Maiden Lane Bridge (carrying York Way), Battlebridge basin opens up on the right. Battlebridge was the old name for King's Cross and is popularly believed to have been the site of Queen Boudicca's defeat of the Romans in AD 61. The name is, in fact, a corruption of Broad Ford Bridge. The ford was a crossing on the River Fleet, which flowed by King's Cross Station to the west. Until early this century ice harvested from Scandinavian lakes was landed at Battlebridge and stored in a specially adapted warehouse. The warehouse, on the east side of the basin, now houses the London Canal Museum Ⓗ.

Into Islington

Beyond the bridge carrying the Caledonian Road, the canal enters the 960-yard (878-metre) Islington Tunnel under Pentonville Hill. Walk up the sloping path to the left. At the top of the path go right and left through a gate to the right of an old wall along a path that winds through the Half Moon Crescent Housing Co-operative. This path leads into Maygood Street. At the far end turn right into Barnsbury Road leading into Penton Street. Opposite is the Penny Farthing pub, formerly the White Conduit House (see name above second storey). Here was founded in 1752 the White Conduit Cricket Club. A Yorkshireman called Thomas Lord was the club's groundsman. Lord later opened his own cricket ground, which became the home of the Marylebone Cricket Club (MCC) and the headquarters of the whole game.

Look out for the Salmon and Compasses pub on the left, then go over the zebra crossing into Chapel Market, a Tuesday to Sunday general market. At the end cross into Parkfield Street turning right at the end into Berners Road. This brings you down past the Business Design Centre (the former Royal Agricultural Hall) to Upper Street, the centre of Islington. Go straight over the zebra crossing into Charlton Place, cutting across Camden Passage and the antiques market. On the right-hand side, No. 32 Charlton Place has a plaque to Caroline Chisholm, called the 'emigrant's friend' because of the voluntary help she gave to emigrants to Australia in the 19th century. She lived in the colony for many years, giving practical help to settlers and leading parties of them into the unexplored interior. At the bottom of Charlton Place turn right into Duncan Terrace, a street of handsome Georgian terraced houses separated from Colebrooke Row by a narrow strip of railed garden. The garden marks the course of the New River, described in more detail in the Islington Walk (see page 93). On reaching Duncan Street, look across to the corner of Vincent Terrace; at this point the canal emerges from the Islington Tunnel and is joined once more by the towpath. From here the walk can be extended to the end of the canal at Limehouse basin on the Thames (about the same distance as the first section of the walk: the canal's overall length is 8½ miles (13.5 kilometres). If you walk to Limehouse, public transport details for your homeward journey can be found under the Wapping to Limehouse walk (see page 117).

Now turn right into Duncan Street. At the main road turn left. Angel Station, where the walk ends, is ahead on the left Ⓣ.

Regent's Park

Summary: Regent's Park and its smaller sister Primrose Hill lie immediately north of Marylebone and the West End. The walk begins in Regent's Park Road, climbs up to the viewpoint at the summit of Primrose Hill (206 feet/62.8 metres above sea-level) and then descends to the 400-acre (162-hectare) Regent's Park directly below. Within Regent's Park the walk passes London Zoo, the London Central Mosque, the boating lake, and Queen Mary's Gardens, Open-Air Theatre and café. The last section of the walk is a close-up view of some of the palatial cream-stuccoed terraces that surround the park. The whole scheme was devised around 1820 by the architect John Nash as part of the grandest town-planning scheme ever executed in central London before or since.

***Start:* Chalk Farm Station (Northern Underground line).**
***Finish:* Regent's Park Station (Bakerloo Underground line).**
***Length:* 3½ miles (5.6 kilometres).**
***Time:* 1½ hours.**
***Refreshments:* The restaurant in the centre of Regent's Park at about the half-way stage is a good place to stop for fuel.**

Turn right out of Chalk Farm Station and cross the road (Adelaide Road) into Bridge Approach. Cross the pedestrians-only bridge over the railway lines and go straight on into Regent's Park Road, the local shopping street. On the left beyond the shops, No. 122 has a plaque in memory of Friedrich Engels. A friend and collaborator of Karl Marx, Engels moved here when he was 50 years old and stayed until he was 74, the year before he died.

A bird's eye view

When you get to Primrose Hill Road on the right, go through the gate into Primrose Hill Park Ⓟ and turn immediately right up the hill. The panorama from the summit includes London Zoo, Regent's Park and the West End straight ahead, and the tower blocks of the City on the left. A metal panel at the summit identifies the position of these and other major landmarks in the view.

Retrace your steps a short distance down the hill and take the first path on the right. When it forks, keep to the right and continue, crossing over all other paths until you come to the south-east corner of the park, opposite London Zoo. Cross the main road here (Prince Albert Road) and turn left. When you reach the church (St Mark's Regent's Park) turn right onto the bridge across the Regent's Canal, signposted to London Zoo.

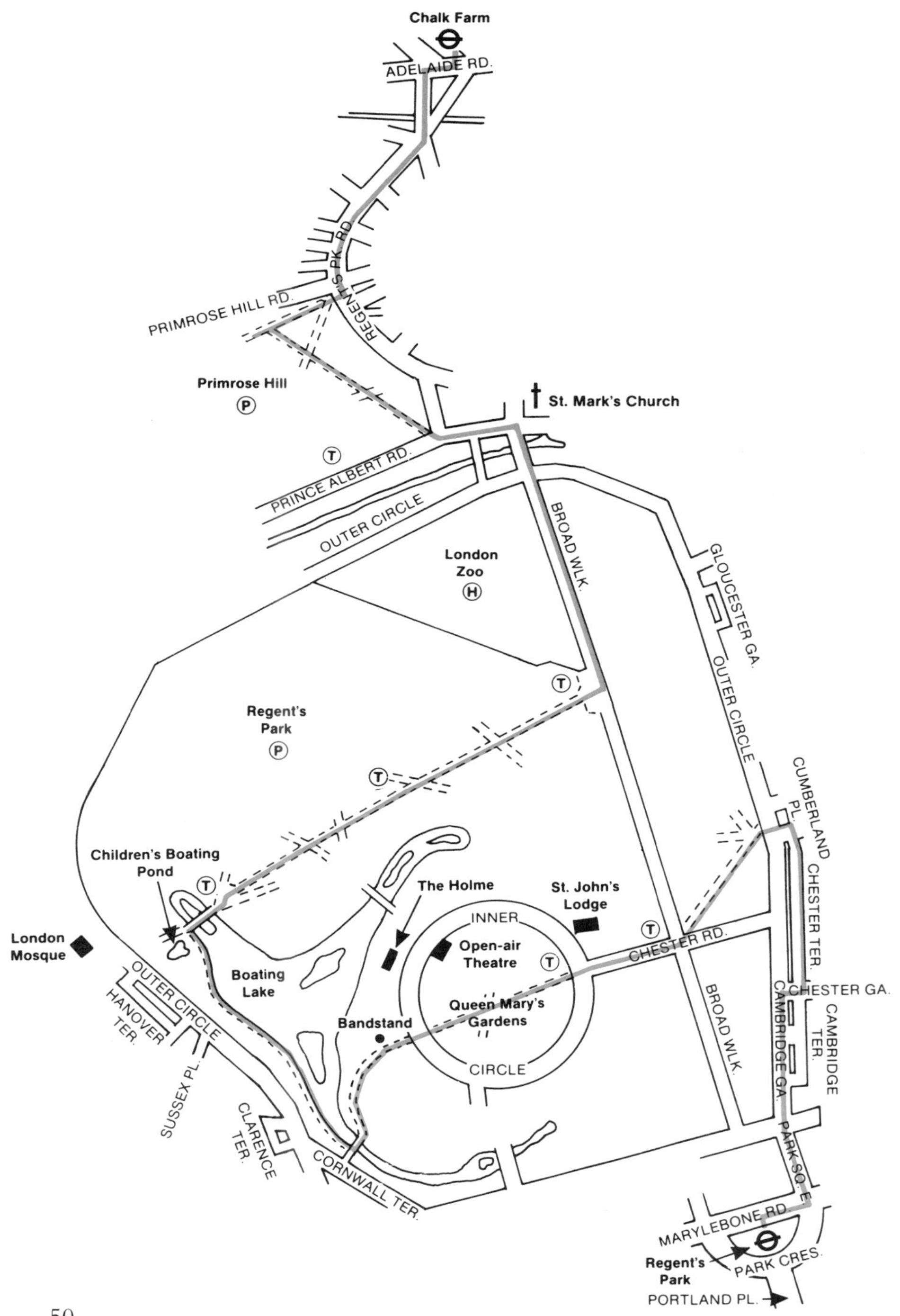

Chalk Farm
ADELAIDE RD.
REGENT'S PK. RD.
PRIMROSE HILL RD.
Primrose Hill
St. Mark's Church
PRINCE ALBERT RD.
OUTER CIRCLE
London Zoo
BROAD WLK.
GLOUCESTER GA.
OUTER CIRCLE
Regent's Park
CUMBERLAND PL.
CHESTER TER.
Children's Boating Pond
The Holme
St. John's Lodge
INNER
London Mosque
Open-air Theatre
CHESTER RD.
Boating Lake
CHESTER GA.
OUTER CIRCLE
HANOVER TER.
Queen Mary's Gardens
Bandstand
BROAD WLK.
CAMBRIDGE GA.
CAMBRIDGE TER.
CIRCLE
SUSSEX PL.
CLARENCE TER.
CORNWALL TER.
PARK SQ. E.
MARYLEBONE RD.
Regent's Park
PARK CRES.
PORTLAND PL.

Go across the bridge and the Outer Circle road into the Broad Walk of Regent's Park Ⓟ and continue past the zoo on your right. Regent's Park and the surrounding palatial terraces were all part of a huge development stretching from this point down to St James's Park by Buckingham Palace. The scheme's sponsor was the Prince Regent, later George IV, who owned much of the land (the park and terraces are still Crown property). Its designer was the Prince's favourite architect, John Nash, one of the handful of architects who have done most to shape the development of London over the centuries.

The essence of Nash's scheme was a park dotted with large detached villas and surrounded by great terraces designed to look like individual mansions but, in fact, incorporating 20 or more separate houses. To the left you can see the beginning of one of these terraces - Gloucester Gate, built in 1827. There were also plans to build similar terraces to your right but the land was assigned instead to the newly-founded Zoological Society for its Zoological Gardens Ⓗ, first opened to the public in 1828.

Some distance ahead you can see a large drinking fountain. Just before the fountain, take the path on the right through the shrubbery Ⓣ, fork left and follow the path round to the right across the middle of the park. Ahead you should be able to see the burnished copper dome of the London Central Mosque. To the left, behind the trees, is St John's Lodge, one of the eight large houses built in the park. Originally Nash planned 56 such mansions – which would of course have ruled out the creation of a public park – but the Crown Estate decided not to build the remaining 48 because it was satisfied with the revenue from the existing villas and terraces. Most of the modern park area was open to public use by 1841.

West-side terraces

When you reach the west side of the park, cross over the bridge Ⓣ and turn left between the children's boating pond and the main boating lake, fed by the River Tyburn. Through the trees to the right you can see the first of the west-side terraces - Hanover Terrace (1822) - with a relief in the pediment picked out in blue and white. Sussex Place (also 1822) is next with its curving ends and pepperpots. On the other side of the boating lake there is a private house called The Holme, another of the eight original villas built in the park. The third terrace is Clarence Terrace, built in 1823 and the smallest of them all. Each terrace in the scheme takes its name from titles held by various members of the royal family during the reign of George IV.

Just before Cornwall Terrace (1821), turn left across the bridge. Turn left again and then follow the path round to the right, going past the bandstand on your left. This was the scene of the IRA bomb attack in 1982 in which seven Royal Greenjackets bandsmen were killed. The building on your right houses a privately-owned American liberal arts college and the European Business School.

When you come to the Inner Circle road (unlike the Outer Circle this is perfectly round) cross over into Queen Mary's Gardens in the middle. Go past the restaurant and then turn left and right around the railings surrounding the sunken garden. To the left across the lawn is the entrance to the Open-Air Theatre. Continue through the gardens towards the wrought-iron gates Ⓣ and go through the gates, across the Inner Circle road again, then into Chester Road.

Half-way along this road, turn left into the Broad Walk again Ⓣ and then take the first path on the right, heading towards the Nash terraces on the east side of the park. Nash did not have time to design all the terraces, but he did personally approve each plan. Continue along the path and go through the gate out of the park. Cross the road (Outer Circle), go into Cumberland Place opposite and turn right into Chester Terrace (1825), its name blazoned across the entrance arch. This terrace is cream-coloured and clean with sharp lines and little ornamentation apart from some fluted pilasters and carved capitals. Near the far end there is a plaque on the former home of Charles Cockerell, architect of the Chilianwallah obelisk (see the Chelsea walk, page 30) and the unfinished National Monument on Edinburgh's Calton Hill. In case you are wondering what the signs with 'CEPC' on them mean, the letters stand for Crown Estate Paving Commissioners, the body responsible for the upkeep of the Regent's Park estate.

Regency entertainment

At the end of Chester Terrace turn right into Chester Gate and then left back onto the Outer Circle road with the park on your right. Cambridge Terrace (1825) is the next terrace on your left; then comes Cambridge Gate. Cambridge Gate was built in 1880 and replaced an unusual feature of the Regency scheme of Nash and George IV - the Colosseum. This was a large domed building with a massive portico, similar to the Pantheon in Rome. Inside was a vast panorama of London painted from drawings made from the top of St Paul's Cathedral. 40,000 square feet (12,192 square metres) in extent, it took years to prepare and cost a huge amount, but it failed to draw the crowds. New attractions were added later, but the Colosseum never made any money and was eventually demolished in 1875. Beyond Cambridge Gate is the modern headquarters of the Royal College of Physicians.

Continue straight ahead into Park Square East. The central section of this terrace was occupied by another kind of entertainment not unlike the Colosseum but more fun. This was the Diorama, its name still visible after 150 years above one of the doors and also at the top of the façade. The 19th-century precursor of the cinema, the Diorama was invented by Frenchman Jacques Daguerre, better known for his later invention of the daguerreotype, the first effective form of photography. In a Diorama the spectators sat in a revolving auditorium while various special effects were used to animate scenes painted on a cotton screen - in this case the interior of Canterbury Cathedral and an alpine valley scene from Switzerland. Like the Colosseum, the Diorama was not a great success and closed down, 25 years after opening, in 1848. The three-storey glass-roofed auditorium still exists in the centre of the building, which is now the headquarters of the Prince of Wales's Princes Trust, an organisation set up to help young people start their own businesses.

Across Marylebone Road, at the bottom of Park Square East, the Nash scheme continues around Park Crescent into Portland Place, and then down to the Mall bordering St James's Park. The walk, however, ends at Regent's Park Station which is to the right on Marylebone Road.

Plate 1: *Chelsea Pensioners parading on Oak Apple Day (see the Chelsea walk, page 28).*

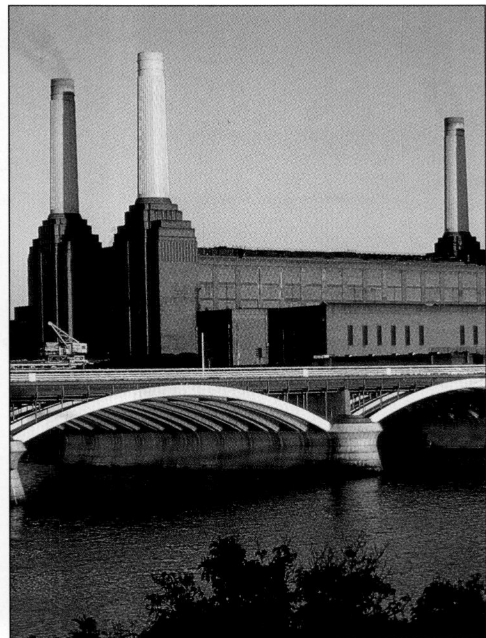

Plate 2: *View to Battersea Power Station (see the Chelsea walk, page 30).*

Plate 3: *Kensington Palace beyond the sunken gardens (see the Bayswater to Belgravia walk, page 33).*

Plate 4: *The Royal Albert Hall* (see *the Bayswater to Belgravia walk, page 34*).

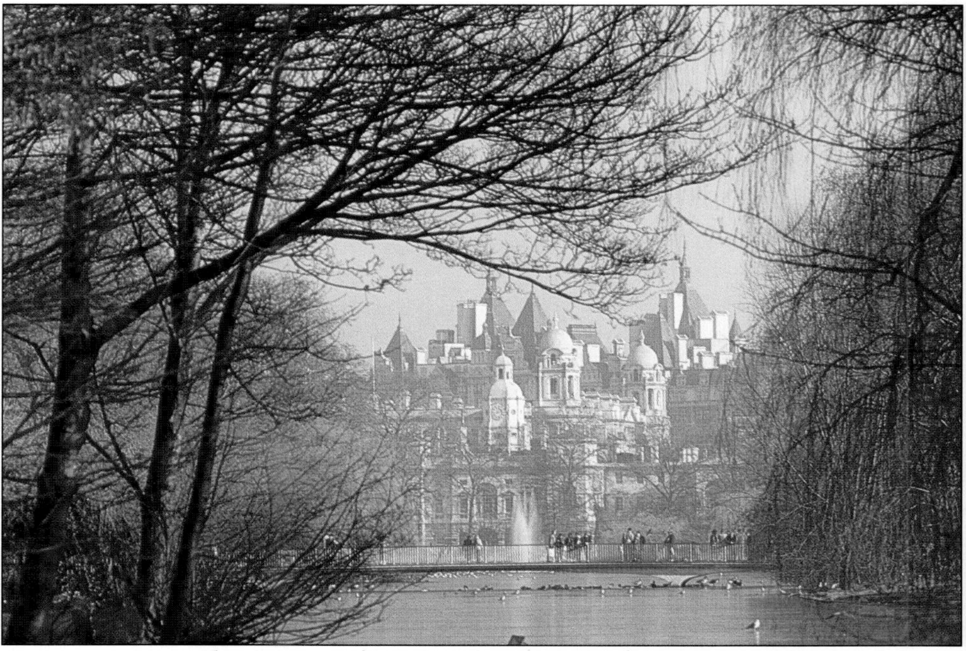

Plate 5: *A view of Horse Guards and Whitehall from St James's Park* (see *the Central Parks walk, page 40*).

Plate 6: *Clarence House, the home of the Queen Mother* (see *the Central Parks walk, page 40*).

Plate 7: *Plane trees and hawthorns in Green Park* (see *the Central Parks walk, page 40*).

Plate 8: *Queen Victoria at Kensington Palace* (see *the Central Parks walk, page 42*).

Marylebone

Summary: Marylebone is just north of Oxford Street in the West End. It was one of the closest villages to central London until two landowners in the area began to lay out the regular grid of impressive streets and squares for which the area is chiefly known today. Many fine houses from that time (the 18th and early 19th centuries) still remain, although most have been converted into offices. Features of the walk include the old High Street and parish church (grave of the hymn-writer Charles Wesley), four squares (including Manchester Square where the Wallace Collection is based), Harley Street, Madame Tussaud's Waxworks, Oxford Street, and the award-winning shopping precinct, St Christopher's Place.

***Start:* Edgware Road Station (Circle, District and Hammersmith & City Underground lines - the Bakerloo Underground line stops at a separate Edgware Road Station close by).**
***Finish:* Baker Street Station (Jubilee, Bakerloo, Metropolitan, Hammersmith & City and Circle Underground lines).**
***Length:* 2½ miles (4 kilometres).**
***Time:* 1½ hours.**
***Refreshments:* Various pubs *en route* plus a wide selection of places in the second half of the walk near Oxford Street and in Marylebone High Street. James Street, just next door to St Christopher's Place, has several pavement restaurants for al-fresco eating.**

Take the main Chapel Street exit out of Edgware Road Station, walking left to the end of the road. Go over Old Marylebone Road and continue into Homer Street, which is named after local landowner Edward Homer not the Greek poet. Turn left along Crawford Street to Wyndham Place. Wyndham Place and St Mary's Church Ⓗ on the left were both part of the development of Bryanston Square on the right and were designed to close the vista north from the country end of Oxford Street, a point now occupied by Marble Arch. Since the development was planned in the 1820s the trees in Bryanston Square have grown to maturity and rather spoilt the effect.

Turn right into Wyndham Place (note the decorative coalhole covers, some of them dated) and go down the right-hand side of Bryanston Square, built on Henry Portman's estate and named after the family seat in Dorset. At the bottom turn left into George Street along the south side of the square, passing on the way the 1862 memorial to William Pitt Byrne, proprietor of the *Morning Post* newspaper (Byrne died at his house in nearby Montagu Street in April 1861). The house in front of

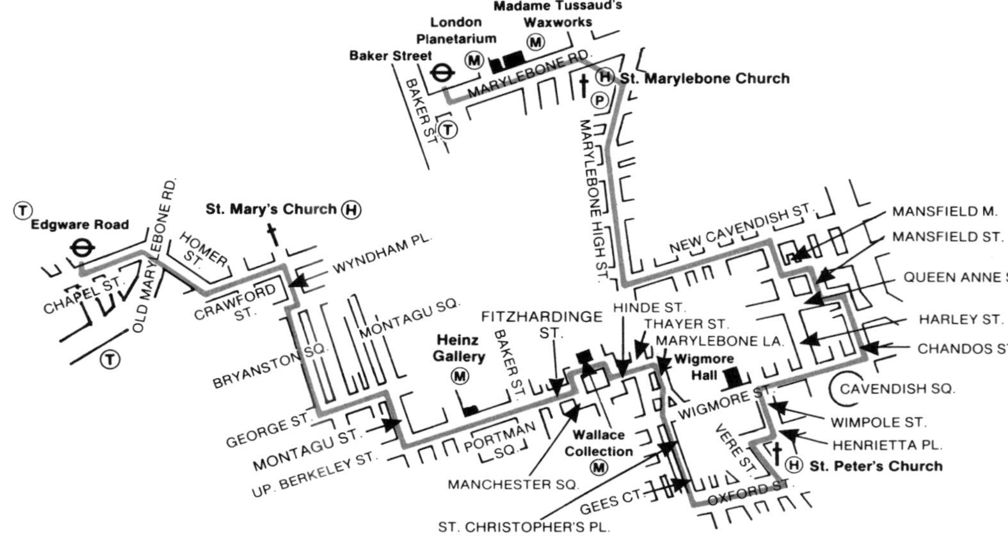

you on the corner of Bryanston Square has a plaque to Mustapha Reschid Pasha (1800-58), the Ottoman Empire's ambassador to Britain in 1836-7 (not 1839 as stated on the plaque).

Blue stockings

When you reach Montagu Square (1811) turn right into Montagu Street and then left into Upper Berkeley Street. The hotel on the left stands on the site of Montagu House, a large mansion destroyed by bombs in World War II. In the 18th century it was the home of Mrs Montagu, one of the cleverest women of her day and hostess of a leading intellectual salon. One regular was a man who wore blue instead of the more normal black stockings, a foible which led observers to label Mrs Montagu and her guests 'bluestockings', hence the colloquial name for an intellecual woman. Walk on into Portman Square, the nucleus of the Portman Estate, completed in 1784. Little remains of its original architecture except for two houses on the corner. No. 21 is the Heinz Gallery of architectural drawings belonging to the Royal Institute of British Architects. No. 20, Home House, was designed in the 1770s by Robert Adam for the Countess of Home and is now a private club.

Continue along the north side of the square, across Baker Street, along Fitzhardinge Street, and into Manchester Square. Completed in 1788, this was the second square to be built on the Portman Estate and is the most attractive in Marylebone. Walk to the left along the north side of the square. This is wholly taken up by Hertford House, home of the Wallace art collection Ⓜ. The collection was assembled by several Marquises of Hertford, the best-known being the third Marquis. Artistically his main interests were Sèvres porcelain and Dutch painting.

Personally he was so unpleasant that the novelist Thackeray used him as a model for the loathsome Lord Steyne in *Vanity Fair*. Sir Richard Wallace, whose wife donated the Wallace Collection to the nation, was the natural son and heir of the fourth Marquis of Hertford.

Slum to shopping mall

Leave Manchester Square opposite Fitzhardinge Street going along Hinde Street. Cross Thayer Street and then turn right into Marylebone Lane, a vestige of the old lane from the West End to Marylebone village. Take the path that branches right at the Button Queen shop (Jason Court) and cross Wigmore Street into St Christopher's Place. This narrow street was a slum for many years, despite the efforts of reformers and local authorities to make improvements. Now, by transforming the street into a fashionable shopping enclave, it seems the property developers have succeeded where social do-gooders failed. At the southern end Ⓣ St Christopher's Place becomes Gees Court and narrows into an archway leading onto Oxford Street.

Turning left into Oxford Street, London's main shopping street, walk past the entrance to Stratford Place to your left. Stratford House at the northern end was built in 1775 for Edward Stratford, second Earl of Aldborough. It is now the Oriental Club. Continue along Oxford Street, crossing Marylebone Lane twice, and turn left into Vere Street. Turn right at St Peter's Church Ⓗ (1724 - see board to left of entrance) into Henrietta Place and then left into Wimpole Street. No. 1 on the right is the Royal Society of Medicine. Take the first turning on the right into Wigmore Street. To the left you can see the entrance to the Wigmore Hall, a well known venue for classical music concerts.

Walk across Harley Street into Cavendish Square, built on land owned by Edward Harley, second Earl of Oxford. Named after the earl's wife, Lady Henrietta Cavendish Holles, Cavendish Square was both the centrepiece of the Portland Estate (which is still owned by descendants of the original owners) and the first stage of the transformation of the rural village of Marylebone into a part of urban London. On the left, beyond the surgeon Sir Jonathan Hutchinson's house, are two survivors from the original Georgian square, much of which has been rebuilt since World War II. The Convent of the Sisters of the Holy Child Jesus used to be based in one of the houses and it was they who in the 1950s commissioned the Jacob Epstein sculpture of the Madonna and Child fixed to the arch over Dean's Mews.

Take the first left turn into Chandos Street. On the left at No. 11 are the original premises of the Medical Society of London, founded in 1773 largely through the efforts of the Quaker physician John Lettsom, a seemingly tireless man who for 19 years never took a holiday and wrote all his letters, lectures and even books while driving around in his carriage visiting patients. Opposite the Medical Society is the back of the Langham, in Victorian times the grandest hotel in London.

Carry on to the end of Chandos Street. The austere, silver-grey house facing you was designed by Robert Adam in 1770 for the Duke of Chandos, whose family owned land here bordering on the Portland Estate. This is actually a side view, for the main front of the house originally faced east across substantial private grounds.

Amongst many original features note the torch snuffers either side of the portico and the rings to stand the torches in.

At Chandos House turn left into Queen Anne Street. Take the first right turn into Mansfield Street (more architecture by the 18th-century Adam brothers), the first left turn into Mansfield Mews and then right into Harley Street, where top medical specialists have their consulting rooms. Almost every door has a collection of brass name-plates. Queen's College to the left is a private girls' school founded in 1848 and the first institution to provide girls with academic qualifications and access to higher education. Straight ahead as you walk up Harley Street is Regent's Park. At the first set of traffic lights turn left into New Cavendish Street. No. 48 on the left is the estate office of the Portland Estate, now called the Howard de Walden Estate because the Howard de Walden family acquired it by a fortunate marriage with the Portlands in 1879.

St Mary-by-the-Bourne

When you get to the end of the road, turn right into Marylebone High Street. This was the main street of the village of Marylebone and still retains a little of its provincial if not rural character. Unlike most of the streets in this part of London, Marylebone High Street is not straight. This is because the High Street and Marylebone Lane developed alongside the winding River Tyburn, long before the property developers arrived with their surveying instruments and grid plans. As well as its form, Marylebone owes its name to the Tyburn. Tyburn was originally spelt Tybourne and St Marylebone was originally St Mary-by-the-Bourne.

The manor house of Marylebone was near the north end of the street, on the right-hand side roughly where Beaumont Street is now. In adjacent fields from 1650 to 1778 were the Marylebone Pleasure Gardens. In 1668 Samuel Pepys described the gardens as 'a pretty place'; a century later Thomas Arne, composer of *Rule Britannia*, was resident conductor of the gardens' orchestra. Opposite the manor house stood the old parish church. Only the graveyard remains, now used as a public garden Ⓟ. Near the pavement is the grave of Charles Wesley, Methodist hymn-writer and brother of John Wesley, the founder of Methodism. A little further on beyond the local school, turn left across the open space towards the new parish church Ⓗ, built in 1817 as part of the Regent's Park development scheme. A notice in the garden has more of its history.

When you reach Marylebone Road in front of the church, turn left and cross the road at the traffic lights. Continue walking to the left and you will come to Madame Tussaud's Waxworks Ⓜ on your right. Marie Tussaud transported her wax figures from France to England in 1802 and exhibited them around the country until 1835 when she settled in nearby Baker Street. Some 30 years after her death in 1850 – by which time her show was already an institution – the figures were installed in this building. The Planetarium Ⓜ with its astrological displays was opened next door in 1958. Beyond the Planetarium is Baker Street Station Ⓣ where the walk ends.

Mayfair

Summary: Mayfair is an exclusive shopping, residential and business district in the heart of the West End. It was developed in the 18th century, mainly by the fabulously wealthy Grosvenor family, which still owns a substantial amount of property in the area. Almost every shop is a household name and nearly every house has had at least one famous occupant. This circular walk passes all of the well-known shops, such as Fortnum and Mason and Tiffany, as well as the homes of people like Beau Brummell and Clive of India. The walk includes Berkeley Square and Grosvenor Square, the Burlington Arcade and Royal Arcade, Bond Street and Savile Row, the Royal Academy and Royal Institution, and last but not least Shepherd Market, Mayfair's own red light district.

Start and finish: **Piccadilly Circus Station (Piccadilly and Bakerloo Underground lines).**
Length: **3 miles (4.8 kilometres).**
Time: **2 hours.**
Refreshments: **Shepherd Market about a third of the way along the route is undoubtedly the best place to stop because of its wide choice of venues (several with seats outside) and its friendly atmosphere. Avery Row, about two-thirds of the way, has several good sandwich bars and is similarly welcoming. Otherwise try a picnic at the half-way stage in delightful Mount Street Gardens.**
Route note: **The Burlington and Royal Arcades are both closed on Sundays.**

Leave Piccadilly Station Ⓣ by the 'Piccadilly (South Side)' exit and walk along Piccadilly away from the Circus. To your left you will soon see St James's Church Ⓗ, designed by Sir Christopher Wren in 1676 as the parish church for the new district of St James's being developed by the Jermyn family, earls of St Albans. The visionary artist and poet William Blake was baptized here in 1757. From Tuesday to Saturday the church forecourt is taken over by a small market selling antiques on Tuesday and clothes, jewellery, prints and souvenirs on the other days. Further along, you come to Hatchard's bookshop and then two other stores, including Fortnum and Mason, the high-class grocers. These shops all bear coats of arms, indicating that they are all official suppliers to various members of the Royal Family. Fortnum and Mason's connections with royalty go back to 1707 when William Fortnum became a footman in the royal household. John Hatchard founded his bookshop in Piccadilly in 1797 with less than £5 capital.

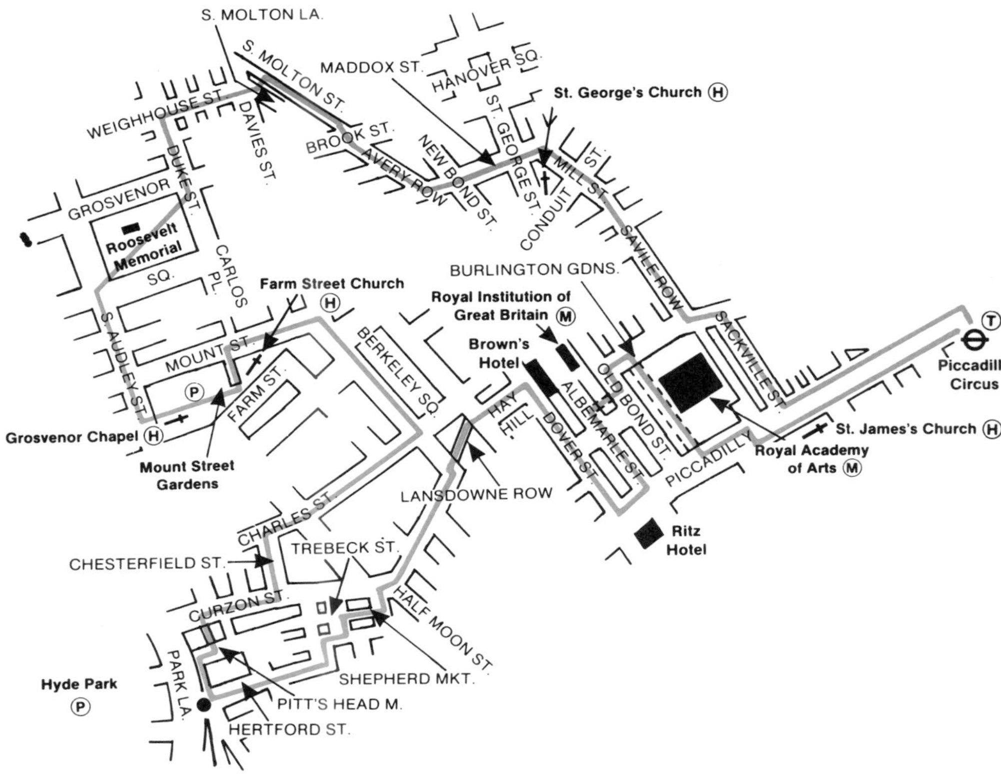

Piccadilly arcades

Opposite Hatchard's, in its own little courtyard, is the Albany, a unique set of bachelors' apartments created in 1802 by architect Henry Holland out of the town house of one of George III's sons, the 'grand old Duke of York' of the nursery rhyme. The apartments are owned by a trust and then let to tenants. Byron was one of the first people to live there; recent occupants include Edward Heath, Prime Minister in the 1970s, and actor Terence Stamp.

Continue along Piccadilly past the entrance to Prince's Arcade. When you get to Duke Street St James's on your left, turn right across Piccadilly and then turn left past the entrance to Burlington House, former town house of the Earls of Burlington and home of the Royal Academy of Arts Ⓜ, founded 1768, since 1868. Five learned societies occupy purpose-built premises around the perimeter of the courtyard. The statue in the middle is of Sir Joshua Reynolds, the first president of the Academy.

Beyond the Academy turn right into Burlington Arcade (1819), second oldest of London's five 19th-century shopping arcades (the oldest is the Royal Opera Arcade: see the Soho to Trafalgar Square walk, page 75). Turn left out of the arcade into

Burlington Gardens. At the end of the road on the left, a plaque records that the corner building was once Atkinson's, a famous perfumier. The carillon is a peal of handbells housed in the black wooden steeple high above. Opposite on the other side of Old Bond Street are two famous jewellers: Tiffany and Cartier. This part of London is the most expensive shopping area in the capital as well as the centre of the fine art trade. Turn left into Old Bond Street and then, a little further on, cross the road into the Royal Arcade. A product of the Victorian age, it lacks the Regency elegance of the Burlington Arcade and, to make matters worse, is painted in a horrible mixture of brown and orange. Standing at the exit of the arcade in Albemarle Street, to your right is the Royal Institution Ⓜ where Michael Faraday carried out his experiments with electricity. Opposite is Brown's Hotel, founded in 1837 by ex-manservant James Brown. Now turn left. No. 50 Albemarle Street, the second from the end on the right-hand side, has been the office of John Murray, the publishers, since 1812. Byron and Jane Austen were two of the firm's earliest authors. Unlike many publishers, the firm has remained independent and is still run by the Murray family. From the end of Albemarle Street there is a good view of the Tudor gatehouse of St James's Palace.

Turn right into Piccadilly and right again opposite the Ritz Hotel into Dover Street. No. 40 on the left is the Arts Club. Founded in 1863, Dickens was an early member. Further on the town house at No. 37 was built in 1772 for the Bishop of Ely (hence the bishop's mitre in the middle roundel above the first-floor windows) and has one of the finest classical façades of any house in Mayfair.

The May Fairs

From Dover Street turn left into Hay Hill, cross the street at the bottom and go through Lansdowne Row into Curzon Street. After Half Moon Street turn left through the arch at No. 47 into Shepherd Market. Edward Shepherd started a twice-weekly cattle market here on the banks of the Tyburn river in 1688. The two-week May fair, from which Mayfair takes its name, began a few years later but was banned in the 18th-century after objections from local residents. By then the market had become a haunt of prostitutes and if you look closely at the doorbells you will see that 'French models' are still plying their time-honoured trade in the area today.

At the Grapes pub turn right and walk as far as Trebeck Street. To the right you can see Crewe House, formerly the town house of Lord Crewe and now the Saudi Arabian embassy. Opposite is Tiddy Dols eating house, named after an 18th-century gingerbread maker who was a well-known figure at the May fairs. As the sign-board on the restaurant's front points out, artist William Hogarth included him in one of his pictures, an enlarged version of which can be seen in a shop window to your left in Trebeck Street.

Go past this shop and then right and left into Hertford Street. On the left at No. 10 lived General Burgoyne, the British general who lost the battle of Saratoga during the American War of Independence. The general was followed by Richard Brinsley Sheridan, the author of two evergreen comedies of the stage, *The Rivals* and *The School for Scandal*. Further along on the left at No. 20 lived Sir George Cayley,

Yorkshire squire and little-known pioneer of aviation. In 1804 he built and flew the world's first flying machine.

Hertford Street ends in a small roundabout with Park Lane on the opposite side and Hyde Park Ⓟ beyond. Turn right here across the forecourt of the Hilton Hotel, right again into Pitt's Head Mews and then immediately left up the steps into Curzon Place. Turn right into Curzon Street. Benjamin Disraeli lived and died at No. 19 on the right. No. 30, also on the right-hand side, houses Crockford's, the famous gambling club founded in St James's Street in 1828.

Mayfair squares

At the Curzon cinema turn left into Chesterfield Street, a virtually intact Georgian street, except for the reconstructed No. 6 on the right, former home of the novelist Somerset Maugham. Two centuries ago the narrow white house next door was the home of Beau Brummell, the famous dandy and style-king of the Regency period. So great was Brummell's influence that he is reputed to have once made the Prince Regent cry by telling him he did not like the cut of his coat. Unfortunately Brummell's finances were not as sure as his taste and he died abroad a fugitive from his creditors.

Turn right into handsome Charles Street, leading down to Berkeley Square. This is the most attractive of Mayfair's three squares, with its 200-year-old plane trees and a fine terrace of Georgian houses along the left-hand (west) side. Walk up this terrace passing No. 45, once the home of Lord Clive, the clerk-turned-soldier whose brilliant generalship established Britain as the dominant power in India in the 18th-century.

At the top of the square turn left into Mount Street. As you do so, you pass from the old Berkeley Estate into the Grosvenor Estate. Walk down to Carlos Place and turn left again into Mount Street Gardens Ⓟ, the former burial ground of St Mary's Hanover Square, seen later on the walk. On the left, the Church of the Immaculate Conception is the headquarters of the English Jesuits. It's popularly known as 'Farm Street' because the main entrance is the other side in Farm Street. Walk straight through the gardens and out by the gates on the opposite side. The church on the left is the Grosvenor Chapel Ⓗ, built in 1730 to serve the developing Grosvenor Estate. Turn right into South Audley Street, passing the famous gunmakers Purdey's on the other side of the road.

At the top of South Audley Street is Grosvenor Square, the centrepiece of the Grosvenor Estate and the third largest square in London (the largest is Ladbroke Square in Notting Hill: see the Notting Hill walk, page 20). Only one of the original Georgian houses has survived, so that the modern square is somewhat featureless and impersonal. The whole of its western side is taken up by the monolithic American Embassy. Cut across the square diagonally to the right. In the centre there is a statue of the American president, Franklin D Roosevelt, and a memorial to the American and British pilots of the RAF's World War II Eagle Squadrons. In the top right corner go across the road to the left into Duke Street and then turn right into Weighhouse Street, by the Ukrainian Catholic Cathedral. Built in 1892, this was originally the King's Weigh House Chapel, and replaced the original Weigh House

Chapel which occupied rooms above the medieval king's weigh house in Eastcheap in the City. Weighhouse Street will bring you to Davies Street and the former toiletware factory of J Bolding, now converted into Gray's Antique Market.

Stylish shopping

Turn right into South Molton Lane, take the immediate left turn into South Molton Passage and then turn right again into pedestrianized South Molton Street. The coat of arms on the front of some of the shops indicates that you are now on land owned (since the 1620s) by the Corporation of London. At the end of South Molton Street cross Brook Street to Colefax and Fowler, leaders in country house interior design. Their shop was once the home of the Regency architect Sir Jeffry Wyatville whose main achievement was turning Windsor Castle into the palace we know today.

Descend narrow Avery Row by the side of Colefax and Fowler. At the end of the Row, which is built over the Tyburn river, turn left and go across New Bond Street into Maddox Street - looking out for Sotheby's to the right on the opposite side of New Bond Street. St George's Church Ⓗ looms up at the end of Maddox Street. This has been one of London's most fashionable churches ever since it was built as part of the Hanover Square development in the 1720s. Hanover Square, the third of Mayfair's three squares, is to the left at the top of St. George Street. The figure at the entrance to the square is of William Pitt, Prime Minister in 1783 at the tender age of 24.

Tailors and painters

Continue along Maddox Street across St George Street and turn to the right around the back of the church into Mill Street. Cross Conduit Street into Savile Row, a street famous for its men's tailors. On the left you pass a monumental building aptly named Fortress House, the headquarters of English Heritage - the organization which manages all the publicly-owned historic buildings and monuments in the country. Further on, some of the 18th-century houses retain their original exterior fixtures. No. 17 with its flagpole, first-floor balcony supported by cast-iron pillars, entrance lanterns, torch snuffers and studded front door, is a fine example. Nineteenth-century architect George Basevi lived here.

At the end of Savile Row you look straight into the rear entrance of the Albany flanked by two small lodges. To the left is the tailor Gieves and Hawkes, uniform maker and another royal supplier. Turn left beside Gieves and Hawkes into Vigo Street and then turn right into Sackville Street. There is a good view here of the former galleries of the Royal Institute of Painters in Water Colours on Piccadilly. The name of the institute is written on the façade above the busts of eight famous water-colour artists of the 18th and 19th centuries (Sandby, Girtin, Cozens, Turner, Cox, De Wint, Barret and Hunt). Founded in 1831, the institute still exists, but it now shares a building with other art societies in Carlton House Terrace.

When you reach Piccadilly, turn left and walk towards Piccadilly Circus and the statue of Eros, a somewhat inappropriate tribute to the 19th-century philanthropist Lord Shaftesbury (of Shaftesbury Avenue fame). The walk ends at Piccadilly Station Ⓣ beneath the statue.

Westminster and St James's

Summary: A circular walk around royal Westminster and aristocratic St James's via Whitehall (a street of government offices), St James's Park/Square/Street/Palace, Buckingham Palace (the Queen's London residence), Westminster Abbey and School and the Houses of Parliament. Other features include Downing Street (No. 10 is the Prime Minister's official residence), Horse Guards Parade (including the Horse Guards and Foot Guards themselves), the gentlemen's clubs of St James's, then Green Park and finally, some of the picturesque streets in the vicinity of Westminster Abbey.

***Start and finish:* Westminster Station (District, Circle and Jubilee Underground lines).**
***Length:* 3 miles (4.8 kilometres).**
***Time:* 2 hours.**
***Refreshments:* Fill up when and where you can because - surprisingly for such a central district - places to stop are relatively scarce and there is nowhere worthy of special recommendation.**

Leave Westminster Station and turn right into Bridge Street with Big Ben and the Houses of Parliament on your left. Pause for a moment at the traffic lights, as you stand at the political heart of the nation. There are statues of six prime ministers around the perimeter of Parliament Square, including, nearest to the Houses of Parliament, a bronze figure of the wartime leader Winston Churchill. On the left-hand side of the square the old parish church of Westminster (St Margaret's Ⓗ) is dwarfed by Westminster Abbey behind. Straight ahead across the square is the former Middlesex Guildhall, now law courts.

Old Whitehall Palace

Now turn right into Parliament Street Ⓣ leading directly into Whitehall further along. Government offices line both sides of this wide road, nearly all the way to Trafalgar Square. First on the left is the Treasury, separated from the Foreign Office by King Charles Street. In the middle of the road stands the Cenotaph, the national memorial to Britain's war dead. Leading off to the right is Richmond Terrace where Henry Stanley, the man who found Livingstone in Africa, lived before it was claimed by the Civil Service. On the right beyond this terrace is the great grey bulk of the Ministry of Defence. The statues on the front lawn are of Second World War military commanders (Montgomery, Alanbrooke and Slim) and Sir Walter Raleigh,

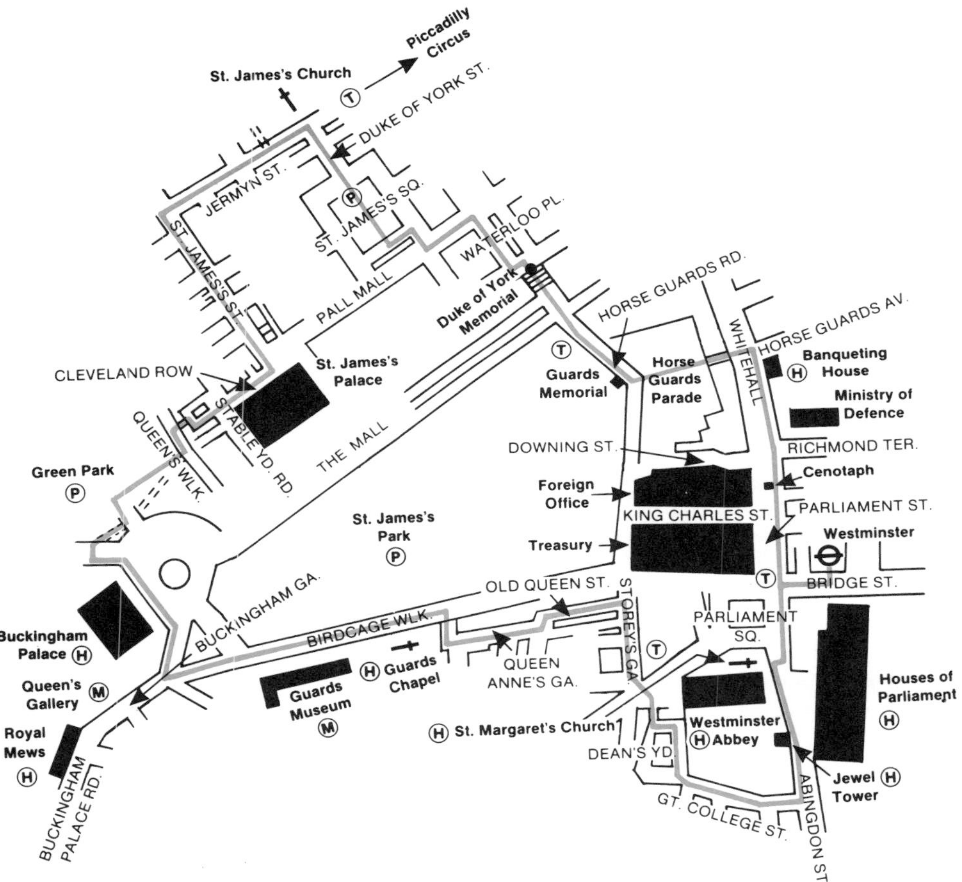

beheaded in 1618 after an abortive expedition in search of the fabled El Dorado.

On the left-hand side of the street again, you will see the gated entrance to Downing Street. No. 10 has been the official residence of the Prime Minister since Sir Robert Walpole, the first Prime Minister, lived here in 1732. The Chancellor of the Exchequer lives next door at No. 11. Government ministers attend cabinet meetings most Thursday mornings in Downing Street: the civil servants who service these meetings work in the Cabinet Office on the corner of Downing Street. The Privy Council, a body of specially-appointed public figures which advises the Crown on matters where it still has some political authority, has the office next to the Cabinet Office. Beyond the Privy Council is the domed entrance to the Scottish Office.

Going back onto the right-hand side of the street, beyond the Ministry of Defence is the Welsh Office. Then comes the magnificent 17th-century Banqueting House Ⓗ, the only surviving building above ground of Whitehall Palace (the old palace wine cellar still exists *beneath* the Ministry of Defence). This 2,000-room royal palace occupied the whole of this area until it was destroyed by fire in 1698. On a cold morning in January 1649 King Charles I was beheaded here after stepping through a window of the Banqueting House onto a specially constructed scaffold. There is a bust of the king and a plaque above the Banqueting House entrance.

Military milieu

Cross Horse Guards Avenue beyond the Banqueting House and then cross Whitehall at the traffic lights to reach Horse Guards Ⓗ. The mounted guards on duty here come from the Household Cavalry, descendants of the original mounted guards for whom the Horse Guards building was constructed in the 1750s. There are notices on the inner wall of the courtyard which will tell you more about the Life Guards and how the guard is mounted. What they do not tell you is that each horse and rider stands guard for one hour only at a time and not the whole day.

Go through the archway into Horse Guards Parade, the former tiltyard or jousting field of Whitehall Palace. Every year in June the square is used for the Trooping the Colour ceremony when two thousand red-coated foot guards together with cavalry and military bands parade their regimental flags during the Queen's birthday parade. To the left you can see the garden of 10 Downing Street. Cross Horse Guards Road at the end of the parade-ground and go into St James's Park Ⓟ, passing on your left the war memorial of the Household Division (the Household Cavalry and the Guards infantry combined). Turn right along the tarmac path Ⓣ. On the right the ivy-covered Citadel was built as a bomb-proof communications centre for the navy in World War II and is still used by the Defence Ministry today.

When you reach the Mall cross over at the traffic lights, admiring the view to the left of Buckingham Palace and to the right of Admiralty Arch. Walk up the steps to the Duke of York's column. The Duke was the second son of George III and commander-in-chief of the British Army at the time of the Battle of Waterloo (1815).

Waterloo Place at the top of the steps contains many statues, including on the left, Sir John Franklin, lost while trying to find the north-west passage round Alaska, and on the right, Captain Scott, the first Englishman to reach the South Pole.

Clubs of Pall Mall

Walk down the left-hand side of Waterloo Place, past the mounting block installed for the Duke of Wellington, the British commander at Waterloo. Cross Pall Mall, which runs centrally through Waterloo Place, and turn left. Named after a game - similar to croquet - imported from France and popularized after 1660 by Charles II, Pall Mall is pre-eminently a street of gentlemen's social clubs. On the left you pass the Athenaeum, Travellers and Reform Clubs, all founded in the 19th century. Take the first right turn opposite the Italian palazzo-style Reform Club into St James's Square. Turn left along the south side of the square and then right by the pavilion into the gardens (open Monday to Friday 10-4.30; skirt round the outside if closed). The square was developed soon after the restoration of the monarchy in 1660 and rapidly became the smartest address in London: around 1720 it was home to no fewer than six dukes and seven earls. By 1796, however, the Wedgwood china company had taken over one of the houses as a showroom and since then business has completed its conquest.

Walk straight through the gardens past the statue of King William III - to your right there is a good view of London's oldest theatre, the Haymarket, built in 1820 - and go up Duke of York Street towards St James's Church at the top. At the church, turn left into Jermyn Street, famous for its shirt shops and men's outfitters. Isaac Newton, discoverer of the law of gravity, lived opposite the entrance to Prince's Arcade on the right.

Continue on to St James's Street and turn left towards Henry VIII's St James's Palace at the foot of the hill. On the left, the balconied house next to the chemist's is Boodle's Club and opposite, the large house with the blue door is Brooks's Club. Both clubs have been operating for well over two hundred years and have seen countless country estates lost and won at their gambling tables. Further down on the left you pass the battered shop front of Berry Brothers and Rudd, wine merchants who have been in business, originally as grocers, since the 1600s. American readers may like to know that Pickering Place, through the archway on the left, was the base of the independent Texan Republic's legation until Texas joined the Union in 1845.

When you come to St James's Palace turn right along Cleveland Row. St James's has not been used as a royal palace since the early 1800s although foreign ambassadors are still officially accredited to the Court of St James's. Some of the Palace's contemporary functions are to provide offices for part of the Royal Household and a London base for the Prince of Wales. Continue past the entrance to Stable Yard on the left and go through the passage to the right of the small car park into Queen's Walk. Here turn left and then almost immediately right into Green Park Ⓟ, opposite Milkmaid's Passage on your left. Take the left-most of the three tarmac paths and then at the crossroads turn left towards Buckingham Palace Ⓗ, the Queen's London home. If the flag is flying, she is in residence.

Home of the monarch

To the left beyond the palace you can see the red and white campanile of the Roman Catholic Westminster Cathedral. Go to the right of the huge wrought-iron gates and cross Constitution Hill at the traffic lights to the palace, the sovereign's main London home since 1837, when Queen Victoria took up residence. Walk along the front of the palace to Buckingham Gate. The entrances to the Queen's Gallery Ⓜ and the Royal Mews Ⓗ are further along the road on the right-hand side. Cross the road and turn left along Birdcage Walk, so called because there was a royal aviary here in the 17th century. On your left is St James's Park Ⓟ and on your right are the Wellington Barracks, used by the various Guards regiments detailed to protect the royal palaces. There are a total of seven regiments of Guards: five infantry (Irish, Scots, Welsh, Coldstream and Grenadier), and two cavalry (Life Guards and Blues and Royals). The two cavalry regiments wear different coloured uniforms; the uniformly red-coated foot guards are identified by different arrangements of tunic buttons. At the far end of the barracks are the modern Guards chapel Ⓗ and the Guards museum Ⓜ. Rising up behind is the modern Home Office building in Queen Anne's Gate.

Walk on past the chapel. When you reach the traffic lights go right into Queen Anne's Gate, architecturally one of London's finest streets. Fittingly, the National Trust, Britain's leading heritage organization, has its headquarters here (on the right as you turn left to walk down the street). Queen Anne's Gate was built in the early 18th century when Queen Anne was on the throne. There is a statue of the queen on the right where the street narrows. Nearly every house seems to have a plaque on it commemorating some worthy politician or other. Carry on to the end of the street and then turn left into Old Queen Street, also built during the 18th century. On the left you pass Cockpit Steps, site of the 17th century royal cockfighting arena.

At the end of Old Queen Street turn right into Storey's Gate, named after Charles II's gamekeeper in St James's Park. On your left now is the new Queen Elizabeth II Conference Centre Ⓣ. Cross over the road to the forecourt of Westminster Abbey Ⓗ, the national church and scene of the coronation of almost every English monarch since William the Conqueror in 1066. Continue on through the archway into Dean's Yard. This was the main abbey courtyard when Westminster was still a monastery: turning left, you will see a gateway ahead leading into the abbey's cloisters and its 900-year-old garden.

Richard the Lionheart

Turn right along the east side of the quadrangle. On the left you pass the old abbey guesthouse, now the office of the cathedral chapter, and the entrance to Little Dean's Yard and Westminster School, once the abbey school and now a leading public school. Go through the archway at the end of Dean's Yard and turn left into Great College Street with the medieval abbey wall on your left. Near the end of the street, turn left along the path through Abingdon Gardens, laid out over an underground car park.

On the right is a bronze sculpture by Henry Moore, *Knife Edge Two Piece* (1962), dwarfed by the massive Victoria Tower of the Houses of Parliament. At the opposite end of the gardens on the left is the Jewel Tower Ⓗ, part of the medieval Palace of Westminster destroyed by fire in 1834 and replaced by the present Houses of Parliament Ⓗ. Opposite the Jewel Tower, the statue of King Richard the Lionheart brandishing his sword stands in Old Palace Yard, outside the House of Lords. Further along - spared by the fire - is the original medieval hall of the Palace of Westminster, its pitched roof, flying buttresses and plain exterior distinguishing it clearly from the ornate 19th-century Parliament building. Interestingly, the style of the new Parliament building mirrors the 15th-century east end of Westminster Abbey opposite. The statue in front of Westminster Hall is of Oliver Cromwell, leader of the Parliamentarians in their fight against King Charles I in the 1640s.

Beyond Westminster Hall, New Palace Yard is the main entrance to the House of Commons for MPs. Cross Bridge Street at the traffic lights on the corner and turn right towards Westminster Station and the end of the walk.

Bloomsbury

Summary: A circular walk around a once-fashionable residential district laid out between the late 17th and early 19th centuries, mainly by the Dukes of Bedford. During the early 1900s the district gave its name to the Bloomsbury Group of artists and writers, several of whom lived in the area. The main features of the walk are London University and the British Museum, six squares including Bloomsbury Square, Queen Square and Bedford Square (the finest surviving Georgian square in London), the Dickens House Museum, The Great Ormond Street Hospital for Sick Children and the Coram Foundation (including the art collection). Bibliophiles will find several second-hand bookshops near the end of the walk around Museum Street.

Start and finish: **Tottenham Court Road Station (Central and Northern Underground lines).**
Length: **2½ miles (4 kilometres).**
Time: **1½ hours.**
Refreshments: **Apart from the open-air café in Russell Square, the first two-thirds of this walk are largely barren of sustenance. In the final third, however, there are plenty of places, first in Lamb's Conduit Street, then in and around Cosmo Place off Queen Square and finally in Pied Bull Yard near the British Museum (wine bar and coffee bar, both with seats outside).**
Route note: **Pied Bull Yard is closed on Sundays but directions for a short diversion are given in the text.**

Take exit 3 from Tottenham Court Road Station, go straight past the Dominion Theatre and turn right into Great Russell Street by the modern YMCA building. Turn left into Adeline Place which brings you into Bedford Square, completed in 1780 as the showpiece of the Bedford Estate and today the finest complete Georgian square in London. Continue along the left-hand side of the square past No. 35 which bears plaques relating to two 19th-century doctors: Thomas Wakley, who in 1823 founded the *Lancet*, today Britain's leading medical journal, and Thomas Hodgkin, who was one of the founders of the Aborigines' Protection Society in 1838 and did a lot of good work on behalf of persecuted Jews and the London poor. All Bedford Square's houses have been converted into offices, many of which – in keeping with the district's literary traditions – were occupied by publishers until the 1980s.

Turn right along the top of the square and go straight on across Gower Street into Montague Place. Further along on the left is Senate House (1932), the main building of London University. Opposite Senate House, on the right, is the rear

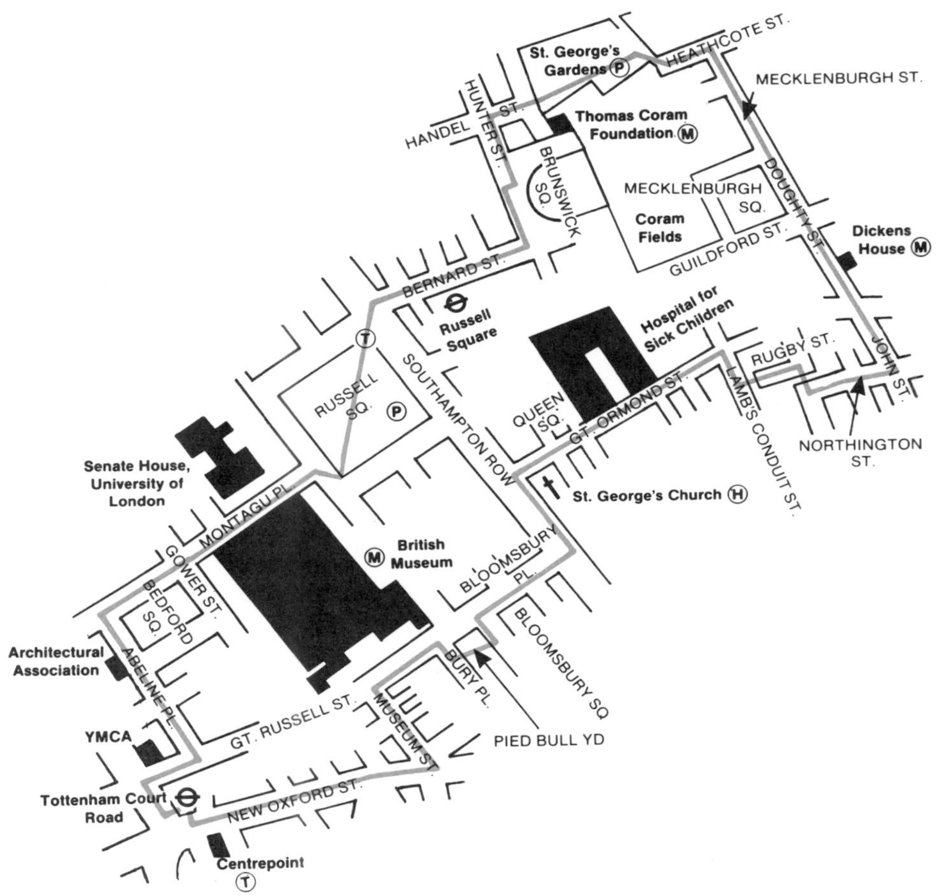

entrance of the British Museum Ⓜ. This great museum was opened in 1759 but the building you see here (the Edward VII galleries) dates from the early 1900s.

At the end of Montague Place, cross into Russell Square gardens Ⓟ using the entrance to the right. Laid out in 1800 and named after the Russells, Dukes of Bedford, there is a statue of the fifth Duke (died 1805) on the right. Follow the main path diagonally across the middle of the garden, past the café, to the opposite corner Ⓣ. Then cross the main road into Bernard Street. Walk past Russell Square Station on the right and the Brunswick Centre (a development of shops and flats built in 1972) on the left and turn left into Brunswick Square. Virginia Woolf, Leonard Woolf, Duncan Grant and John Maynard Keynes - all members of the so-called Bloomsbury Group, an association of writers, artists and intellectuals - shared a house here in the 1900s. Since then the square has been completely redeveloped.

Handel's orphan concerts

Carry on past the entrance to the Renoir cinema. If you look right down the north side of Brunswick Square you can see at the far end a statue of Captain Thomas Coram, an eighteenth-century sea-captain turned philanthropist. To the left of the statue is the Coram Foundation, the descendant of the orphans' home (known as the Foundling Hospital) which Thomas Coram founded in 1742. The old hospital building, which stood behind the statue, was demolished in the 1920s. The modern foundation continues the hospital's work, but sponsors fostering rather than looking after orphans itself. The foundation's famous art collection Ⓜ – composed of pictures donated to the Hospital by 18th-century painters like Hogarth, Reynolds and Gainsborough – is usually open to the public.

Walk on to Hunter Street and take the first right turn into Handel Street, so named because Handel gave performances of his *Messiah* in the Foundling Hospital chapel to raise money for the orphans. At the end of Handel Street go into St George's Gardens Ⓟ. This public garden was once the burial ground of St George's Church, seen later in the walk. Follow the main path through the garden, bearing right about two-thirds of the way along. Anna Gibson, Oliver Cromwell's granddaughter, lies in the tomb on the right with the pyramid-shaped top. Go through the gate at the right-hand corner of the garden, then turn left and right into Mecklenburgh Street, leading into Mecklenburgh Square. Both this square - named after George III's wife, Princess Charlotte of Mecklenburgh-Strelitz - and the original Brunswick Square were built in the 18th century on the Foundling Hospital estate, with the hospital building in the middle.

Dickens of Doughty Street

Walk straight on along the left-hand side of Mecklenburgh Square into Doughty Street, built around 1800. Go across Guildford Street. Clergyman and famous wit Sydney Smith (1771-1845) lived at No. 14 on the right. 'I never read a book before reviewing it; it prejudices one so' was one of his cracks. On the left, No. 48 Doughty Street is the Dickens House museum Ⓜ. Charles Dickens lived here from 1837 for three years and completed his first three novels here (*Pickwick Papers*, *Oliver Twist* and *Nicholas Nickleby*).

Continue up the slope into John Street and turn right into Northington Street. At the end of the street, turn right and left into Rugby Street, built around 1680 on land owned by Rugby School in Warwickshire. On the left a plaque on No. 13 records the location of the White Conduit, part of the medieval water supply of Greyfriars monastery, which was near St Paul's in the City.

At the end of Rugby Street turn right into Lamb's Conduit Street. After Greyfriars monastery was shut down in the mid 16th-century, the conduit fell into disrepair. However in 1577 it was rebuilt by William Lamb, a chorister in the Chapel Royal. The site of his conduit is marked by a stone plaque at the entrance to Long Yard near the far end of the street. Right at the end of the street there is still a drinking fountain. At this point you can also see the original main entrance to the old Foundling Hospital, now a children's playground known as Coram's Fields.

Half way down Lamb's Conduit Street turn left into Great Ormond Street, completed in 1720. On the left, No. 23 has a plaque to John Howard, an 18th-century High Sheriff of Bedfordshire who spent a lifetime visiting prisons in Britain and on the continent in a pioneering attempt to improve prisoners' conditions. Apparently, the only prison Howard was unable to enter was the Bastille in Paris, though, as he said in one of his books, he 'knocked hard at the outer gate'. Howard's work is still carried on today by the Howard League for Penal Reform.

The right-hand side of Great Ormond Street is mostly taken up by the famous Hospital for Sick Children. Dr Charles West and other doctors founded it in 1852 after research had revealed that there were no hospital places for children in London, even though over 20,000 London children aged ten or under were dying each year.

Walk along Great Ormond Street into Queen Square, built early in the 18th century during the reign of Queen Anne. Various medical institutions are based in this square, including on the left the private Italian Hospital. This was started in 1884 in a private house as a hospital for poor Italians. London's Italian community was at that time concentrated in nearby Holborn.

The church of the 'climbing boys'

Cross the square and go into Cosmo Place. On one side is the Queen's Larder pub apparently named after a cellar where Queen Charlotte stored delicacies for her deranged husband, George III, while he was being treated by his doctor in Queen Square. On the other side is St George's Church Ⓗ, built in 1706 and once known as the sweeps'church due to a parishioner's benefaction providing Christmas dinners for one hundred chimney sweeps' apprentices. Called climbing boys, these children were sent up chimneys to dislodge soot and clean flues until the practice was outlawed in 1875.

From Cosmo Place turn left onto Southampton Row and then first right into Bloomsbury Place, leading to Bloomsbury Square, originally built in the 1660s. Sir Hans Sloane, the physician who features in the Chelsea walk (see page 28), lived at No. 4 for almost 50 years. Under the terms of his will in 1753 his enormous collections of books, manuscripts and natural history items were sold to the government for a modest sum. They subsequently formed the basic stock of the new British Museum.

Carry on along the top side of Bloomsbury Square (passing the statue of Whig politician Charles James Fox, who died in 1806) and then turn left down the far side next to No. 17, the former headquarters of the Pharmaceutical Society (note the words carved high up on the façade). Just beyond No. 15, turn right into Pied Bull Yard where you will find a café, wine bar and some interesting specialist shops. Go straight through the gate in the far right corner and turn right and then left into Great Russell Street (if the Yard is closed, carry straight on from Bloomsbury Square into Great Russell Street). The imposing main entrance of the British Museum is now on your right.

Opposite the main gates to the museum, turn left into Museum Street and at the end of the street turn right into New Oxford Street. Walk towards the Centrepoint tower block (1967) Ⓣ and Tottenham Court Road Station, where the walk ends.

Soho to Trafalgar Square

Summary: Soho's image as London's red-light district is fading but sex is still a major enterprise in the area. The other industries are films, music, eating and drinking - all of which reflect the cosmopolitan mix of people (mainly French Huguenots) who have lived in Soho since the first houses were built in the 1670s. The main features of the walk in Soho are its two squares (Soho and Golden), Berwick Street Market, Broadwick Street (a landmark in medical history), the birthplace of the poet William Blake and the Sixties' hangover, Carnaby Street. During the walk, you will also see Pollock's Toy Museum, Chinatown, John Nash's Haymarket Theatre and Royal Opera Arcade, the National Gallery and Nelson's Column, as well as the smallest police station in the country.

Start: **Goodge Street Station (Northern Underground line).**
Finish: **Charing Cross Station (Northern, Bakerloo and Jubilee Underground lines).**
Length: **2½ miles (4 kilometres).**
Time: **1½ -2 hours.**
Refreshments: **Plenty of places *en route*, particularly at the half-way stage around Soho and Chinatown. These are *par excellence* places for eating and drinking, so take your pick. There are several pavement restaurants in Charlotte Street just before you enter Soho proper.**
Route note: **The Royal Opera Arcade is closed on Sundays, in which case carry on past the entrance, turn left into Regent Street and then turn left at the bottom of the street into Pall Mall.**

Turn left out of Goodge Street Station and then left again opposite Heal's into Tottenham Street. The five-storey mural on the right, commissioned by the local council and painted in 1980, depicts characters and scenes from the local Fitzrovia community, named after Fitzroy Square to the right, near Euston Road. Rising up behind the mural is the BT telecommunications tower.

Take the first turning on the left into Whitfield Street. On the right now are Pollock's Theatrical Print Warehouse and, next to it in a crazy old house on the corner of Scala Street, Pollock's Toy Museum Ⓜ. Benjamin Pollock, who died in 1937, was one of the last producers of toy theatre scenery. The museum was added in the 1950s as an attraction to the shop and is worth seeing both for its contents and for its original 1760s' interior.

Walk along Whitfield Street past Cyberia, Britain's first internet café, and cross Goodge Street. Turn right by the garden into Colville Place and then left into

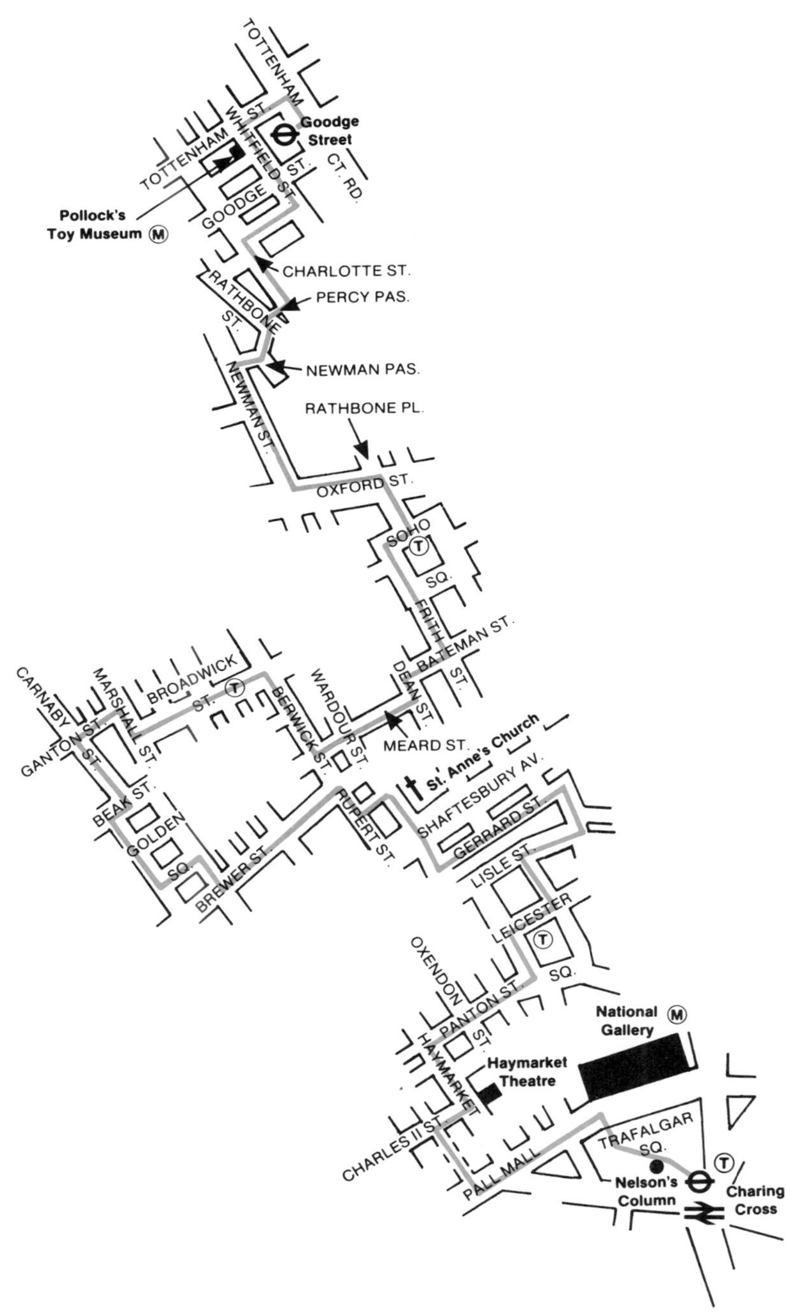
TOTTENHAM
Goodge Street
TOTTENHAM
WHITFIELD ST.
ST.
CT. RD.
Pollock's Toy Museum
GOODGE
CHARLOTTE ST.
PERCY PAS.
RATHBONE ST.
NEWMAN PAS.
NEWMAN ST.
RATHBONE PL.
OXFORD ST.
SOHO SQ.
FRITH
BATEMAN ST.
CARNABY
MARSHALL ST.
BROADWICK ST.
BERWICK ST.
WARDOUR ST.
DEAN ST.
GANTON ST.
MEARD ST.
St. Anne's Church
SHAFTESBURY AV.
BEAK ST.
GOLDEN SQ.
BREWER ST.
RUPERT ST.
GERRARD ST.
LISLE ST.
LEICESTER SQ.
OXENDON
PANTON ST.
National Gallery
HAYMARKET
Haymarket Theatre
CHARLES II ST.
PALL MALL
TRAFALGAR SQ.
Nelson's Column
Charing Cross

Charlotte Street, which is lined with restaurants and wine bars, much like Soho. Just beyond Windmill Street on the left, turn right into Percy Passage, cross Rathbone Street and enter Newman Passage next to the Newman Arms pub.

The sights of Soho

At the end of Newman Passage turn left into Newman Street, centre of the textile and fashion industries, and walk down to the junction with Oxford Street. Turn left here. When you get to Rathbone Place on the left (notice the street sign dated 1718) turn right into Soho Street and then right again into Soho Square Ⓣ. This is one of two squares in Soho and was built in the 1680s in open fields on the northern boundary of London. The area was once a royal hunting ground and 'Soho' was an old hunting cry. The first residents of the square were aristocrats like the Earl of Carlisle. Soon, however, Huguenot refugees from France invaded the area, the first of a series of foreign influxes which have made Soho the colourful and cosmopolitan quarter it is today.

The French Protestant Church on your right has been the centre of Huguenot life since the first refugees arrived in London in the 1550s, although the congregation did not physically come to the square until 1893. Walk around the square crossing Carlisle Street. On the right in the corner ahead there is a stone in the wall marking the site of a house where a group of early botanists once lived, and where the Linnean Society (a botanical society founded in 1788 and still active today) met from 1821 to 1857. Twentieth-Century Fox now has offices on this site.

Continue around the square and turn right into Frith Street, the first of the two streets leading out of the south side of the square. The other is Greek Street, named after the Greek Christians who settled in Soho in the 17th century. On the left Hazlitt's Hotel is the house where writer William Hazlitt died in 1830.

When you get to Bateman Street, at the end of Frith Street, look to the left at Portland House, the white house facing you. Wedgwood, makers of the famous blue china, had their London showroom here from 1774 until 1795, when they moved to more up-market premises in St James's Square. Now turn right into Bateman Street, left into Dean Street and then right again into Meard Street, built in the 1720s though its original street sign is dated 1732.

Votes for kisses

Go across Wardour Street, the centre of the film and music business, into Peter Street. The Intrepid Fox pub on the corner bears a large relief of a scene from the fiercely contested Westminster election of 1784, with the charismatic Charles James Fox (son of a lord and champion of the people) as the candidate, and honest Sam House, the pub's landlord, as his enthusiastic supporter. Fox only won the election after enlisting the help of the beautiful Duchess of Devonshire and other great ladies who gave kisses to all the tradesmen in return for their votes. Turn first right out of Peter Street into Berwick Street.

Berwick Street Market (Monday to Saturday) is reputed to have the best-quality fruit and vegetables of any street market in London. Turn left at the end of the market into Broadwick Street Ⓣ. Formerly called Broad Street, this was the centre of an outbreak of cholera in 1854 which killed over ten thousand people, including the occupants of 37 out of the 49 houses in this street. Many more people would have died had not the local medical officer, Dr John Snow, realized that all victims of the disease had been drinking from the same street pump. When the pump handle was removed the death rate promptly fell. Snow's discovery - that cholera is water-borne - is one of the most important in medical history. A replica of the pump stands at the junction with Poland Street and a reddish kerbstone outside the John Snow pub ahead marks the pump's actual site.

Blake's birthplace

Opposite the pub No. 54 has a plaque to Charles Bridgman, gardener to the first two King Georges and inventor of the ha-ha, a type of sunken fence. Continue along Broadwick Street and at Marshall Street turn right. A large sign on the right marks the place of birth in 1757 of the poet and visionary artist, William Blake. Turn first left into Ganton Street and go past the entrance to cobbled Newburgh Street. Then turn left into Carnaby Street, still home to the boutiques that made it the centre of Swinging London in the '60s.

From Carnaby Street, turn right into Beak Street and first left into Upper John Street. This leads into Golden Square, its name a corruption of 'gelding'; geldings were once grazed in fields on this site. Walk along the right-hand side of the square, which was popular with embassies in the 18th century. The Portuguese embassy was at Nos. 23 and 24 on the right during the 1740s and the embassy chapel (accessed from Warwick Street) is still a Roman Catholic church.

Follow the square around to the left (the statue in the middle is of George II) and then turn right into Lower James Street. Turn left into Brewer Street, walking along until you come to Rupert Street Market. Turn right here and then take the second turning on the left into Winnett Street. From here, turn right into Wardour Street, passing on the left St Anne's, the parish church of Soho, only the tower of which escaped bombing in World War II. Over ten thousand corpses in the disused graveyard have raised it as much as 6 feet (2 metres) above the pavement.

Oriental history

At the bottom of Wardour Street cross Shaftesbury Avenue, leaving Soho and entering London's Chinatown. Take the second turning on the left into Chinatown's main street, Gerrard Street, with its Chinese entrance arches, street names in Chinese characters and oriental-style telephone booths.

Leave Gerrard Street, turning right into Newport Place and then right again into Lisle Street. When you reach the Chinese supermarket on the right, look up to the pediment above. 'New Lisle Street' and the 1791 date refer to the extension of existing Lisle Street in that year, made possible by the demolition of Leicester House, one of London's largest houses. As you turn left into Leicester Place, leading to Leicester Square, you are actually walking through the marble-floored hall of the house, out of the front door, and across the gravelled forecourt into what was then called Leicester Fields. During the 1700s George, Prince of Wales, lived in Leicester House having been evicted from St James's Palace after a quarrel with his father.

Hay and straw market

Turn right into Leicester Square Ⓣ. For a century this has been a major centre of popular entertainment, first music halls and now clubs and cinemas. Turn left down the west side: Sir Joshua Reynolds, England's leading portrait painter in the 18th century, lived at No. 48. Leave the square from the bottom right-hand corner. Walk along Panton Street, crossing Whitcomb Street and Oxendon Street, and then turn left down Haymarket. Until 1830 Haymarket was, quite literally, the site of a hay and straw market supplying nearby stables and the Royal Mews. Towards the bottom on the left is the Haymarket Theatre, with its grand portico jutting out over the pavement. Designed by John Nash in 1820, this is the oldest theatre in London.

Opposite the theatre, turn right into Charles II Street. Half-way along cross over and go through the archway at the back of Her Majesty's Theatre into the Royal Opera Arcade. Built 1816-18 by Nash along the back of what was then the main opera house in London, this is the oldest of London's five 19th-century shopping arcades. Around the other three sides of the theatre were colonnades open to the street. A fire in 1867 seriously damaged the theatre and in 1891 it was demolished, with only Nash's arcade, which had survived the fire, being retained. By this time Covent Garden had established itself as London's new royal opera house (see the Covent Garden walk, page 79).

Turn left out of the arcade onto Pall Mall. Opposite is the Nash-designed Institute of Directors, a businessmen's association, with a fine frieze beautifully set off by its blue background. Walk along Pall Mall towards the domed National Gallery Ⓜ, built in 1838 on the site of the old Royal Mews. St Martin's-in-the-Fields Church is beyond. Cross the road at the traffic lights beside the new Sainsbury wing of the National Gallery and go into Trafalgar Square, also dating from 1838. Admiral Nelson, victor of the Battle of Trafalgar in 1805, gazes towards Big Ben and the central spire of the Houses of Parliament from the top of his 145-foot (44 metre) granite column, erected in 1842. In front, isolated on a tiny traffic island, King Charles I on horseback also faces down Whitehall, but he is looking straight at the Banqueting House where, in 1649, he was beheaded. To the right, Admiralty Arch marks the beginning of the Mall leading to Buckingham Palace. Both the Arch and the Mall are part of the national memorial to Queen Victoria, who died in 1901. To your left, the Strand connects with Charing Cross Road at the point from which all road distances to and from central London are measured. On the Trafalgar Square side of the junction you can see a small round building with a lamp on top. This is Britain's smallest police station, with its own telephone line to Scotland Yard. Nearby is a subway leading to Charing Cross Station Ⓣ where the walk ends.

Covent Garden

Summary: North of the Strand, between the West End and the City, Covent Garden is a fashionable, vibrant and youthful quarter centred on a converted 1830s fruit and vegetable market. This circular walk includes the central market piazza (cafés, wine bars, interesting shops and street performers), Neal Street and Neal's Yard, Seven Dials, the Drury Lane Theatre and the Royal Opera House and various places associated with the Bow Street Runners and writers such as Dickens, Johnson, Boswell and Thomas de Quincey. There is also a section to the south of the Strand featuring relics of former riverside mansions (York House Watergate, Savoy Chapel), the Savoy Hotel, the Adelphi, and houses connected with Pepys, Kipling and Peter the Great of Russia.

***Start and Finish:* Leicester Square Station (Piccadilly and Northern Underground lines).**
***Length:* 2 miles (3.2 kilometres).**
***Time:* 2 hours.**
***Refreshments:* All kinds of places *en route*, but Covent Garden itself, conveniently situated half-way through the walk, will probably be the choice for most walkers, especially for visitors to London. Neal's Yard a little further on is well-known for its organic and vegetarian foods.**

Take the 'Charing Cross Road (South)' exit from Leicester Square Station and turn left along Charing Cross Road past Wyndham's Theatre. Take the second turning on the left into Cecil Court, a pedestrian precinct lined with secondhand shops specializing in books, prints, maps, stamps and posters. When you get to St Martin's Lane, cross over and turn right. Ahead on the left, the white building with the globe on top is the Coliseum Theatre, housing the English National Opera. After passing the theatre, cross William IV Street at the traffic lights. To your right is the memorial to Edith Cavell, a British nurse executed during World War I for helping allied soldiers stranded after the German occupation of Belgium. Just before St Martins-in-the-Fields Church Ⓗ, designed by James Gibbs in 1724, turn left, with the railings and market on your right.

Beyond the market turn right into Adelaide Street Ⓣ and then cross Duncannon Street and the Strand to reach the forecourt of Charing Cross Station Ⓣ. In the centre stands a 19th century replica of the medieval Charing Cross, one of twelve erected by Edward I to mark the stopping places of his wife's funeral cortège as it journeyed from Lincoln to Westminster Abbey in 1290. The original cross stood in Trafalgar Square near Nelson's column, a point still officially called Charing Cross.

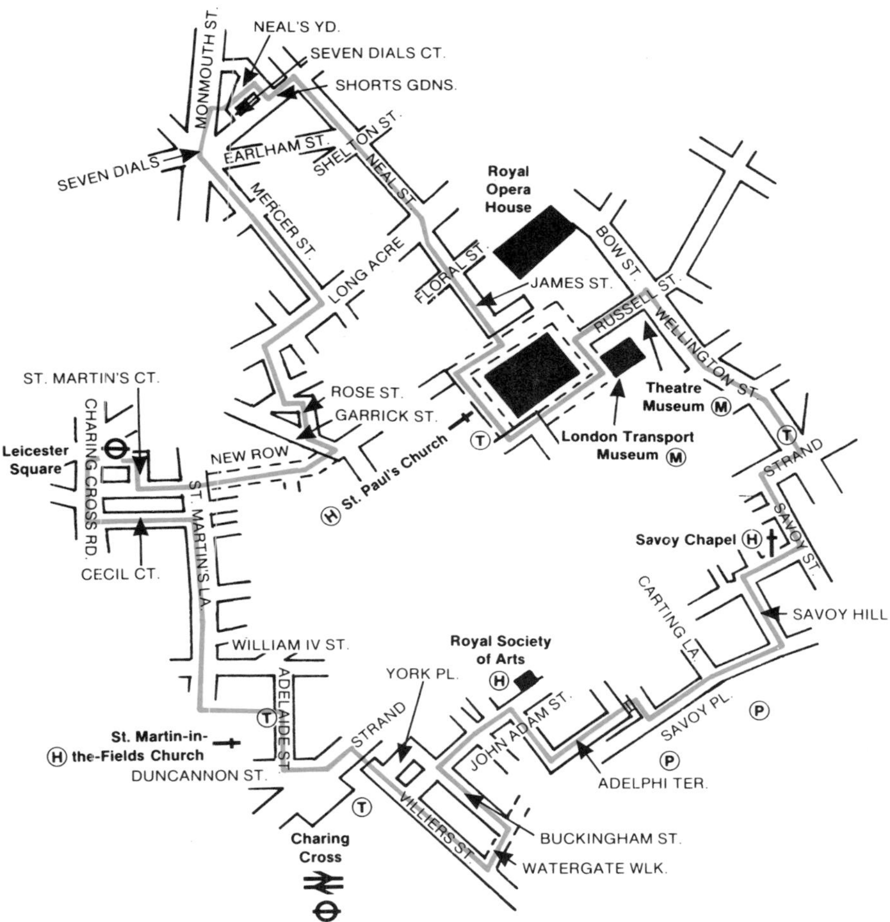

Riverside relics

In front of the station turn left and then right into Villiers Street, leading down the hill towards the river. Look out on the left for York Place, formerly Of Alley. In the 1600s there was a large mansion here called York House, the town house of the Villiers family, Dukes of Buckingham. When the second Duke sold it for redevelopment in the 1670s he insisted that every part of his name and title be used in the naming of the new streets, including the 'of' in Duke of Buckingham. Hence Of Alley.

The arches underneath Charing Cross station house the Players' Theatre, where the traditions of the Victorian music hall are maintained with full audience participation and dining during performances. On the left, the last house before Embankment Gardens (No. 43) is where the 24-year-old Rudyard Kipling lived on his return from India after seven years working as a journalist. It was here that he wrote his first novel, *The Light that Failed* (1890). Soon after this he married and left for America.

Turn left here through the gate and go down the steps into Watergate Walk, which takes its name from the former York House gateway on the right. When the Thames was London's main highway all the big riverside houses along the Strand had their own river gates or stairs. This gateway, built in 1626, is the only one to survive. Until 1870, when the embankment was built, it stood right on the riverside. The Latin inscription along the top (*Fidei Coticula Crux* - the touchstone of faith is the cross) was the motto of the Villiers family.

Russian connections

Ascend the steps to the left into Buckingham Street. Samuel Pepys lived in this street for over 20 years, arriving in 1679 at the age of 46, when he was the senior civil servant in the Admiralty. He lived first at No. 12 (the third house on the left) and then at No. 14 (the first house on the left). He still had a house here in 1698 when Peter the Great of Russia arrived on his famous study tour of England and Holland. The Czar stayed on the right at No. 15.

At the top of the street turn right into John Adam Street. On the left, Durham House (built on the site of the original Durham House, the London house of the Bishops of Durham) has a plaque to the caricaturist Thomas Rowlandson, whose comic pictures of English life around 1800 are still widely known today. Beyond, the fine house with the flagpole and columns (No. 8) is the Royal Society of Arts Ⓗ, founded in 1754 as the Society for the Encouragement of Arts, Manufactures and Commerce. The Society organized the country's first art exhibition in 1760 and first photography exhibition in 1852. Its home was purpose-built in 1774 by the Adam brothers as part of their Adelphi residential development ('adelphi' is Greek for brothers). The Adelphi consisted of 24 terraced houses built high above the river over huge vaults. Most of the houses were demolished before World War II, although the dark-brick house with cream stucco work which you can see at the far end of John Adam Street is original, and the vaults (not accessible from this point) still exist. The Adelphi office block of 1938 now covers most of the site.

Life of luxury

Just before the RSA, turn right into Robert Street. Famous former residents of this street include Robert Adam, and the writers Thomas Hood, John Galsworthy and J M Barrie. Turn left along Adelphi Terrace, looking out over Victoria Embankment Gardens. Go down the steps at the end of the terrace into Savoy Place and turn left through the colonnade underneath Shell-Mex House. Cross Carting Lane. Now you pass the rear entrance to the Savoy Hotel. Richard D'Oyly Carte started the hotel over a century ago, intending it to be the last word in luxury. The showers in the bathrooms had 12-inch (30 centimetre) shower heads and the huge baths could be filled in 12 seconds from 1½-inch (4-centimetre) water pipes. César Ritz of Ritz Hotel fame was its first manager and the legendary Auguste Escoffier its first chef. On the right, the small garden Ⓟ with seats, flower basin and sundial was given to

London in 1989 by the hotel to mark its centenary. Beyond in the main garden Ⓟ there is a bust of the composer, Sir Arthur Sullivan - of the Gilbert and Sullivan duo. D'Oyly Carte, a theatrical impresario by profession, discovered Gilbert and Sullivan and had already built the Savoy Theatre for the sole purpose of staging their work before he began work on the adjacent hotel.

Take the first turning on the left into Savoy Hill, following the road round to the right to the Savoy Chapel Ⓗ, relic of the medieval Savoy Palace. The residence in the 13th century of Count Peter of Savoy, uncle of Henry III's queen, the palace was later used as a prison and hospital before being demolished in 1820 to make way for the new Waterloo Bridge. The old chapel is owned by the Queen as part of the Duchy of Lancaster estate and is also known as the Queen's Chapel of the Savoy. As such it serves as the official Chapel of the Royal Victorian Order.

Walk past the chapel, turn left into Savoy Street and at the top of the street turn right onto the Strand. Go across the Strand at the traffic lights. Turn right and then left into Wellington Street (Ⓣ men only) passing on the left the famous Lyceum Theatre founded by actor Sir Henry Irving. At the junction with Tavistock Street, the building on the right is where Charles Dickens edited his magazine *All The Year Round* for 11 years until his death in 1870. Round the corner at No. 36 Tavistock Street, Thomas de Quincey wrote *Confessions of an English Opium Eater* (1821) in a lonely little back room.

Continue walking along Wellington Street to the junction with Russell Street. To the right you can see the Theatre Royal, Drury Lane, with its long colonnade on Russell Street. Drury Lane is one of England's oldest and most famous theatres: the actress Nell Gwyn, better known as Charles II's mistress, made her debut in a previous building on this site in 1665. David Garrick, the 18th century's most distinguished actor, first appeared at this theatre in 1742. He was also manager here, as was Richard Brinsley Sheridan - author of *The School for Scandal* - after him. Ahead in Bow Street, a continuation of Wellington Street, is the Royal Opera House, originally opened as the Covent Garden Theatre in 1732. It became the Royal Opera House in 1847 when Italian composer Guiseppe Persiani took it over after the then opera house (now Her Majesty's Theatre - see the Soho to Trafalgar Square Walk, page 75) refused to stage one of his works. Facing the Royal Opera House are Bow Street magistrates' court and adjacent police buildings. These are descendants of the original Bow Street court-house where, in 1749, the novelist-magistrate Henry Fielding (*Tom Jones* is his best-known work) recruited the first Bow Street Runners, ancestors of the Metropolitan Police Force.

Biographer of Dr Johnson

Turn left into Russell Street, passing on the left the Theatre Museum Ⓜ and then the Boswell Coffee House where, in 1763, Dr Johnson had his first meeting with his future biographer James Boswell. It was not actually a coffee house then, although at that time Covent Garden was famous for its coffee houses where all the great literary men of the day met and talked. Ahead is Covent Garden, originally a *convent* garden. The old market building, London's main fruit, vegetable and flower market until 1974, fills the centre of Inigo Jones's 17th-century square. Around the perimeter, starting on your left, are the London Transport Museum Ⓜ, the Jubilee Market Hall and Sports Centre, and St Paul's Church Ⓗ, known as the actors' church Ⓣ, the entrance to which is reached via archways in King Street and Henrietta Street. At the beginning of King Street there is a house with a plaque in memory of Admiral Edward Russell. It was his uncle, the first Duke of Bedford, who started Covent Garden Market in 1670.

Turn right in front of the house and then left into James Street. Go across Floral Street and Long Acre into Neal Street. This is the main street of the regenerated warehouse area to the north of the old market, and is a curious mixture of avant-garde fashion and environmentalism. Cross Shelton Street and the entrance to Earlham Street and then turn left into Short's Gardens. On the right, the water-powered clock on the front of the Wholefood Warehouse is well worth watching if the hour is about to strike.

The sins of Seven Dials

From here turn right into the organic enclave of Neal's Yard, where you can buy bread, organic fruit and vegetables, wholefood and herbal remedies. Turn left through the yard and go through the gate into the little mall leading to Monmouth Street. Turn left to Seven Dials, the meeting point of seven roads. (If it is a Sunday and the gate from Neal's Yard into the little mall is shut, retrace your steps to Short's Gardens and then turn right.) The column in the centre of Seven Dials is a modern replica of the original which was taken down as long ago as 1773 after it had become a notorious rendezvous for thieves and prostitutes. Thomas Neale, Master of the Royal Mint, started the building of the Seven Dials area in the 1690s, hence Neal Street and Neal's Yard.

Take the third turning on the left into Mercer Street, go across Shelton Street again, and turn right into Long Acre. Cross over when you see Stanford's famous map shop on the opposite side and go through the arch on the right into Rose Street. Go across Floral Street and follow Rose Street round to the left and right, past the 1623 Lamb and Flag pub (where the poet Dryden was once famously beaten up) into Garrick Street. To your right, the large stone building with flagpole is the Garrick Club, founded in 1831 to promote social contact between actors and artists and the upper classes. Both club and street are named after the 18th-century actor, David Garrick.

Cross over the road to the Roundhouse pub and go round the corner into New Row. On the left, look out for the interesting scientific instrument shop on the corner of Bedfordbury. At the end of New Row cross St Martin's Lane by the Albery Theatre and go into St Martin's Court. Half-way along, turn right by the public telephone boxes and follow the court round to the left to Leicester Square Station where the walk ends.

Lambeth and the South Bank

Summary: The first part of this walk takes you round the back of Waterloo Station through Lower Marsh (Monday to Saturday market for household items) to Archbishop's Park and the ancient palace of the Archbishops of Canterbury at Lambeth (the Museum of Garden History is next to the palace). The next section is along the riverside embankment to the South Bank arts complex, passing on the opposite bank, the Houses of Parliament, Whitehall and Cleopatra's Needle. Finally, the walk crosses Waterloo Bridge (best bridge view of Westminster and the City) to Somerset House, St Mary-le-Strand Church and the Surrey Street 'Roman' bath on the north bank.

Start: **Waterloo Station (Northern, Bakerloo, Jubilee and Waterloo & City Underground lines; trains from the south and west).**
Finish: **Temple Station (District and Circle Underground lines). On Sundays when Temple Station is closed use Blackfriars instead.**
Length: **2½ miles (4 kilometres).**
Time: **1½ hours.**
Refreshments: **Apart from the station area at the start of the walk and cafés and pubs in Lower Marsh, there is nowhere to stop until you get to the riverside bars and restaurants in the South Bank arts complex in the walk's closing stages.**

Take the 'South Bank' or 'County Hall' exit from Waterloo Underground Station, cross York Road and turn left towards the bridge. Go straight over the entrance to the road on the right, which slopes upwards to the main entrance to Waterloo Station Ⓣ, and turn right into Mepham Street immediately before the bridge. When you reach the main road (Waterloo Road), turn right and walk past the ground-level entrance to Waterloo Station.

'Home of Shakespeare'

The Old Vic Theatre stands to your left on the corner of The Cut. Built in 1818 and later named after Queen Victoria, this famous old theatre enjoyed its heyday under the management of Lilian Baylis. Taking over from her social-reformer aunt, Emma Cons, in 1912, Baylis transformed the theatre from an alcohol-free music hall with religious overtones into the 'home of Shakespeare' in London and a popular opera house, all without losing its local (mostly working-class) audience. In 1982 the theatre was again revamped and relaunched by the Canadian entrepreneur Ed Mirvish.

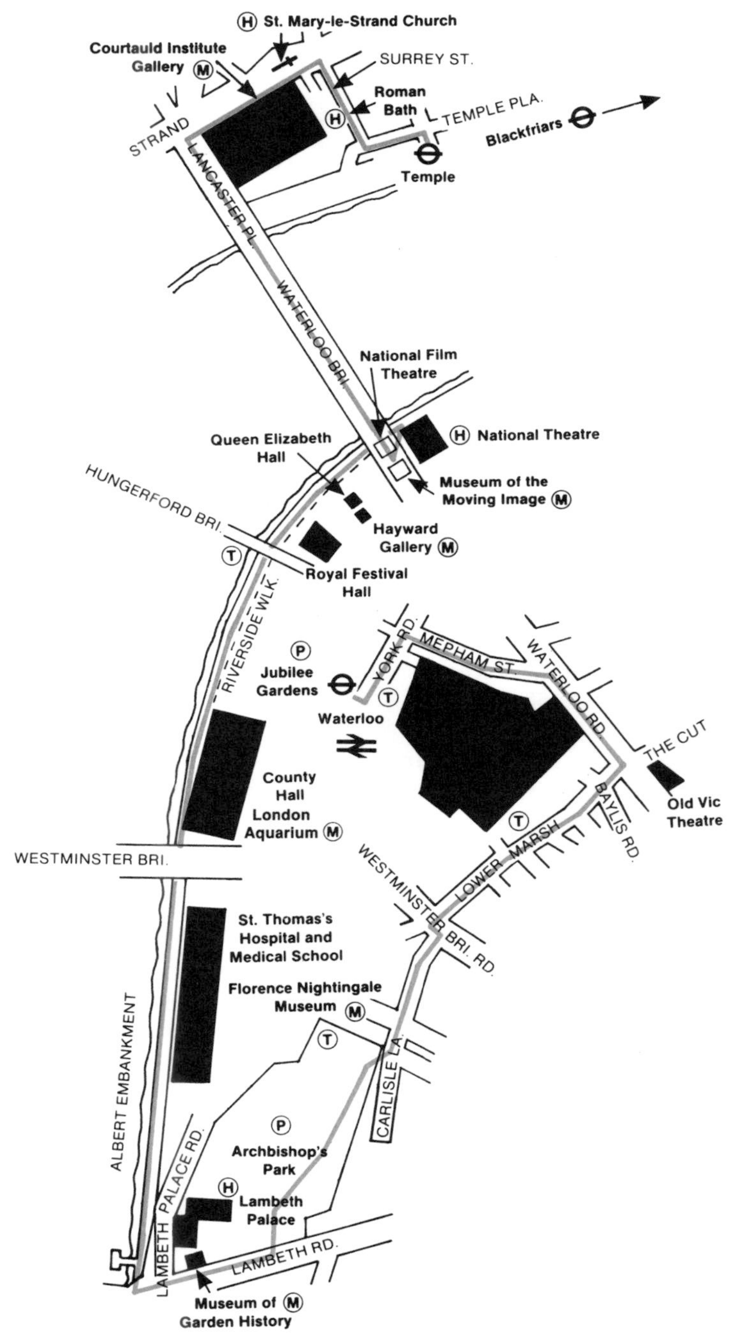

St. Mary-le-Strand Church
Courtauld Institute Gallery
SURREY ST.
Roman Bath
TEMPLE PLA.
Blackfriars
STRAND
Temple
LANCASTER PL.
WATERLOO BRI.
National Film Theatre
National Theatre
Queen Elizabeth Hall
HUNGERFORD BRI.
Museum of the Moving Image
Hayward Gallery
Royal Festival Hall
RIVERSIDE WLK.
YORK RD.
MEPHAM ST.
WATERLOO RD.
Jubilee Gardens
Waterloo
THE CUT
County Hall
London Aquarium
Old Vic Theatre
BAYLIS RD.
LOWER MARSH
WESTMINSTER BRI.
WESTMINSTER BRI. RD.
St. Thomas's Hospital and Medical School
Florence Nightingale Museum
ALBERT EMBANKMENT
CARLISLE LA.
Archbishop's Park
LAMBETH PALACE RD.
Lambeth Palace
LAMBETH RD.
Museum of Garden History

Walk to the right into Baylis Road, and keep right into Lower Marsh and its small market Ⓣ. Until the 19th century, when it was drained and developed, this area was marshland much prized for duck shooting, hence the street name.

At the end of Lower Marsh cross Westminster Bridge Road and go straight on into Carlisle Lane. Continue under the railway bridge, going past the car park on the right, and turn right into Archbishop's Park Ⓟ Ⓣ. Even though it is open to the public, this park is still owned by the Archbishops of Canterbury and was once part of the grounds of Lambeth Palace which you can see behind the trees in the opposite corner. Further round to the right you can see the top of the Victoria Tower in the Houses of Parliament rising up over the medical school of St Thomas's Hospital.

Follow the path to the end of the park and when it curves to the right, walk straight ahead into the alley and out into Lambeth Road. Turn right here along the side of the former Archbishop Tait's Infants' School and various precincts of Lambeth Palace. When you get to St Mary-at-Lambeth Church on the right, go into the churchyard.

The redundant church and part of the churchyard now house the Museum of Garden History Ⓜ operated by the Tradescant Trust. John Tradescant and his son were famous professional gardeners in the 17th-century and were employed both by James I and his son Charles I. They were also great travellers and brought many new plants back to England, including lilac, evening primrose, Virginia creeper and the parent of the London plane. Their home was in Lambeth where they had a famous museum called 'Tradescant's Ark' containing 'all things strange and rare' including a 'natural dragon' and 'blood that rained in the Isle of Wight'. The Tradescants are buried in the museum part of the churchyard. Also buried here is Admiral William Bligh, better known as Captain Bligh of *Mutiny on the Bounty* fame. His harsh discipline provoked his crew into mutiny in 1789. With only 18 loyal crewmen he was set adrift in a small boat in the middle of the Pacific but still made it to land after an heroic 4000-mile journey. Bligh lived at No. 100 Lambeth Road.

Leave the churchyard and go across the forecourt of the Tudor gatehouse of Lambeth Palace Ⓗ. The Archbishops of Canterbury acquired the manor of Lambeth in 1197, conveniently close to the royal palace at Westminster across the river, and have had their main palace here ever since. Cross Lambeth Palace Road to Lambeth Pier and turn right along the Albert Embankment. There is a fine view of the Houses of Parliament on the opposite bank, including the riverside terrace, which is invisible from the Westminster bank.

The Albert Embankment was completed in 1870, as you can see from the date on the base of the ornate lamp-posts. Subsequently the embankment wall was raised by 18 inches (45 centimetres) in order to protect the city from rising flood tide levels. At the same time the embankment seats were raised on plinths to preserve the view. Recently a special Thames barrier was built to protect London from floods. In view of this the extra blocks on top of the wall have been removed, but the benches have been allowed to stay on their plinths.

Riverside nightingales

When you come to the wall on the right, note the plaque to Lt-Col John By, builder of the Rideau canal in Canada. The wall belongs to St Thomas's Hospital and its medical school. The hospital was founded around 1200 at the Southwark side of London Bridge (see the Bankside and Southwark walk, page 110) and then in 1871 it moved to what was then the more peaceful location of Lambeth. The first training school for nurses, inspired by the pioneering work of Florence Nightingale, was founded at St Thomas's in 1860 and there is now a Florence Nightingale Museum Ⓜ in the hospital.

Go through the subway under Westminster Bridge. As you emerge, look back and up at the huge stone lion. A well-known riverside feature since 1837, it used to stand a little further downstream by Hungerford Bridge, over the entrance to the Lion Brewery. The Brewery was demolished in 1949 and the lion was moved to this position in 1966. It is made of Coade Stone, the most weatherproof artificial stone ever made, but the stone's formula was lost when the Coade factory, founded in the 1760s by Mrs Eleanor Coade, closed in 1840. The Coade factory stood just here where County Hall now stands. County Hall was the headquarters of the London County Council and then the Greater London Council until the latter's abolition in 1986. The building has since been converted into a hotel, conference centre, offices, shops, restaurants and the London Aquarium Ⓜ.

South Bank celebrations

Continue along the riverside walk. Beyond County Hall on the right is the Shell Centre building, separated from the river by the Jubilee Gardens Ⓟ, laid out to mark the Queen's Silver Jubilee in 1977. Previously the site had been used for the 1951 Festival of Britain, a celebration of national achievements a century after the 1851 Great Exhibition, designed to lift the spirits of the nation after six years of post-war austerity. Near the Jubilee Oracle sculpture look out for two verses inscribed in the pavement: a humorous piece about swans and buses from comedian Spike Milligan and something rather more elegaic from 19th-century poet and designer, William Morris:

'Forget six counties overhung with smoke
Forget the snorting steam and piston stroke,
Forget the spreading of the hideous town;
Think rather of the pack-horse on the down,
And dream of London, small, and white, and clean,
The clear Thames bordered by its gardens green.'

Nearby, there is an immense flagpole cut from the forests of British Columbia especially for the Festival of Britain. After the Festival the flagpole was taken down but then re-erected by the British Columbian government to mark the Queen's Silver Jubilee. On the north bank in front of the Ministry of Defence there is a gold eagle on a large pedestal; this is the Royal Air Force war memorial for World Wars I and II.

Continue along the embankment and under Hungerford Bridge Ⓣ. On the right, the Royal Festival Hall, built for the Festival of Britain, marks the start of the South Bank arts complex, which itself grew out of the Festival. Next on the right is the

Queen Elizabeth Hall and the Purcell Room, with the Hayward Gallery Ⓜ behind. On the other side of the river you can see Cleopatra's Needle, an ancient Egyptian obelisk given to Britain in 1819 by Egypt's Turkish overlords and floated here in 1878 from Alexandria. The National Film Theatre and Museum of the Moving Image Ⓜ are underneath Waterloo Bridge and beyond the bridge is the National Theatre Ⓗ, incorporating three separate theatres – the Olivier, the Lyttelton and the Cottesloe. The appearance of these South Bank concrete blockhouses has provoked growing criticism in recent years, but so far none of the various proposals put forward for improving them (including a transparent roof covering the whole complex) has satisfied the often-conflicting criteria of public approval and affordability.

The north bank

Go under Waterloo Bridge, turn immediately right up the steps and then turn right again over the bridge, towards Somerset House on the north bank. Somerset House, the most important 18th century public building in London, was built in 1775 for various government departments, primarily the Navy Office. Then for years it was the place to go for birth certificates and wills. Half-way between the City and Westminster, the bridge provides superb views in both directions (the main landmarks are identified on panels half-way across the bridge). When you come to the end of the bridge, continue into Lancaster Place, passing the west wing of Somerset House, until you come to the junction with the Strand. Turn right onto the Strand, passing on the right the main entrance to Somerset House and the Courtauld Institute Gallery Ⓜ and then King's College, part of London University. On the left is St Mary-le-Strand Church Ⓗ, built in 1717, with Bush House behind, occupied by BBC Radio and its World Service.

Take the first turning on the right into Surrey Street, walking down towards the river. Look out for Surrey Steps, half-way along the street on the right. These steps lead to an alley called Surrey Lane where there is what is traditionally claimed to be a Roman bath Ⓗ - now owned by the National Trust - in a basement of a King's College building. You can view the bath from outside through a window and there is an information board which will tell you more about its possible origins (probably not Roman). At the end of Surrey Street turn left along Temple Place to Temple Station where the walk ends. (If the station is closed, continue along the embankment to Blackfriars Station.)

Inns of Court

Summary: This is a circular walk through the heart of legal London featuring the capital's four ancient Inns of Court where barristers (i.e. advocates) first train and then practise. These four Inns (in the order in which they are covered by the walk) are: Gray's Inn, Lincoln's Inn, Middle Temple and Inner Temple. Apart from the inns and their old courts and quiet gardens, features of the walk include St Clement Danes Church, the law courts in the Strand, Dickens's Old Curiosity Shop, Lincoln's Inn Fields, Staple Inn, Chancery Lane and the London Silver Vaults.

***Start and finish:* Temple Station (District and Circle Underground lines) On Sundays when Temple Station is closed use Blackfriars instead.**
***Length:* 2 miles (3.2 kilometres).**
***Time:* 1-1½ hours.**
***Refreshments:* Plenty of pubs, wine bars and sandwich bars *en route* between the Inns.**
***Route note:* This walk needs to be done on a weekday because the Inns are closed at weekends.**

Leave Temple Station, turn left up the steps and then right into Temple Place. When the road curves to the right, turn left into Milford Lane and climb the steps into Essex Street. Middle Temple lies on the right-hand side behind the houses. Shortage of space in the Inns, including Middle Temple, has forced many barristers to seek offices (known as chambers) in nearby streets, not because the Inns are too small, but because some chambers have been let out to members of other professions, like solicitors and surveyors. Several Middle Temple barristers have their chambers in this street. Look out for No. 11 on the left, an old house with the Middle Temple coat of arms above the door. It's easy for the tenants of these chambers to get to their Inn because there is a handy back entrance at the end of Devereux Court (opposite, by the Edgar Wallace pub).

The Young Pretender

Further along the street is Essex Hall, the main church and central office of the General Assembly of Unitarian and Free Christian Churches (Unitarianism is a liberal tendency which differs from more 'Establishment' creeds by putting reason and the individual conscience before dogma). The Hall is post-war, but the first Unitarian chapel was founded here in 1774. A stone by the door of the Temple bookshop on the left is inscribed with more details of Essex Street's 300-year history, including Bonnie Prince Charlie's five-day secret visit to London five years after the abortive Jacobite rising of 1745. The stone also records the existence of Dr Johnson's club at the Essex Head pub, now the Edgar Wallace.

You emerge from Essex Street at the east end of the Strand. St Clement Danes

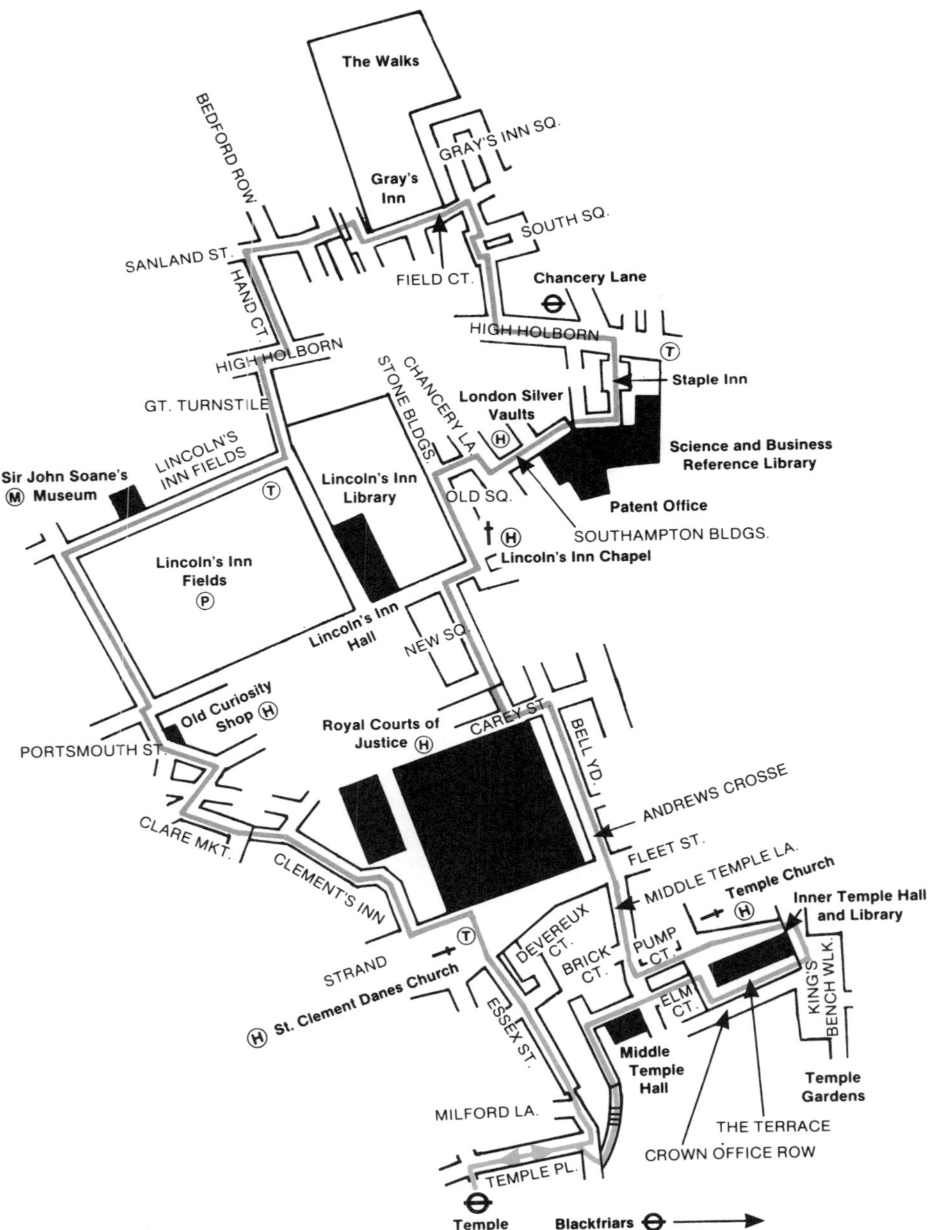

Church Ⓗ) stands on an island site in the middle of the road with a figure of Dr Johnson in the grass at its east end. The opposite side of the street here consists entirely of the Royal Courts of Justice Ⓗ. Go over the Strand at the zebra crossing to the right Ⓣ and turn left. There are about 60 courtrooms altogether, most of which hear only civil cases: serious criminal cases are dealt with at the Old Bailey in the City.

At the end of the wrought-iron screen that masks the administrative offices of the courts, turn right through the gate into Clement's Inn. The Inn, now an enclave of office blocks, was once one of about eight Inns of Chancery that existed side by side with the Inns of Court. Although the Inns of Chancery were able to educate budding lawyers, unlike the Inns of Court they could not qualify their students to become barristers and practise at the bar and as a result they eventually died out. This Inn was finally demolished in 1891 after a 400-year existence.

Walk along the path between the office blocks and go up the steps into Clement's Inn Passage, leading into Clare Market. Until the beginning of this century there was a market here but today the campus of the London School of Economics covers the area. Turn right beyond the bookshop and second left by the pub into Portsmouth Street. On the right, looking quite out of place, is the Old Curiosity Shop Ⓗ. Apart from being reckoned the oldest shop in London, it is also said to be the original of Dickens's eponymous novel - the one where Little Nell and her grandfather the shop-keeper are hounded by the money-lender Quilp.

Students' playground

Continue along Portsmouth Street into Lincoln's Inn Fields Ⓟ, the second largest square in London. Away to the right you can see the gateway into Lincoln's Inn. Walk along the left-hand side of the square. As its name suggests' it was open ground before building started in the 1600s. The only original house left is at Nos. 59-60 on this side, painted red and white and retaining the high railings and the iron cradles for torches and lanterns used before the days of street lighting. Spencer Perceval once lived here. The only British prime minister to have been assassinated, he was shot in 1812 by John Bellingham, a deranged bankrupt convinced that Perceval was at the root of his problems.

The penultimate house on the left, No. 65, was the home of William Marsden, founder of both the Royal Free Hospital ('free' because it didn't charge for its services) and the Cancer Hospital, now the Royal Marsden Hospital. Next door at No. 66 are the offices of Farrer and Co, solicitors to the Queen.

Turn right along the top of the square. No. 13 in the middle is the former home of Sir John Soane, architect of the Bank of England Ⓜ. Soane married the daughter of a wealthy builder and created a collection of historical and architectural curiosities and works of art, including many drawings and pictures. In accordance with his wishes the house was turned into a public museum after his death in 1837. It has remained virtually unchanged since and is now one of the most extraordinary time-capsule interiors in London.

Turn left at the corner opposite the 'Camdonian' sculpture Ⓣ, walk along Newman's Row and go through Great Turnstile (there was a turnstile here in the

1600s) into High Holborn. Go across High Holborn at the traffic lights, turn right and then left into Hand Court, an alley next to the Bung Hole wine bar. At the end turn right along Sandland Street past the entrance to Bedford Row, historically a favourite address for solicitors. Quiet and spacious, the Row has classic town architecture and a hint of the exotic in the robinia trees. Continue past the old water pump and go through the gate in the wall into Gray's Inn, the first of the four Inns of Court. This Inn is named after Reginald le Grey, Chief Justice of Chester, whose London house became the original Gray's Inn after his death in 1308.

The shame of Gray's Inn

Follow the path to the right between the buildings into Gray's Inn Place. Ahead is the Inns of Court School of Law, where trainee barristers study for their formal qualifications. Turn left into Field Court, facing the gardens which are known as The Walks (open weekday lunchtimes). Walk through the arch ahead into Gray's Inn Square and turn immediately right into South Square. The figure away to the left is Francis Bacon, one of the Inn's most famous, or infamous, old members: as Lord Chancellor in 1621 he was convicted of taking bribes, fined £40,000 and imprisoned in the Tower of London. Continue through the next two archways and you find yourself back on High Holborn.

Turn left and walk down to the traffic lights Ⓣ. Go across High Holborn here and turn left past the griffin on its pedestal marking the boundary of the City of London. On the right, Staple Inn, one of the old Inns of Chancery, is one of the few timber-framed buildings to have survived the Great Fire in 1666. Turn right through the archway into the shady cobbled courtyard of the Inn and go through the next archway into the small, immaculate gardens in front of the old hall. Follow the path round to the right, climb the steps and go into Southampton Buildings. On the left is the Patent Office where new inventions are registered. On the right a little further along are the London Silver Vaults Ⓗ, large safes once used by a safe deposit company and now converted into a subterranean arcade of silverware shops.

Cross Chancery Lane, turn right and then go left through the gates into Lincoln's Inn, the second of the Inns of Court. Stone Buildings on the right was added to the Inn around 1780. Turn left into Old Square and walk to the right of the vaulted undercroft underneath the 17th-century chapel Ⓗ. As you pass the corner of the building notice on the wall the plaque recording the dropping of a bomb from a German airship in 1915. The undercroft floor is made up of the gravestones of people buried in Lincoln's Inn, one of whom was the puritan writer, William Prynne, who died in 1669 and whose scurrilous writings during his lifetime caused him first to lose both his ears and then to be branded 'S L' as a seditious libeller. Such were the perils of free expression in those days. (There is a list of the gravestones and a key showing their location inside the undercroft. Prynne's is no. 44.)

Walk past the undercroft and chapel entrance towards the old hall of Lincoln's Inn and then turn right to the war memorial. Ahead you can see the other side of the gateway you saw from Lincoln Inn's Fields, to the right the Inn's new hall, library and garden (open weekday lunchtimes), and to the left, New Square, three hundred years old despite the name.

Turn along the left-hand side of New Square. At the end go through the archway and turn left into Carey Street. Ahead now is the former Public Record Office, Britain's first purpose-built national archive, opened in the 1860s and closed in 1996 following the final transfer of documents to a new building in Kew in south-west London. Take the first turning on the right into Bell Yard alongside the law courts. This leads into Andrews Crosse. At the end you emerge at the point where Fleet Street meets the Strand, which is also the point where the City of London meets the City of Westminster. Originally a gate called Temple Bar stood here but it was removed because it held up traffic. It now stands forgotten in the grounds of a country house north of London. The griffin marks the site. If the sovereign wishes to enter the City of London, he or she must stop here and ask permission of the Lord Mayor. The Lord Mayor in return offers his Sword of State as a sign of the City's loyalty to the sovereign. In the past, particularly at the time of the Civil War, this was not always forthcoming.

Knights Templar

The orange-brick building opposite is the main entrance to Middle Temple (1684), the third of the Inns of Court. Go across the road using the lights left and through the gate into the Inn. Walk down Middle Temple Lane past Brick Court on the right and turn left through the archway with the lantern above it into Pump Court. Pass through the cloisters at the end into the open court where Lamb Buildings stood until they were destroyed by bombs in 1941. You are now in Inner Temple, the fourth and final Inn of Court. In the Middle Ages, both Inner and Middle Temple were part of the monastery of the military monks known as the Knights Templar. The Order was suppressed in 1312 and most of their premises (except for the Outer Temple which is now Essex Street) taken over by lawyers. On the left is the 12th-century Templars' church Ⓗ. Inner and Middle Temple separated in 1732.

Walk along to the end of the courtyard (on the left is the house of the Master of the Inn), through the archway and out into King's Bench Walk stretching down the hill towards the river. Turn right here and then right again into Crown Office Row. On your left are Paper Buildings ('paper' is an old term for a house built of wood and plaster rather than stone or bricks) and Temple Gardens with their gates dating from 1730. Follow the raised terrace to the right and go through the narrow gap in the angle of the Row. This brings you into Elm Court by the side of the old buttery of the Templars on the right. A plaque on the buttery wall records the existence of vanished Fig Tree Court, first burnt in the Great Fire (1666) and then finally destroyed by bombing in World War II. Turn left here, go through the archway and cross Middle Temple Lane into Middle Temple's Fountain Court. On the left is Middle Temple Hall where Shakespeare's *Twelfth Night* was first performed - at Candlemas (2nd February) 1601. To the right are New Court and Devereux Chambers, and the other side of the gateway you saw earlier on from Essex Street.

Turn left down the steps by Middle Temple gardens (open weekday lunchtimes May-September) and follow the path out of the Inn and back into Milford Lane. From here retrace your steps the short distance to Temple Station and the end of the walk.

Islington

Summary: Islington lies to the north of the City, with Clerkenwell in between. This walk starts at the historic Angel road junction and then makes its way north and uphill through the antiques market to the Canonbury Estate and Highbury Fields at the top of the hill. The middle section of the walk follows the course of the now filled-in New River, London's main water supply from 1613 until the 1980s. The 16th-century Canonbury Tower is the centrepiece of the Canonbury Estate. Other features of the walk include Charles Lamb's house and Walter Sickert's art school.

Start: **Angel Station (Northern Underground line).**
Finish: **Holloway Road Station (Piccadilly Underground line).**
Alternative finishes: **Highbury and Islington Station (Victoria Underground line, Silverlink Metro and trains from Moorgate). Drayton Park (trains from Moorgate).**
Length: **3 miles (4.8 kilometres).**
Time: **2½ hours.**
Refreshments: **Plenty of pubs and take-away cafés/restaurants at the start of the walk in Islington and at the end (lower quality) in Holloway Road. Otherwise a few pubs *en route* and a few cafés around Highbury and Islington Station.**
Route note: **This walk is best done when the Camden Passage market is open: Wednesday and Saturday (antiques), Thursday (books).**

Come out of Angel Station onto Islington High Street. To the left the Angel road junction is the meeting place of five major roads. Historically, the Angel was the starting point of the Great North Road, the main road from London to York. Entering central London, the road split at the Angel: one road went to the City, another to Smithfield Market. The domed building on the right hand side of the junction stands on the site of the Angel coaching inn, which gave its name to the junction. The inn was the first staging post on the road to the north.

Turn right along Islington High Street. Before the property developers took over, Islington was a great dairying centre, supplying the capital with much of its fresh milk. To Londoners it was also 'merry Islington', an area vying with Clerkenwell to the south as a playground for city-dwellers in search of fresh air, exercise and entertainment. Cricket grounds, bowling greens, tea gardens and spas could all be found in Islington in the 18th century. Over 100 ft above sea level, the village was a welcome refuge from the fogs and smogs of the city.

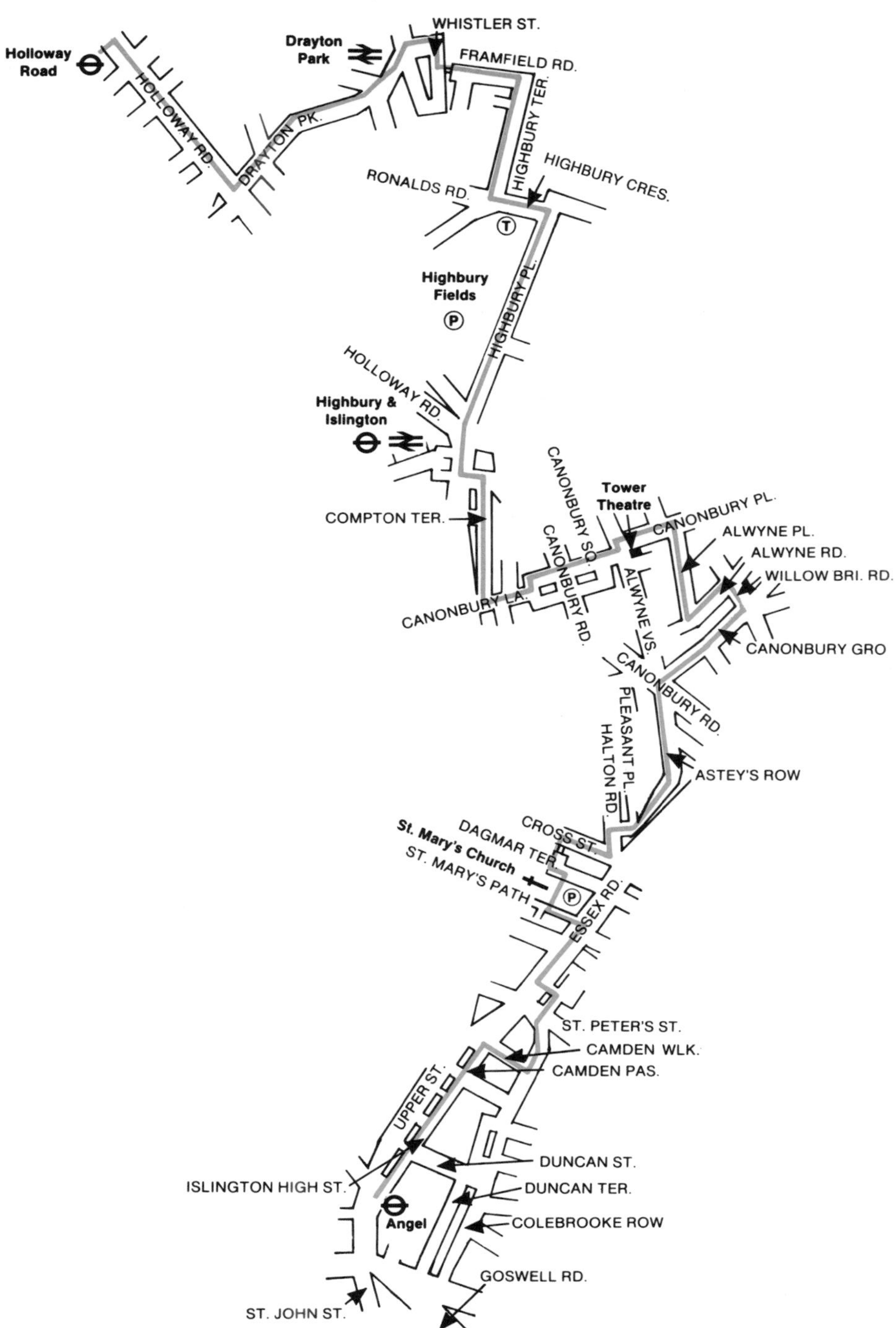
Holloway Road
HOLLOWAY RD.
DRAYTON PK.
Drayton Park
WHISTLER ST.
FRAMFIELD RD.
HIGHBURY TER.
HIGHBURY CRES.
RONALDS RD.
Highbury Fields
HIGHBURY PL.
HOLLOWAY RD.
Highbury & Islington
COMPTON TER.
CANONBURY SQ.
Tower Theatre
CANONBURY PL.
ALWYNE PL.
ALWYNE RD.
WILLOW BRI. RD.
CANONBURY RD.
CANONBURY LA.
ALWYNE VS.
CANONBURY GRO
CANONBURY RD.
PLEASANT PL.
HALTON RD.
ASTEY'S ROW
CROSS ST.
DAGMAR TER.
St. Mary's Church
ST. MARY'S PATH
ESSEX RD.
ST. PETER'S ST.
CAMDEN WLK.
CAMDEN PAS.
UPPER ST.
DUNCAN ST.
ISLINGTON HIGH ST.
DUNCAN TER.
Angel
COLEBROOKE ROW
GOSWELL RD.
ST. JOHN ST.

Antique activities

Keep to the right of the High Street and follow it when it veers to the right away from the main road, which becomes Upper Street. The High Street, together with Camden Passage ahead, is the nucleus of the antiques market. The market began in the early 1960s when antique collecting first became a popular activity. On the left, just before the passage widens in front of the Camden Head pub, No. 45 Camden Passage has a bust and a plaque dedicated to an eccentric scholar and bookseller called Alexander Cruden. *The Biblical Concordance* he produced in 1761 - a system of finding a particular text in the Bible by means of a key word - is still a standard work of reference.

When you reach the Camden Head pub, turn right into the Colinsdale Estate, go left down either a ramp or steps, and then turn right through the car park and turn left. This side of the street is called Duncan Terrace after Admiral Duncan, fleet commander at the Battle of Camperdown in 1797 when the Dutch lost nine ships and the British none. The other side of the street (built around 1768, some decades before Duncan Terrace), is called Colebrooke Row after the Colebrooke family who were lords of the manor in the middle of the 18th century. The New River ran between these terraces, first as an open channel and then from 1861 in underground pipes. The river's course is marked by a series of strip gardens at the south end of the road behind you.

At the end of Duncan Terrace on the left, there is a small white house with a plaque to Charles Lamb, East India Company official, critic and essayist, best known today for his *Essays of Elia*. The year these essays were published (1823) Lamb moved here to be near to his sister who had been committed to the Islington mad house after fatally stabbing their mother in a fit of insanity. Lamb was her legal guardian and occasionally had her at home with him whenever she was well enough to leave the asylum.

Cross St Peter's Street and follow Colebrooke Row round to the left onto Essex Road. Here turn right and walk along to the King's Head pub on the left. Go over the zebra crossing and walk up St Mary's Path by the side of the pub. Just before Church Cottage, turn right into the gardens Ⓟ behind St Mary's, the parish church of Islington.

Walk straight through the gardens into Dagmar Terrace, go through the archway and turn right into Cross Street, built around 1780. At Halton Road turn left and then first right into Halton Cross Street. Turn left into Astey's Row just before the Thatched House pub. Now you pick up the course of the New River once again.

The tale of the New River

The New River was a man-made channel, 10 feet (3 metres) wide and four feet (1 metre) deep, which conveyed fresh spring water from villages near Ware in Hertfordshire to the City. Completed in 1613 it was the main source of drinking water for north London and the City until superseded around 1990 by the London Tunnel Ring Main. Originally, the New River fed reservoirs at New River Head (see the Clerkenwell walk, page 98) but after World War II it was shut off just north of Islington at Stoke Newington. Long before then sections of the river running through newly-developed Islington were piped in and covered up. This section by Astey's Row was enclosed in 1893. When the flow was disconnected the pipes were dug up and the ground made into gardens, as in Colebrooke Row. The man behind this early example of commercial enterprise and civil engineering skill was City banker and MP Hugh Myddelton (there is a statue of him on Islington Green). At first capital proved hard to raise and King James I had to take a 50 per cent share in the New River Company to get the project going. But over the long term shareholders made fortunes. In 1893 one of the original 72 shares was sold for nearly £95,000. The operations of the New River Company were transferred to the Metropolitan Water Board in 1904.

When you get to Canonbury Road walk over the zebra crossing by the Myddleton (*sic*) Arms and go into Canonbury Grove, built in 1823. Here the strip gardens by the New River resume, but they are better landscaped and far better kept than the section by Astey's Row. Turn into the gardens and walk along the meandering path by the side of the river (actually duck ponds made to look like the river).

Monks and merchants

At the end of Canonbury Grove the gardens continue in Douglas Road but the walk turns left over Willow Bridge (Canonbury Grove used to be called Willow Cottages and Willow Terrace) and left again into Alwyne Road. Turn right into Alwyne Place, its entrance flanked by white and pink cottages. All the houses here were built in the 1840s and 1850s on Canonbury Field. At the top of Alwyne Place, turn left into Canonbury Place and walk along to an old house on the left called Canonbury Tower, on the corner with Alwyne Villas. Alwyne was one of the names of the second Marquess of Northampton (more about the Northamptons in a minute).

Now leased to a theatre company, the Canonbury Tower once stood on its own on the top of a hill and for centuries was an important local landmark. In the Middle Ages the estate was owned by the Augustinian canons of St Bartholomew's Priory in Clerkenwell, after whom Canonbury is named. William Bolton, last prior of St Bartholomew's, built the Tower in the early 1500s as a manor house. After the Priory was dissolved in 1539 the estate was bought by Sir John Spencer, a rich but mean City cloth merchant who was Lord Mayor in 1594. Spencer's daughter and heiress Elizabeth eloped from the Tower with Lord Compton after being lowered from an upper-storey window in a bread basket. Lord Compton's descendants, the Marquesses of Northampton, still own the Tower, even though they have not lived here since the 1600s. Around 1770 a stockbroker called John Dawes was tenant of the Tower. He demolished some of the monastic buildings and built Canonbury House round the corner, as well as Nos. 1-5 in Canonbury Place on the far side of Canonbury House (the date 1780 is visible at the top of their drainpipes).

Continue along Canonbury Place and enter Canonbury Square: Evelyn Waugh lived here in 1928, as did George Orwell in 1945. Walk along the right-hand side of the square and follow it round to the left. Turn right into Canonbury Lane and then take the second turning on the right into Compton Terrace. Canonbury Square and Compton Terrace were built soon after 1800 by Henry Leroux. Go down the steps at the end of the terrace, go over the zebra crossing to the left and then turn right. Highbury and Islington Station is round the corner to the left in Holloway Road.

All ranks and degrees

Cross Holloway Road into Highbury Place and walk along the broad walk parallel with the row of Georgian terraced houses on the right (built in 1774-79). No. 1 is where the British Impressionist painter Walter Sickert ran his painting and engraving school in the 1920s and 1930s. John Nichols, historian of literary life in the 18th century, lived at No. 14 from 1803 until his death in 1820. No. 15 was the home of Joseph Chamberlain, father of 1930s prime minister Neville Chamberlain. After the Great Fire of 1666 the diarist John Evelyn saw in Highbury Fields Ⓟ (the park on the left) a crowd of as many as '200,000 people of all ranks and degrees dispersed and lying along by their heapes of what they could save from the fire, deploring their losses, and though ready to perish for hunger and destitution, yet not asking one penny for relief'.

When you get to Highbury Crescent bisecting Highbury Fields turn left Ⓣ and then right along hilltop Highbury Terrace, built in 1789. From the top of Framfield Road at the end of Highbury Terrace you can see right across the 'hollow way' of Holloway to the wooded heights of Hampstead Heath beyond.

From this point there are two ways to finish the walk. You can continue to Drayton Park Station (5 minutes' walk) or Holloway Road Station (15 minutes' walk). Alternatively you can retrace your steps to Highbury and Islington Station. To get to Drayton Park Station and Holloway Station go down Framfield Road and through the passage at the end. Then turn right and left in Whistler Street and left onto Drayton Park. Drayton Park Station is opposite. Follow the road round as it bends left and right as far as the junction with Holloway Road. Then turn right and walk towards the bridge. Holloway Road Station is underneath the bridge.

Clerkenwell

Summary: Close to the St Paul's Cathedral end of the City, Clerkenwell is particularly rich in historical features, including the remains of three medieval monasteries (St Bartholomew's, Charterhouse and the Priory of St John of Jerusalem), London's oldest church (St Bartholomew-the-Great), London's oldest hospital (St Bartholomew's), a centuries-old market (Smithfield), a medieval well (the Clerks' Well), an old prison (Clerkenwell House of Detention), a village green (now tarmac rather than grass), an historic theatre (Sadler's Wells) and two Georgian squares (Claremont and Myddelton). As if this were not enough, it also has connections with historic events like the Peasants' Revolt, the Reformation and the Spa Fields Riots.

Start: **Angel Station (Northern Underground line).**
Finish: **Barbican Station (Circle, Metropolitan and Hammersmith & City Underground lines).**
Length: **2 miles (3.2 kilometres).**
Time: **1½ hours.**
Refreshments: **Pubs, sandwich bars and restaurants *en route* in Exmouth Market (a third of the way along the route), Clerkenwell Green (two-thirds of the way and the nicest place to stop) and Smithfield (near the end of the walk).**
Route note: **By doing this walk in the morning you could combine it with an afternoon visit to the Musuem of London, which is just a short distance from the end of the walk.**

Turn left out of Angel Station and walk down to the traffic lights. Turn right into Pentonville Road, cross over at the lights and take the first turning on the left into Claremont Square. The embankment in the centre of the square hides the upper of the two reservoirs constructed to collect water from the New River (see the Islington walk, page 93). This one dates from 1709. Walk straight down Mylne Street into the west side of Myddelton Square. Both squares were developed in the 1820s by the New River Company.

Spas and wells

At the bottom of the square cross River Street and go into Myddelton Passage. Follow this road round to the left and then turn right into Arlington Way. On your left is the back of Sadler's Wells Theatre. On your right is New River Head, the original termination of the New River, an artificial watercourse which from 1613 brought water to London from springs 20 miles (32 kilometres) away in

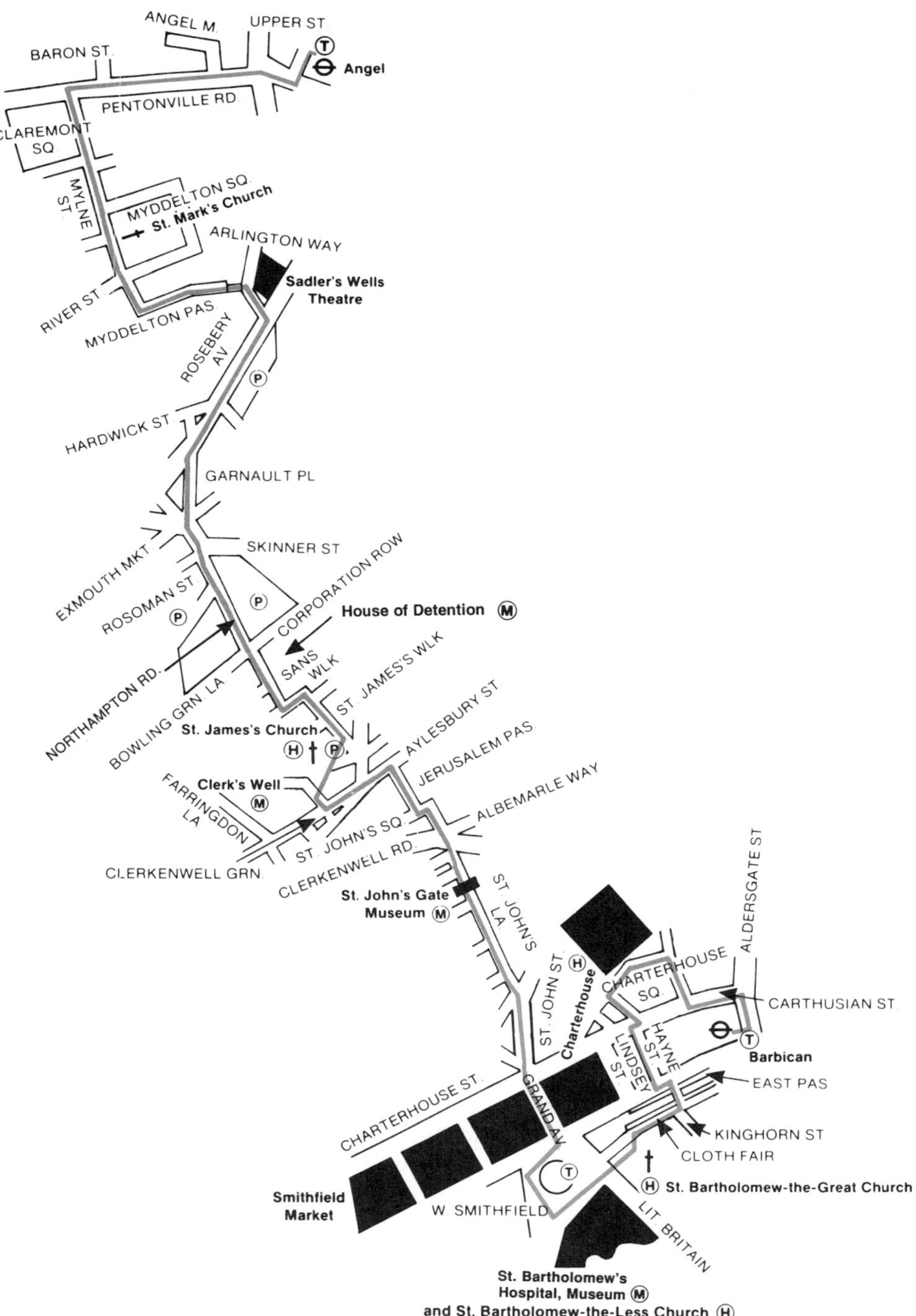
ANGEL M.
UPPER ST.
BARON ST.
Angel
PENTONVILLE RD.
CLAREMONT SQ.
MYLNE ST.
MYDDELTON SQ.
St. Mark's Church
ARLINGTON WAY
Sadler's Wells Theatre
RIVER ST.
MYDDELTON PAS.
ROSEBERY AV.
HARDWICK ST.
GARNAULT PL.
SKINNER ST.
EXMOUTH MKT.
ROSOMAN ST.
CORPORATION ROW
House of Detention
SANS WLK.
ST. JAMES'S WLK.
NORTHAMPTON RD.
BOWLING GRN. LA.
St. James's Church
AYLESBURY ST.
JERUSALEM PAS.
Clerk's Well
FARRINGDON LA.
ALBEMARLE WAY
ST. JOHN'S SQ.
CLERKENWELL RD.
CLERKENWELL GRN.
St. John's Gate Museum
ST. JOHN'S LA.
ALDERSGATE ST.
ST. JOHN ST.
Charterhouse
CHARTERHOUSE SQ.
CARTHUSIAN ST.
HAYNE ST.
LINDSEY ST.
Barbican
EAST PAS.
CHARTERHOUSE ST.
GRAND AV.
KINGHORN ST.
CLOTH FAIR
St. Bartholomew-the-Great Church
Smithfield Market
W. SMITHFIELD
LIT. BRITAIN
St. Bartholomew's Hospital, Museum
and St. Bartholomew-the-Less Church

Hertfordshire. Looking right, through the fountain gardens, you can see remains of the old waterworks, including the base of the windmill which from the early 18th-century was used to pump water up to the reservoir in Claremont Square. From there gravity-fed pipes carried it to customers. In the 1680s natural springs around the reservoirs were found to have medicinal properties and at least a dozen were developed into commercial spas. Thomas Sadler built the original Sadler's Wells Theatre in 1683 as an attraction to his spa.

From Arlington Way turn right onto Rosebery Avenue, transferring to the other side of the road when you get to the zebra crossing. The statue in the gardens Ⓟ on this side of the road is part of the Finsbury war memorial. Continue along Rosebery Avenue and take the next turning on the left into Garnault Place. Then go over the zebra crossings to get to the London Spa pub by Exmouth Market opposite. The London Spa was another of the local spas.

When you reach the London Spa, turn left into Rosoman Street and walk straight on between the gardens Ⓟ when the road bends to the left. The open space around here is known as Spa Fields and it was here that the patrons of the spas danced, played games and strolled through shady walks. In 1816 the Spa Fields Riots took place here when a parliamentary reform meeting got out of hand and an attempt was made to seize the Tower of London.

Keep going straight on down Northampton Road towards Clerkenwell church, past the sunken playground on the left. Beyond the playground, slum clearance and rebuilding - following World War II bombing raids - have done away with the old streets and replaced them with one huge and unattractive housing estate. Cross the junction of Corporation Row (left) and Bowling Green Lane (right). There was once a bowling green here - one of Clerkenwell's many attractions for the City dwellers to the south. Once again, walk straight ahead when the road bends to the right. On the left now is the former Hugh Myddelton School, now Kingsway College. Before the school a prison called the Clerkenwell House of Detention was here. Some of the subterranean cells have been converted into a spooky museum Ⓜ. To the right you can see evidence of recent rebuilding in Clerkenwell. Many of the new developments consist of workshops and industrial units for craftspeople and small-scale manufacturers, the aim being to support Clerkenwell's craft tradition, historically centred on clock and watch-making.

Religious and radical movements

Turn left into Sans Walk, right into St James's Walk and half-way along right again into the graveyard garden Ⓟ of St James's Ⓗ, the parish church of Clerkenwell. Go round to the left of the church to the main entrance. Inside there are memorials to the Protestant martyrs of the Reformation (many of whom were burnt at Smithfield, seen later on the walk) and to the victims of the 1867 explosion at the aforementioned House of Detention when members of the Fenian Conspiracy (forerunner of the IRA) blew a hole in the wall in an attempt to release two of their compatriots.

Turn left through the gate out of the churchyard into triangular Clerkenwell Green, historically an open space between St John's Priory (of which more later) and St Mary's Nunnery to the north. At the base of the triangle stands the old

Middlesex Sessions House, built as a court-house in 1782, used until 1920 and now occupied by freemasons. To the right of the Sessions House round the corner in Farringdon Lane is Well Court, an office block built over the Clerks' Well after which Clerkenwell is named. The well in turn is thought to have been named after London's parish clerks who gathered here annually in the Middle Ages to perform mystery plays. The well was rediscovered in 1924 and has been preserved in a small room in the office block, which is visible from the street outside Ⓜ.

Nearby on the right at No. 37a, in a former charity school dating from 1737, is the Marx Memorial Library. After the Spa Fields Riots Clerkenwell became a popular meeting place for radical movements and earned itself a reputation as 'the headquarters of republicanism and revolution'. Various radical organizations made use of the old charity school building and Lenin even edited one of his revolutionary papers here. The library and research centre, specialising in the labour movement, was founded in 1933.

Leave the Green by turning left into Aylesbury Street and then right into Jerusalem Passage, the northern entrance to the medieval Priory of St John of Jerusalem. On the corner there is a plaque to Thomas Britton (1644-1714), a charcoal dealer and music scholar who held weekly concerts in the room above his warehouse where musicians of the stature of Handel regularly played. Jerusalem Passage leads into St John's Square, the main courtyard of the priory. The Knights of St John, along with the Knights Templar, were military monks charged with protecting pilgrims in the Holy Land. In 1539 the English section of the order was abolished by Henry VIII. In 1831 it was refounded as a Protestant organization and set up its headquarters in the new priory on the left of the square. In 1873 it acquired St John's Gate ahead, the 1504 southern entrance to the old priory and now a Hospitaller museum Ⓜ. The new order launched the St John's Ambulance Brigade here in 1877.

The meat market

Now cross Clerkenwell Road - driven through the square in 1878 - and go straight through the gate. Continue along St John's Lane to the junction with St John's Street. The road bellies out here because Hick's Hall, the predecessor of the Middlesex Sessions House on Clerkenwell Green, was built in the middle of the road in 1612. After that time the cattle, sheep and pigs destined for Smithfield market just passed by on either side.

Turn right along St John's Street into the Grand Avenue of Smithfield Market. At the end of the avenue turn right and walk in an anti-clockwise direction around the central gardens, a relic of old Smithfield, originally called Smoothfield. This open space has a long history going back to the early Middle Ages. Just outside the City wall, it was used for jousts, tournaments, fairs and meetings. St Bartholomew's Fair was held here from 1123 to 1855. During the Peasants' Revolt of 1381 the rebels were confronted by young King Richard II here and their leader, Wat Tyler, was stabbed by Lord Mayor William Walworth. Smithfield was also a place of execution; criminals were hanged while traitors, heretics and others were roasted, boiled or burnt. Over 200 Protestants were burned alive here during the six years of Queen Mary's reign in the 1550s. Smithfield was used for a regular Friday horse market as early as 1200. In 1638 a live cattle market was started. As houses surrounded the field, the market became such a nuisance that it was closed and then in 1855 moved to Islington. The dead meat market, still flourishing today, opened in 1868.

Walk around the gardens until you come to St Bartholomew's Hospital Ⓜ. Founded in 1123 as part of St Bartholomew's Augustinian priory, also founded in that year, this is the oldest hospital in London. In 1381 Wat Tyler was brought into the hospital after being stabbed by the Lord Mayor, but soldiers dragged him back outside and decapitated him on the spot. Behind the hospital's main gate, rebuilt in 1702 with a statue of Henry VIII in the niche above the arch, you can see the tower and roof of the hospital chapel. After Henry VIII closed the medieval priory in 1538, he allowed the hospital not only to survive but to become a new parish in its own right. The old hospital chapel became the new parish church of St Bartholomew the Less Ⓗ while the old priory church became the parish church of St Bartholomew the Great.

Continue around the square Ⓣ to the archway beneath the black and white half-timbered building straight ahead. At second-floor level there is a statue of St Bartholomew holding the knife with which he was supposedly flayed alive while on a missionary journey to Armenia. The gateway leads to the parish church of St Bartholomew-the-Great Ⓗ, London's oldest church and, apart from the St Bart's hospital chapel, the only surviving part of the original Augustinian priory.

Commercial cloth

Cross over the churchyard to the gate in the opposite left corner and turn right into Cloth Fair, part of a maze of narrow streets and passageways surrounding the church. In the 15th and 16th centuries cloth was the main source of England's wealth and St Bartholomew's Fair (held over three days around St Bartholomew's Day - 24 August) was the country's biggest cloth trade fair. Merchants came from all parts of Europe to buy the famous English broadcloth. Walk along the side of the church. When you get to Kinghorn Street on the right, turn left to Ye Olde Red Cow pub. Go through the archway, across the road into Hayne Street, and then across Charterhouse Street into Charterhouse Square. Turn right past the arched entrance to Charterhouse Ⓗ.

Charterhouse was a Carthusian monastery founded in 1370. After its closure in 1537 and the execution of 20 monks, including the prior, the building was put to a variety of uses, including storing the royal hunting tents. In 1611 Thomas Sutton, the 'richest commoner in England', bought Charterhouse and converted it into a school and an almshouse. The school became one of England's best-known public schools and still exists at Godalming in Surrey, where it moved about a hundred years ago. The almshouses are still in the Charterhouse.

Walk along the top of the square, passing the Charterhouse chapel behind the railings. In the corner on the left, Rutland Place leads to St Bartholomew's Hospital Medical School, built over the Great Cloister and other parts of Charterhouse destroyed in World War II bombing raids. Turn right here and then left out of the gates into Carthusian Street and walk towards the Barbican. At the main road (Aldersgate Street) turn right to Barbican Station. The walk ends here, but signs point the short distance to the Museum of London Ⓜ for those who have the energy and desire to find out more about London's past.

Plate 9: *Fortnum and Mason of Piccadilly* (see *the Mayfair walk, page 57*).

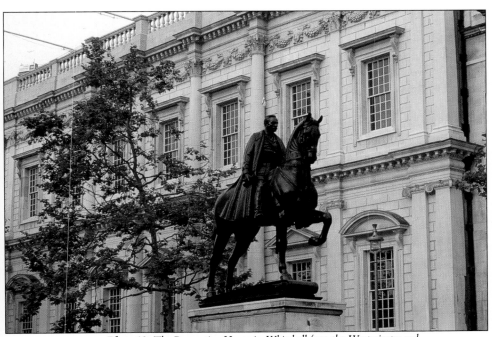

Plate 10: *The Banqueting House in Whitehall* (see *the Westminster and St James's walk, page 63*).

Plate 11: *Buckingham Palace (see the Westminster and St James's walk, page 65).*

Plate 12: *The domed National Gallery in Trafalgar Square (see the Soho to Trafalgar Square walk, page 75).*

Plate 13: *A fine view of the Houses of Parliament from the South Bank* (see *the Lambeth to South Bank walk, page 83*).

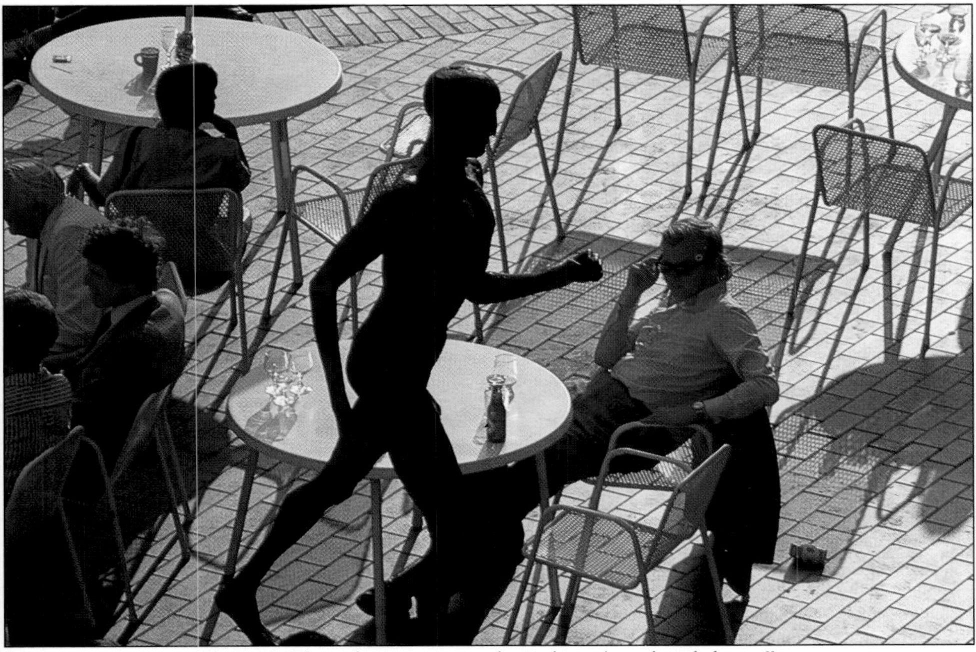

Plate 14: *The sculpture terrace at the Barbican* (see *the Clerkenwell walk, page 100*).

Plate 15: *A floodlit St Paul's Cathedral* (see *the Fleet Street and St Paul's walk, page 101*).

Plate 16: *The stout Black Friar in the City* (see *the Fleet Street and St Paul's walk, page 104*).

Plate 17: *HMS Belfast moored below London Bridge* (see *the Bankside and Southwark walk, page 110*).

Fleet Street and St Paul's (The City West)

Summary: Until quite recently the western part of the City was the traditional centre of London's printing, publishing and newspaper industries. This circular walk includes many places associated with the area's literary past, such as St Paul's Churchyard and Fleet Street, the printers' church of St Bride's, Stationer's Hall and Dr Johnson's House. The walk's other main features include the Old Bailey courthouse together with Newgate and Bridewell prisons, the College of Arms, the site of Blackfriars Monastery, St Paul's Cathedral and other Wren churches, and Playhouse Yard, site of Shakespeare's Blackfriars Playhouse.

Start and finish: **St Paul's Station (Central Underground line).**
Length: **2 miles (3.2 kilometres).**
Time: **1½ hours.**
Refreshments: **Various places *en route*, but there are two pubs worth visiting, both mentioned in the text: Ye Olde Cheshire Cheese in Vine Office Court off Fleet Street (just over half-way round the walk) and the Blackfriar near Blackfriars Bridge (about two-thirds of the way round the walk).**

Take the 'St Paul's' exit from St Paul's Station, turn left and make a U-turn back towards the cathedral. St Paul's Ⓗ is the major work of London's greatest architect, Sir Christopher Wren. The foundation stone was laid in 1675 when Wren was 43 years old and the last stone was put in place by his son 35 years later. Although Wren visited the site weekly, daily supervision was provided throughout the whole period by just one master-builder, Thomas Strong, of a well-known family of Cotswold masons. The original Norman cathedral, destroyed in the Great Fire, was even larger than Wren's new building and must have dwarfed the medieval city.

Turn right along the churchyard railings towards the deanery and chapter house. A plaque on the wall on the right commemorates John Newbery, the first children's book publisher. *Little Goody Two Shoes* is probably his best-known production. In the middle of the 18th century, St Paul's Churchyard was the centre of the London book trade, as it had been for hundreds of years, even before printing arrived in England in 1476. 'Churchyard' was really a loose term for the precincts of the cathedral which over the years had become crowded with shops and houses.

The Paternoster Square debate

Go past the deanery and neighbouring office block and turn right up the steps into Paternoster Square Ⓣ. The square was built on a bomb site and is named after near-

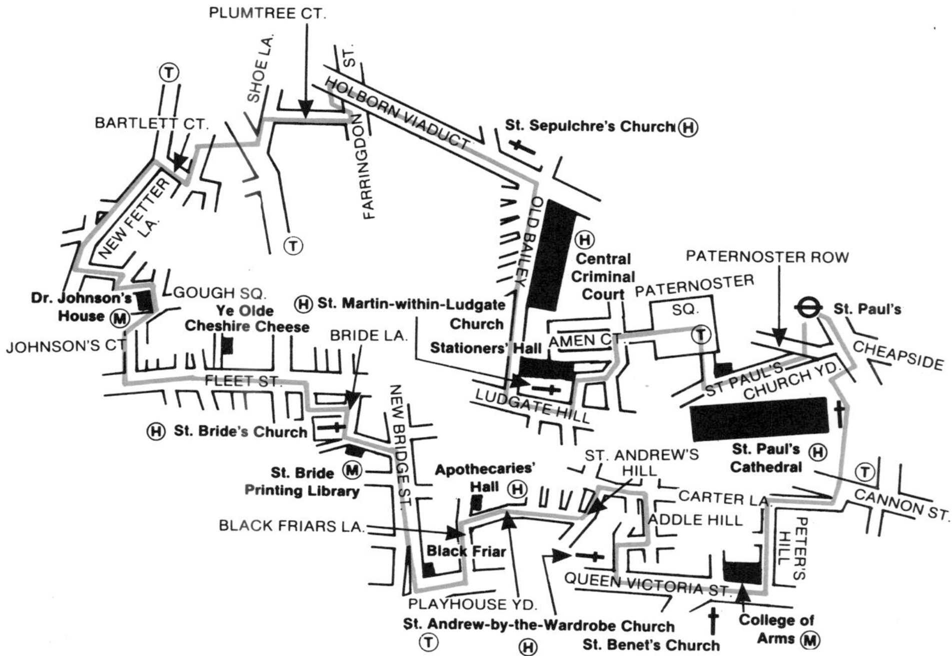

by Paternoster Row, an ancient street where strings of prayer beads (known as paternosters) were made before the Reformation. The modern Paternoster Square is a windy, cheap and dismal place, unpopular with almost everybody. The trouble is that no one can agree on an alternative plan. Should it be traditional? Should it be modern? The debate goes on.

Cross the square to the left and descend the ramp towards the gateway into Amen Court. Go to the left of the gateway and under the modern office building into the forecourt of Stationers' Hall, the livery hall of the Stationers' and Newspaper Makers' Company. In the 16th and 17th centuries the Company effectively controlled the printing and publishing trades, and until as late as 1911 all new books had to be registered at Stationers' Hall. On the front of the hall there is a plaque to Wynkyn de Worde, 'Father of Fleet Street'. We will catch up with this oddly-named person later in the walk.

Go straight past the hall and the gateway into the courtyard; along the alley called Stationers' Hall Court; and right into Ludgate Hill. On your right is the inconspicuous entrance to Wren's church of St Martin-within-Ludgate Ⓗ, situated just inside the Lud Gate of the old city. Beyond the church, turn right into Old Bailey which runs just inside the line of the old city wall. At the end of the street the Central Criminal Court, popularly known as the Old Bailey Ⓗ, is on the right. Built in 1902, the court partially replaced the infamous Newgate Prison where in May 1868 the last public hanging in Britain took place. The victim was Michael Barrett, one of a group of Irish terrorists who had killed six innocent people in a bomb outrage the previous year (see the Clerkenwell walk, page 98). Over the road from the Old

Bailey is St Sepulchre's Church Ⓗ. Originally dedicated to the martyred King Edmund, it acquired its unusual name in the Middle Ages when crusading knights heading off to the Holy Land to fight for the Holy Sepulchre in Jerusalem took to starting their journeys here.

From Old Bailey turn left into Holborn Viaduct. Built in 1869, Holborn Viaduct spans Farringdon Street some way below. Beneath Farringdon Street flows the Fleet River which rises on Hampstead Heath and joins the Thames nearby. For hundreds of years the Fleet was a stinking open sewer and dump for butchers' offal, even after Wren made this section into a decent canal, flanked by 30-feet (9-metre) wide wharves. It was eventually piped in and covered over in 1766. The Fleet still flows into the Thames under Blackfriars Bridge.

Wilkes' battle for liberty

After crossing the viaduct, turn left down the stairs and take two right turns into Plumtree Court. Turn left into Shoe Lane, cross the road ahead and climb the steps on the other side, going through the modern office block. At the top of the steps keep to the right, ascend another short flight of steps and then turn left and right into Bartlett Court. This brings you to New Fetter Lane where you turn left. On the right at the junction with Fetter Lane stands a statue of John Wilkes, 'champion of English freedom'. In the 1760s, Wilkes fought the Government when it tried to close his newspaper and imprison him for sedition. The Government also tried to stop him taking his seat in Parliament after his election as an MP, but violent 'Wilkes and Liberty' riots forced it to concede. The common people loved Wilkes, especially in the City where he was elected Lord Mayor in 1774. The building on the right just beyond the Wilkes statue is the former Public Record Office. Britain's national archives are now stored in a modern building in Kew.

When you come to West Harding Street, turn left and follow the signs to Dr Johnson's House Ⓜ in Gough Square (that is, branch right into Pemberton Row and then right again under the arch). Johnson moved to Gough Square in 1746 and immediately set to work on the great dictionary which was to make his name - though not his fortune - when it was published nine years later. In 1759 he moved to lodgings in the Temple. This house, which he rented for £30 a year, was opened as a Johnson museum in 1914. Over at the far end of the square is a statue of Johnson's beloved cat, Hodge.

Go past the front of the house into Johnson's Court (named after a different Johnson) and follow it to Fleet Street. Turn left here towards St Paul's Cathedral, high on Ludgate Hill on the far side of the Fleet valley. The second court on the left, Bolt Court, is where Johnson died in 1784. The fourth court, Wine Office Court, was the site of an office where licences to sell wine were issued. No doubt the clerks in the office were regulars at Ye Olde Cheshire Cheese pub here. They would have seen Johnson most evenings (he once said, 'a tavern chair is the throne of human felicity'), and many other famous literary men.

Further along Fleet Street you come to the former offices of two famous newspapers: the *Daily Telegraph* (Peterborough Court, Nos. 133-141) and *Daily Express* (building with the black glass front). Fleet Street has been synonymous with newspapers since the first daily newspaper, the *Daily Courant*, was produced here in 1702. Now all the big national newspapers have moved elsewhere, although the world's most famous news agency, Reuters, is still based here. The exodus was prompted by a revolution in printing technology and began amid acrimonious disputes in 1986 when the *Sun* and *News of the World* moved to Wapping.

The Father of Fleet Street

Go across Fleet Street to Wren's St Bride's Church Ⓗ, known as the printers' church. Now we catch up with the Alsatian printer Wynkyn de Worde for it was here, opposite the entrance to Shoe Lane, that in about 1500 he got himself a small house and workshop, and set up the first printing press in Fleet Street. He had previously been working in Westminster, first as assistant to William Caxton (the man who brought printing to England in 1476) and then as proprietor of the business after Caxton's death. It was the increasing competition in the printing world that forced him to move closer to the main book market in St Paul's Churchyard.

Turn left alongside St Bride's. Go down the steps and turn right into Bride Lane and follow the lane past the entrance to St Bride's Institute and Printing Library Ⓜ. In the library exhibition room there is an old wooden hand press, of the sort widely used from the 1400s until around 1800. When you get to New Bridge Street cross over and turn right towards Blackfriars Bridge.

The building on the right with the flagpole on the front (No. 14) is the 1802 gatehouse of the old Bridewell House of Correction. Formerly a medieval riverside palace beside the Thames, the prison was opened around 1555 and closed 300 years later when the women-only Holloway Prison was built in north London. To start with, vagrants and unruly orphaned apprentices were its main clientele. Later large numbers of prostitutes were sent here. For many years a popular amusement for male Londoners was a visit to Bridewell to see the twice-weekly whipping of prostitutes stripped to the waist in the black-draped 'correction' room.

Memorials to the Black Friar

When you get to the Blackfriar pub - decorated in art nouveau style and the only one like it in London - turn left round the corner under the figure of the stout Black Friar and go under the railway bridge. Then turn left into Black Friars Lane. These names all come from the Black Friars (ie Dominican) monastery which stood here from 1278 until its dissolution in 1538. Most of the buildings were then demolished but some parts survived until the Great Fire.

Ahead the building on the right hand corner is Apothecaries' Hall, built in 1688 as the livery hall of the Apothecaries' Company, one of the City livery companies Ⓗ. Just before the hall, turn right into Playhouse Yard, site of the former refectory of the monastery. In Shakespeare's time the refectory was converted into the Blackfriars Playhouse, an indoor theatre (unusual for the time) with three galleries and 600 seats. Shakespeare was a partner in the theatre, and it was used in the winter by his company, the King's Men. In summer the company used their other premises, the famous open-air Globe Theatre on Bankside (see the Bankside and Southwark walk, page 107). Both theatres were closed by the Puritans in the 1640s.

Continue straight on past Church Entry into Ireland Yard. A haberdasher called William Ireland kept a shop here in the ground floor of the old monastery gatehouse. In 1613 Shakespeare bought the shop and then left it to his daughter Susannah when he died three years later. On the left, the little courtyard is part of the churchyard of St Ann Blackfriars which was burnt in the Great Fire. Part of a wall from the monastery still stands just inside the churchyard gate.

The Dragon, the King and the Wardrobe

At the end of this alley, turn left along St Andrew's Hill and then right into Carter Lane. On the right, opposite the youth hostel, an archway leads into Wardrobe Place where the king's Master of the Wardrobe had his office and storeroom from 1359 until the Great Fire. This official was responsible for looking after all the king's ceremonial robes and spare cloth. In 1604 Shakespeare was issued with 4½ yards (4 metres) of scarlet cloth from the Wardrobe so that he could make himself a new suit for James I's state entry into London.

Take the next turning on the right into Addle Hill. Near the bottom of the lane go right into Wardrobe Terrace which takes you round the back of St Andrew-by-the-Wardrobe Ⓗ, Wren's last City church, finished in 1695. On the main road (Queen Victoria Street), turn left. On the right beyond Baynard House are Wren's Benet's Church and the City of London School. On this side of the road is the College of Arms Ⓗ - the office (and for some also the home) of the royal heralds who arrange all the great state occasions like coronations and state openings of Parliament. They also devise new coats of arms (for a fee) and undertake genealogical work. Heralds have picturesque names like Garter King of Arms, Bluemantle and Rouge Dragon, and this college was built for them after the Great Fire on a site - handy for Wardrobe - which they had occupied since 1555.

On the other side of the college, turn left up Peter's Hill towards St Paul's and then, just before the main road at the top, right into Carter Lane. At the end of the lane, cross Cannon Street and walk to the left of the garden through the gate into St Paul's Churchyard. Follow the path round the end of the cathedral, passing St Paul's Choir School on the right. This is a remnant of St Paul's School which was here from 1512 until 1884 when it moved out to Hammersmith. On the far side of the cathedral is Paul's Cross, a column marking the site of an open-air pulpit which was used until 1643 for making public announcements and reading royal proclamations. The historian Carlyle called the cross 'the *Times* newspaper of the Middle Ages'. Turn right here out of the churchyard and follow the road (Change Alley) to the left to St Paul's Station where the walk ends.

Bankside and Southwark

Summary: Bankside and Southwark lie on the south bank of the Thames opposite the City. Historically, they were always part of the City and vie with it in terms of atmosphere and historical appeal. The main features of the walk are: *in Bankside*, the reconstructed Shakespeare's Globe and the sites of three Elizabethan theatres (including the original Globe); *in Southwark,* the Clink Prison, the Bishop of Winchester's medieval palace, St Mary Overy Dock, Southwark Cathedral, the George Inn, the site of Chaucer's Tabard tavern and the old operating theatre-cum-herb garret of St Thomas's Hospital; and in the final section of the walk through the new *London Bridge City*, Hay's Galleria, HMS *Belfast* and Tower Bridge. There are splendid views of the City throughout the walk.

Start: **Blackfriars Station (District and Circle Underground lines and trains).**
Finish: **Tower Hill Station (District and Circle Underground lines). Fenchurch Street Railway Station and the Docklands Light Rail's Tower Gateway Station are both nearby.**
Length: **2½ miles (4 kilometres).**
Time: **2 hours.**
Refreshments: **Riverside pubs on Bankside and pubs and restaurants in Hay's Galleria. Two famous historic pubs worth trying are the Anchor situated on Bankside, just before Clink Street, and the George in Borough High Street, a little further on and about half-way along the route. Both are mentioned in the text.**

Take exit 3 from Blackfriars Station and cross Blackfriars Bridge Ⓣ, the third bridge over the River Thames to be built in central London. This bridge was erected in 1869, though the first Blackfriars Bridge, known as William Pitt Bridge, was built a century earlier. Next to the road bridge is one Victorian railway bridge and the piers of another. Both bridges were built for the London, Chatham and Dover Railway Company, the dismantled one being the first railway bridge across the Thames.

Down to the river
Over the bridge, turn left between the bollards and go down the steps. (In the underpass left are some old views of the railway bridges and the first Blackfriars Bridge.) Turn right through the gate and follow the riverside walk. Beyond the railway bridges Ⓣ there is a fine view of the City. In the east the International Financial Centre is the tallest building, while the western end of the City is still dominated

by St Paul's Cathedral. Until the Hilton Hotel was built in 1963 St Paul's was the tallest building in London. Even now, planning controls dictate that the buildings around the cathedral must be no higher than around 130 feet (40 metres). St Paul's itself is 365 feet (111 metres) high.

Go past the Founders Arms, built on the site of the foundry where all the iron work for St Paul's was forged. On the right is the 1980 Bankside Gallery Ⓜ, home of the Royal Societies of Painters in Watercolours and Painter-Etchers and Engravers. Next on the riverside is the former Bankside Power Station, completed in 1947 and converted in the 1990s into a gallery housing the Tate Gallery's collection of international modern art Ⓜ. In Tudor times (16th century) there were fish ponds here supplying pike to local religious houses and the royal palaces across the river. Beyond the power station, Cardinal's Wharf retains some of its old houses. The house on the left has a plaque recording that Sir Christopher Wren lived here while St Paul's was being built, though there is no evidence to prove this. On the right, Provost's Lodging belongs to the Provost of Southwark Cathedral, which you come to later in the walk.

In between the houses is Cardinal Cap Alley which once led to a tavern and brothel called the Cardinal's Hat. Until the 1600s Bankside was - as a royal proclamation of 1547 put it - a 'naughty place', full of taverns, brothels (called 'stews' from the stewhouses, which were steam baths doubling as brothels), bear and bull-baiting pits and, in the time of Shakespeare, public theatres. These were all enormously popular forms of entertainment but the prudish City authorities refused to tolerate them within their own jurisdiction on the north bank of the river. Ironically, they all flourished here in Bankside, even though part of this area, known as the Liberty of the Clink, was under the control of the Bishops of Winchester, whose London palace was nearby. The other part of the area was called Paris Garden, 'better termed a foule den than a faire garden' as one writer referred to it in 1632. In 1556 the City authorities gained control of the area but conditions did not really change. It was the 17th-century Puritans who really put an end to Bankside's debauchery and dissipation by closing down the theatres during the Commonwealth.

Global development

Next to Cardinal's Wharf is the new International Shakespeare Globe Centre. This enormous project is the fruit of 20 years' hard lobbying by the late American actor and director, Sam Wanamaker, and features a reconstructed Globe Theatre, complete with thatched roof, in which 1500 people can watch performances of Shakespeare's plays in a partly open-air setting, just as they were staged four centuries ago. The season is May to September.

Take the second turning on the right after the Globe Centre into cobbled Bear Gardens, the site of Bankside's bear-baiting arena. At the end on the left the Globe Education Centre marks the position more exactly. In 1613 the bear pit was replaced by the Hope Theatre after the nearby Globe Theatre had burned down (the Hope Theatre's owner, Philip Henslowe, was a business rival of Cuthbert and Richard Burbage, who ran the Globe). Although it was the most modern of the four Bankside theatres in Shakespeare's time, the Hope only survived for three years as a

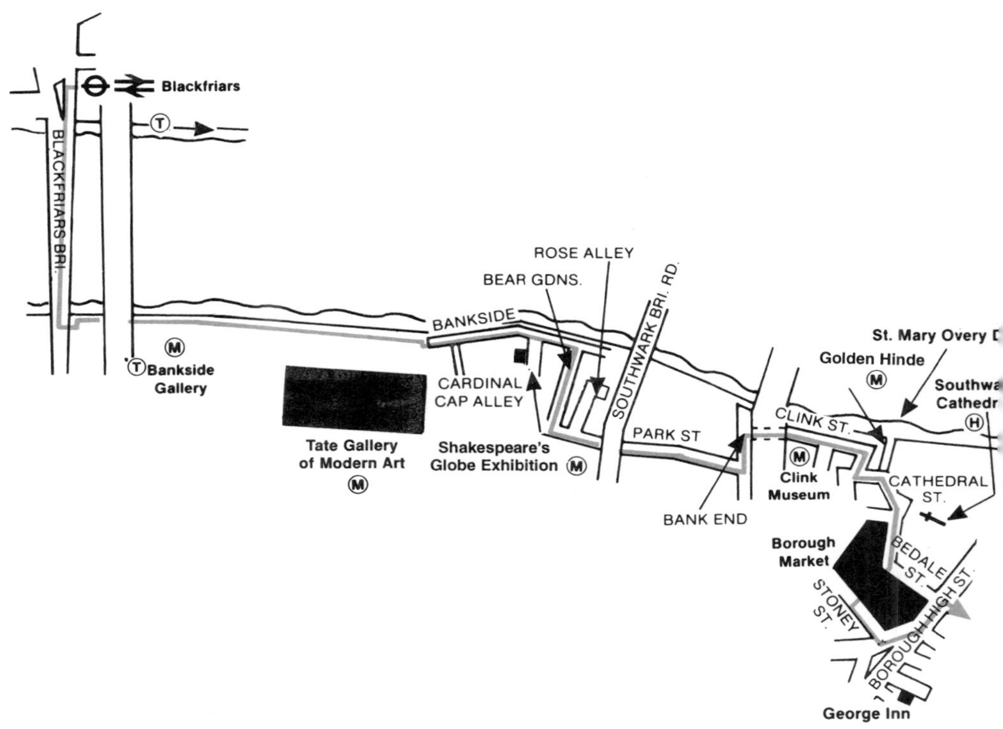

playhouse. Bear-baiting - presumably more profitable - was then resumed. In 1656 the Hope was demolished and, as the plaque on the wall of the centre records, was replaced by the Davies Amphitheatre, the last bear-baiting ring built on Bankside. Bear-baiting and bull-baiting were both finally banned in 1835.

Turn left out of Bear Gardens into Park Street, formerly called Maiden Lane because it was a red light area. The next street on the left is Rose Alley with the site of the Rose Theatre on the corner nearest to the bridge. This theatre, built in 1587, was the first theatre on Bankside and (like the Hope Theatre) was built by Henslowe. Edward Alleyn, founder of Dulwich College and the most famous actor of his day, made his name here, and Shakespeare's *Henry VI* and *Titus Andronicus* were first performed here. Peer through the windows of the modern office block now covering the site and you will see the remains of the Rose's foundations, revealed during excavations for the building in 1989 and preserved after a vigorous campaign by thespians and archaeologists. Eventually the remains may be put on public display.

Continue along Park Street, going underneath the approach to Southwark Bridge. On the left are the offices of the *Financial Times* newspaper. Opposite is the actual site of Shakespeare's Globe (the 'wooden O' as he called it in *Henry V*) with information about the excavations carried out here in the 1990s. What remains were discovered at that time were preserved and then sealed beneath the ground. Shakespeare was both an actor and a shareholder in the Globe, which was built in

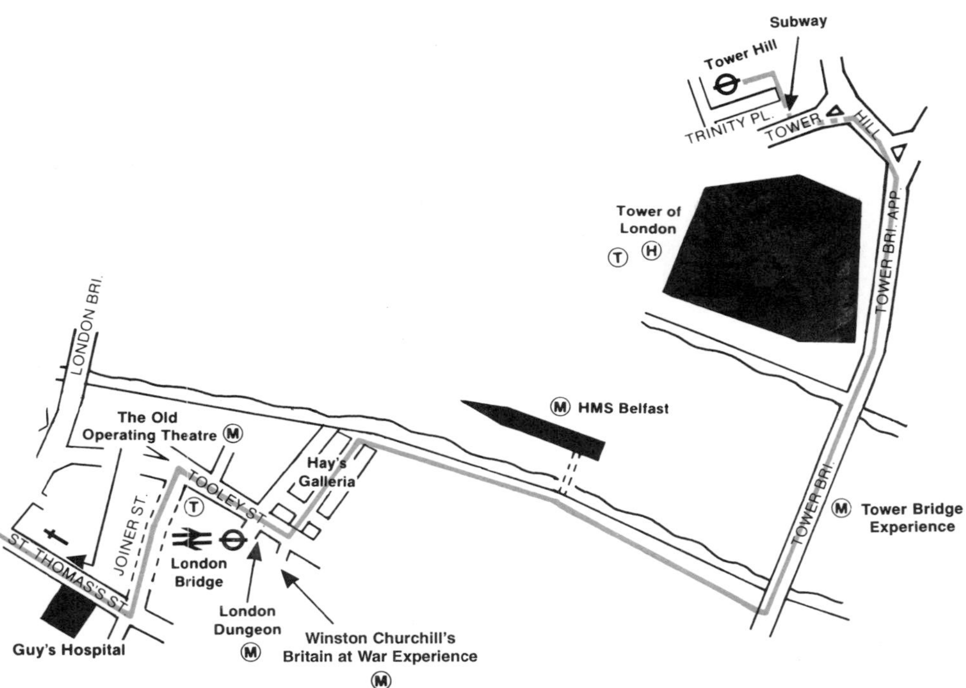

1599 by the Burbages using materials from their old theatre in Shoreditch. The Puritans closed the theatre in 1642 and in 1644 it was demolished to make room for houses. In the 18th century there was a brewery on the site owned by the Thrale family (see plaque on right further on). The Thrales were good friends of another literary giant, Dr Samuel Johnson, who had his own room here at their house next to the brewery. One cannot help wondering whether he ever knew that his illustrious predecessor once trod the boards here. The fourth Bankside theatre was the Swan, built in 1595 near Blackfriars Bridge.

The Liberty of the Clink

At the end of Park Street turn left into Bank End and then right at the Anchor Inn, dating from around 1775, into Clink Street with its old warehouses and derelict sites. This part of Southwark retains many features - and much of the atmosphere – of its recent commercial past. The Clink debtors' prison (the origin of the slang word 'clink' meaning prison) stood here until it was set on fire and destroyed during the Gordon Riots in 1780. On the right, in an old warehouse, there is a museum Ⓜ about Bankside, including the Clink and the 'Liberty' around it which was controlled by the Bishop of Winchester.

Further along on the same side of the road are the remains of Winchester Palace, the London house of the Bishops of Winchester from about 1150 to the mid 17th-century. There is very little to see apart from the foundations, although the west wall with its 14th-century rose window is still standing. On the left, Pickford's Wharf has been renovated as part of the redevelopment of Southwark's ancient dock, St Mary Overy. *The Golden Hinde* Ⓜ, a full-sized reconstruction of the ship in which Sir Francis Drake became the first Englishman to circumnavigate the globe, is now moored here. To the left there is another good view of the City and a key to the landmarks.

Follow the road round to the right and then cross over Cathedral Street to get to Southwark Cathedral Ⓗ. The building dates from 1220 and is full of historic monuments and tombs, including that of John Gower (died 1408), the poet and friend of Chaucer. At that time the church was part of the Priory of St Mary Overy, where Gower lived for the last 20 years of his life. Also buried in the cathedral are Edmund Shakespeare, William's youngest brother, and the dramatists Fletcher and Massinger. John Harvard, founder of Harvard University, was born in Southwark and baptized here in 1607.

Walk past the entrance to the churchyard on the left. Underneath the railway bridge turn right into the covered Borough Market, probably London's oldest fruit and vegetable market on its original site, and immediately fork left. Having crossed the central alley of the market, turn left out of the market into Stoney Street and then cross the road to the traffic lights in front of the Midland Bank. You are now on Borough High Street.

Borough High Street leads to London Bridge on the left. Until 1750 London Bridge was the only way across the Thames in London, so Borough High Street was the main road to the south and the English Channel. Inns for travellers entering and leaving the City lined the length of the street. One actually survives - the George, a galleried inn dating from 1677. You can see the entrance to its yard across the road to the right next to Lloyd's Bank. Further on from the George, Talbot Yard marks the site of the Tabard where Chaucer stayed before setting out on his pilgrimage to Canterbury. In the introduction to the *Canterbury Tales* he says: 'In Southwerk at the Tabard as I lay, Ready to wenden on my pilgrimage to Caunterbury . . .'. Further still down the High Street were two notorious debtors' prisons, the King's Bench and the Marshalsea. Charles Dickens set much of his novel *Little Dorrit* in the Marshalsea after his father had been imprisoned there in 1824. Later, imprisonment for debt was abolished and both prisons were closed.

Hospital to horror house

Now cross Borough High Street and turn left away from the George, and then right into St Thomas's Street. On the left is St Thomas's Church, once a parish church within medieval St Thomas's Hospital and also the hospital chapel. In 1865 the hospital moved to Lambeth (see the Lambeth and the South Bank walk, page 83) to make way for London Bridge Station. The church meanwhile has become the chapter house of Southwark Cathedral. The church loft, which was used both as a storehouse for medicinal herbs and as an operating theatre for the hospital, was rediscovered in 1956 and opened as a museum Ⓜ. Beyond the church, the row of Georgian houses was built for the use of various hospital officials. Nos. 11-19 are still occupied by local health officials.

Opposite is the 1725 entrance court of Guy's Hospital with a statue of its founder, Thomas Guy, MP and a wealthy printer and publisher, in the middle. It was here that John Keats spent a year training to be a surgeon before giving up medicine for poetry.

Turn left into Joiner Street and go through the tunnel under London Bridge Station, opened in 1837 as London's first railway terminus. Cross Tooley Street to the London Bridge Hospital and turn right past the London Dungeon Ⓜ. Opposite Winston Churchill's Britain at War Experience Ⓜ turn left into Hay's Galleria, converted from the warehouses on the former Hay's Wharf - the biggest wharf in the Pool of London - as part of the London Bridge City redevelopment scheme. Walk over the filled-in dock to the riverside terrace: the Custom House is opposite and the former Billingsgate fish market next to it. Turn right here to HMS *Belfast* Ⓜ, the largest cruiser ever built for the Royal Navy - weighing in at 11,000 tons (11,220 tonnes) - and now the only one of its old big-gun ships in existence. The ship was built in 1938, taken out of service in 1965 and opened as a museum in 1971.

Walk on past the entrance to the ship and continue along the riverside walk. The area on the right awaits development as part of London Bridge City. To the left is a fine view of the Tower of London. When you get to Tower Bridge Ⓜ, climb the steps and turn left, crossing the river using the left-hand pavement. Completed in 1894, when tall ships still used the Pool of London just below London Bridge, Tower Bridge was provided with a central section which could be opened to let high-masted ships through, and an overhead walkway so that pedestrians could use the bridge even when it was closed to road traffic. The walkway is now included in the bridge museum.

Once over the bridge, continue along Tower Bridge Approach round behind the Tower to the bus stop. Here, take the subway to Tower Hill Station, which is where the walk ends.

The City (East)

Summary: The eastern half of the City is both the oldest part and the financial centre of modern London. This circular walk sticks mainly to the City's many narrow lanes and alleys, but still manages to cover all the main institutions such as Lloyd's, the Royal Exchange, the Stock Exchange, the Bank of England, the Guildhall, Mansion House and Custom House, as well as other features such as the site of Dick Whittington's house, the Great Fire Monument, the Tower of London, Bow Bells, Leadenhall Market, the old Billingsgate Market, many City churches and livery halls as well as several traditional City pubs and eating houses.

Start and finish: **Tower Hill Station (District and Circle Underground lines). Fenchurch Street Railway Station and the Docklands Light Rail's Tower Gateway Station are both nearby.**
Length: **2½ miles (4 kilometres).**
Time: **1¾ hours.**
Refreshments: **No shortage of pubs, restaurants, wine bars and sandwich bars *en route* plus several old-fashioned City watering holes spread out along the course of the walk and all mentioned in the text (the Jamaica Wine House, the George and Vulture - ties compulsory - the Old Dr Butler's Head, Williamson's Tavern, the Olde Wine Shades).**

Leave Tower Hill Station by the 'Fenchurch Street' exit and walk round the top of Trinity Square between, on the left, Trinity Square gardens Ⓟ, where prisoners from the Tower of London were executed, usually by decapitation, and on the right, Trinity House, headquarters of the 16th century Trinity House Corporation, which is responsible for the lighthouses on the coasts of England and Wales.

Beyond Trinity House turn right into Savage Gardens, left into Pepys Street and then right into Seething Lane. In the 17th-century Samuel Pepys lived and worked in the Navy Office here, and worshipped regularly in St Olave's Church Ⓗ during the period covered by his diary. He was also buried in the church after his death in 1703. St Olave's is in the City's Tower Ward and a noticeboard to the right of the churchyard gate lists the ward's alderman and common councillors. The City is divided into 26 wards, each of which elects a number of common councillors and an alderman who together form the City Corporation, presided over by the Lord Mayor.

The legend of Lloyd's

At the end of Seething Lane turn left and then right into New London Street. Go up the steps, walk straight across the forecourt of Fenchurch Street Station Ⓣ (to the left

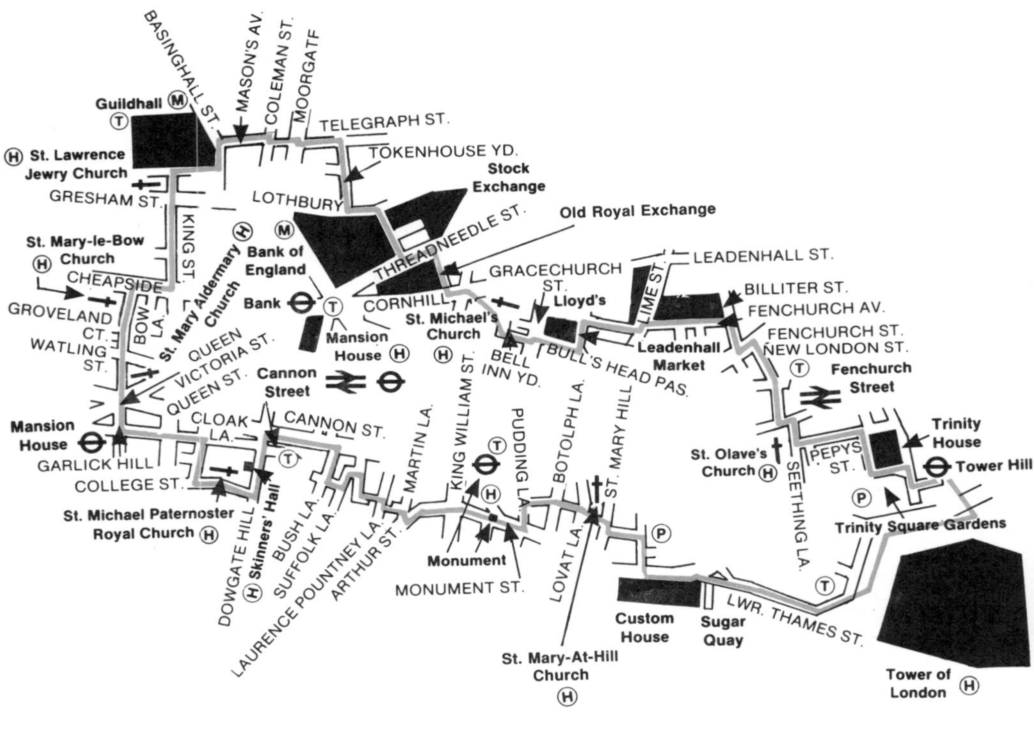

you can see the remains of All Hallows Staining) and then go across Fenchurch Street into Billiter Street to the left. Take the first turning on the left into Fenchurch Avenue. Ahead is the new high-tech headquarters of Lloyd's, the world-famous insurance market originally started in Edward Lloyd's coffee house in Tower Street in the 1680s.

Turn left and right by Lloyd's into Leadenhall Food Market (weekdays only), established here in the 1300s and rebuilt in 1881. Turn left at the central crossroads, take the second turning on the right into Bull's Head Passage by Kent's the fruiterers and then cross Gracechurch Street and go into Bell Inn Yard ahead on the left. Bell Inn was a casualty of the Great Fire of 1666.

Turn right into St Michael's Alley at the end of the yard and go into the former churchyard of St Michael Cornhill with Christopher Wren's church Ⓗ on the far side. Turn left here and go as far as the first crossroads in this maze of narrow passages. On the right is the Jamaica Wine House, built on the site of London's first coffee house, the Sign of the Pasqua Rosee's Head, opened in 1652. In the 1670s it became the Jamaica Coffee House, an unofficial post office for letters to the West Indies and a general rendezvous for merchants and sea captains involved in the Jamaica trade. On the left, the George and Vulture, a traditional City pub and chop house (ties compulsory), has been serving bankers, brokers, merchants and clerks for the best part of 300 years.

Walk on past the jeweller's shop into Castle Court. Turn right into Ball Court at the sign pointing to Simpson's Tavern (opened 1757). On Cornhill, turn left and cross the road at the traffic lights. Go left again and then right into the open space of Royal Exchange Buildings. The Royal Exchange on the left was founded in 1570 by Sir Thomas Gresham as a meeting place for merchants. This is the third building on the site and it was last used for its original purpose in 1939.

Home of the Old Lady

At the end of Royal Exchange Buildings is a statue of George Peabody, the American-born founder of the 19th century Peabody housing trust. Peabody Buildings are still a common sight in London and the City recognized his work on behalf of the poor by making him a freeman. Standing by the statue, you can see to the right the former Stock Exchange, made redundant by the introduction of electronic trading in 1987, and the International Financial Centre - at 600 feet (183 metres) the tallest building in central London.

Turn left now and cross Threadneedle Street into Bartholomew Lane. As you do so look left to the porticoed façade of the 18th century Mansion House Ⓗ, official residence of the City's Lord Mayor during his (or her) one-year term of office. On the left now is the back of the Bank of England Ⓜ, its 18th-century walls windowless for extra security. Familiarly known as the Old Lady of Threadneedle Street and founded in 1694 to raise money for war, the bank now issues banknotes, stores the national gold reserves and supervises financial activities in the City.

At the end of Bartholomew Lane, turn left into Lothbury and then right into Tokenhouse Yard. In the 1600s tokens were minted and issued here whenever coin of the realm was in short supply. Most of the buildings at the end of the yard are occupied by Cazenove's, the most fashionable of the old stock-broking firms in the City and one of the few to remain independent following deregulation of the City's financial markets in 1987.

Shock treatment

Go straight through the passage under Cazenove's and turn left into Telegraph Street. Cross Moorgate - a road that led north towards one of the old City gates - into Great Bell Alley. Then cross Coleman Street into Mason's Avenue. The Old Dr Butler's Head here was one of several pubs founded around 1616 to sell a successful brand of medicinal ale concocted by Dr William Butler, the king's physician. Dr Butler's speciality was shock treatment: he once cured a patient by having him thrown out of a window into the Thames!

Mason's Avenue leads to Basinghall Street where Hugh Myddelton had his office (see the Islington walk, page 93). Turn left here and then first right past the Mayor's and City of London Court (the Lord Mayor is also the City's chief magistrate) into Guildhall Yard where the City Corporation does its work. On the right-hand side is the 15th-century Guildhall Ⓜ, much repaired after the Great Fire and the Blitz. Opposite stands St Lawrence Jewry Church Ⓗ, so named because in medieval times it stood in the Jewish quarter of the City. It now serves as the official church of the Corporation of London.

Turn left by the church and cross Gresham Street into King Street. Turn right into Cheapside and then left into Bow Lane by Wren's St Mary-le-Bow Church Ⓗ. Traditionally, anyone born within the sound of Bow bells was said to be a true Cockney, or pure Londoner. That was in the days when the City was densely populated. Today only a few thousand actually live here: most people simply commute in to work.

Continue along Bow Lane. To the right in Groveland Court is Williamson's Tavern, started in 1739 by Robert Williamson in what had previously been the Lord Mayor's house. The gates at the end were presented to the then Lord Mayor by William III and Queen Mary after a visit to the City. Go across Watling Street, the Roman road from Dover in Kent to Shropshire on the Welsh border. Wren is said to have built what is now Ye Olde Watling pub and to have worked here while St Paul's Cathedral (visible to the right) was being built. Walk past St Aldermary Church Ⓗ and cross Queen Victoria Street into Garlick Hill by Mansion House Station, where the ground begins to drop steeply away towards the river. Garlic was once sold in this district; more recently it was the centre of the fur and skin trade. Take the first turning on the left into Great St Thomas Apostle Street; at the end you pass the site of St Thomas the Apostle church and some handsome merchants' houses. Go across Queen Street into Cloak Lane. The view right is of Southwark Bridge and the *Financial Times* building on the south side of the Thames.

Pantomime hero

From Cloak Lane take the first turning on the right down College Hill. Here on the left lived Richard Whittington, the most famous of all London's citizens. The youngest son of a Gloucestershire landowner, Whittington made his fortune as a mercer (dealer in textiles) and was Lord Mayor four times between 1397 and 1419. Although he married, he died childless so he left most of his enormous wealth to various charities. His generosity made him a popular hero and he is still celebrated in children's stories and Christmas pantomimes.

At the bottom of College Hill is the church of St Michael Paternoster Royal Ⓗ: Whittington was buried in its pre-Great Fire predecessor in 1423. Turn left along winding College Street past the livery hall of the Innholders' Company. Then turn left again into Dowgate Hill past three more livery halls: first, the Dyers' Company; second, the Skinners' Company (a fine Georgian stuccoed building of 1778 - the actual hall Ⓗ is in a courtyard to the rear); and third, the Tallow Chandlers' Company (only the gate is visible - again the hall is in a rear courtyard). The oldest City livery companies (modern creations have taken the total to over 100) are the descendants of the trade guilds which controlled all business life in the medieval City. Today they are mainly charitable and social bodies. All livery men are freemen and all vote in the Lord Mayor's election.

At the top of the hill turn right past Cannon Street Station Ⓣ and then right again into Bush Lane. Then take the first turning on the left into Gophir Lane and turn left again into cobbled Suffolk Lane. Follow this round to the right and turn right into Laurence Pountney Hill. On the right now are two merchants' houses, built in 1703 and the finest houses of their date in the City. In the little square turn left along the sunken path between the two churchyard gardens. Here stood Laurence Pountney Church and Corpus Christi College, both destroyed in the Great Fire. They were founded by Sir John de Pulteney, a Drapers' Company man and Lord Mayor in the 1330s. His house, which was later inhabited by the Black Prince, eldest son of Edward III, stood on the site of the two merchants' houses.

Continue straight across Laurence Pountney Lane and through the small car park to Martin Lane. On the left corner is the Olde Wine Shades, started just before the Great Fire and one of only a couple of City taverns to have survived the conflagration. Turn right here and then immediately left into Arthur Street. Then cross King William Street (subway to left) to the Monument Ⓗ, built by Wren in 1677 as the City's memorial to the Great Fire of 1666 (see the panel on the base for more history). The panorama from the top is well worth the climb up the spiral staircase inside.

The City ablaze

Go past the Monument along Monument Street and take the first turning on the left into Pudding Lane. The Great Fire started here during the night of 2nd September 1666 in the ovens of the king's baker - aptly named Faryner ('farine' is French for flour). Take the first turning on the right into St George's Lane and go straight across Botolph Lane and through Botolph Alley to St Mary-at-Hill Church Ⓗ in Lovat Lane. This church was gutted in 1986 by a fire, a more than usually sad event because it was the only Wren City church to have retained its original interior more or less as the architect designed it. Go through the passage to the right of the church to St Mary At Hill (the church entrance is through a doorway up the hill to the left) and then turn right and left into cobbled St Dunstan's Lane. With the exception of its tower, now used as a chapel, Wren's church of St Dunstan-in-the-East at the end of the lane was largely destroyed during World War II. It has since been converted into a public garden Ⓟ.

Turn right here and cross over the main road (Lower Thames Street) to the Custom House, where customs duties on all goods imported into London have been collected since at least the 1200s. To the right is the former Billingsgate fish market, which was used from the early Middle Ages until the market moved to a new docklands site in 1982. Turn left along Lower Thames Street, and walk straight on when the road bends left up the hill. On the right is Sugar Quay where the great sugar firm of Tate and Lyle have their offices. Turn right on to the quayside (a dead-end) to see the 1200 foot- (366 metre-) long river frontage of the Custom House.

Retrace your steps back to where you turned right onto the quayside, and turn right. This brings you to Tower Pier Ⓣ and the entrance to the 900-year-old Tower of London Ⓗ, built just outside the City boundary by William the Conqueror to overawe the potentially troublesome citizens. Go through the gates by the ticket office and along the moat-side walk. Turn left into the subway under the road and climb the steps to Tower Hill Station where the walk ends.

Plate 18: *A London bus crosses Tower Bridge* (see *the Bankside and Southwark walk, page 111*).

Plate 19: *Officers of the Court of Common Council at the Guildhall* (see *the City [East] walk, page 114*).

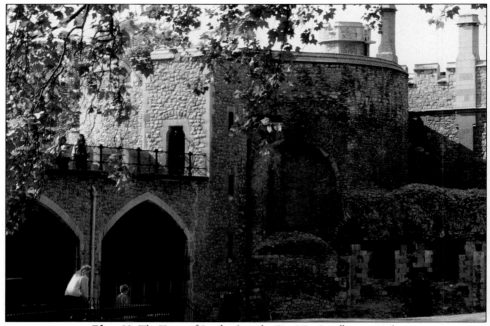

Plate 20: *The Tower of London* (see *the City [East] walk, page 116).*

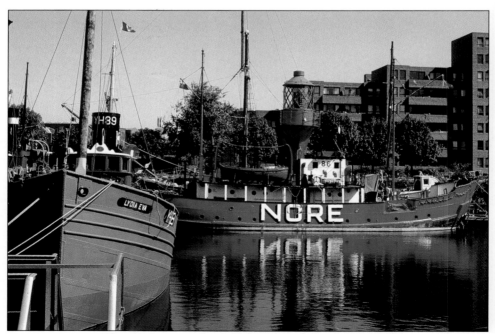

Plate 21: *Boats moored at St Katharine's Dock* (see *the Wapping to Limehouse walk, page 117).*

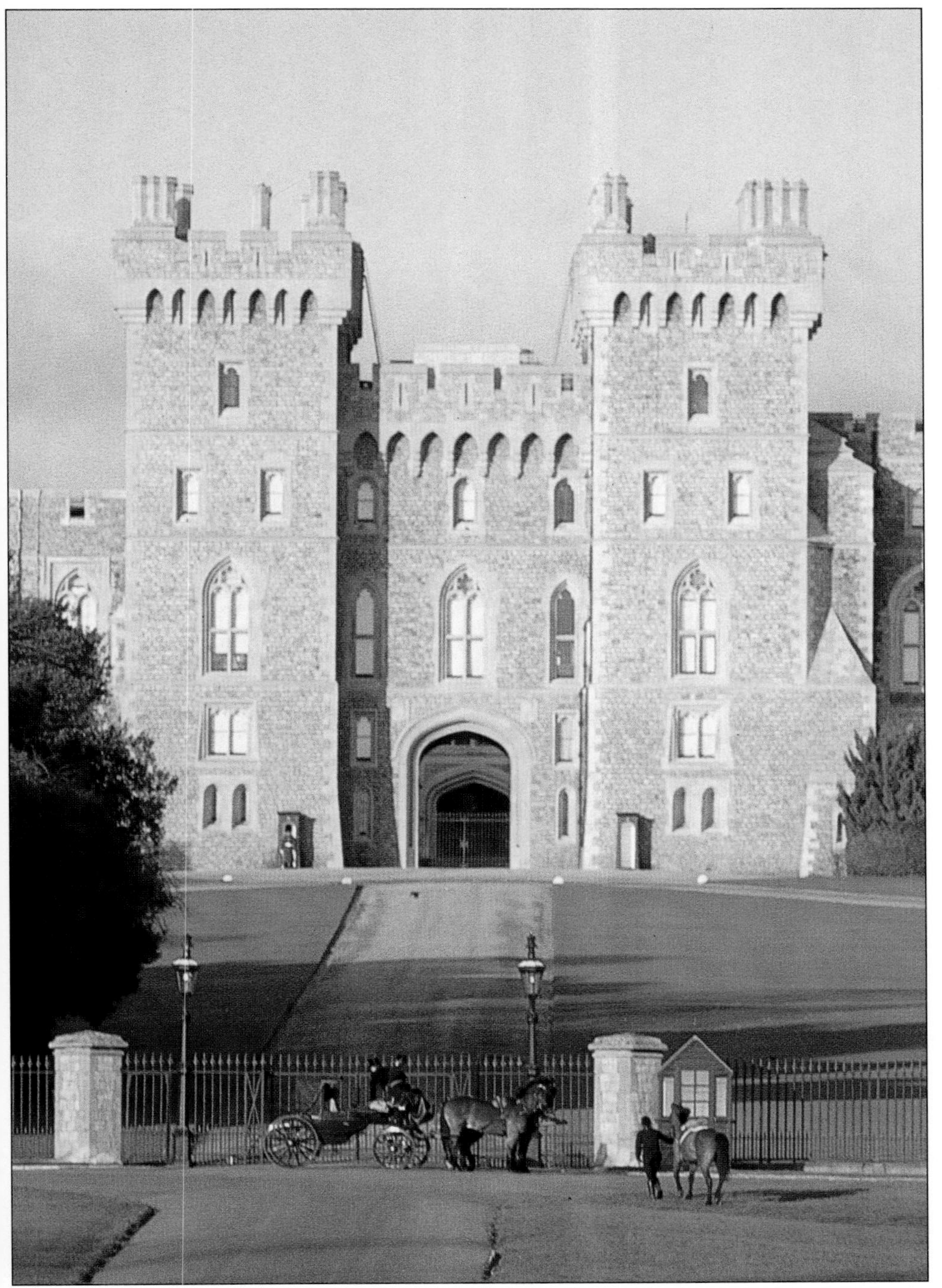

Plate 22: *Windsor Castle* (see *the Windsor and Eton walk, page 122*).

Plate 23: *The tomb of Queen Victoria and Prince Albert in the Royal Mausoleum (see the Windsor and Eton walk, page 124).*

Plate 24: *Schoolboys at Eton in the 4th of June procession of boats (see the Windsor and Eton walk, page 125).*

Wapping to Limehouse

Summary: This walk goes straight along the riverside through the old dockland areas of Wapping, Shadwell and Limehouse, the original Tower Hamlets immediately east of the City. These districts are all at various stages of redevelopment following the wholesale closure of London's moribund docks in the late 1960s. The walk starts at St Katharine's Dock by Tower Bridge. Wapping High Street and Pier Head follow; then Wapping Wall, Shadwell Basin and Park, Narrow Street, Limehouse Basin and Limehouse's famous parish church of St Anne's. Other features are three old docklands pubs and views of the river from stairs, wharves and waterfront parks.

Start: **Tower Hill Station (District and Circle Underground lines). Fenchurch Street Railway Station and the Docklands Light Rail's Tower Gateway Station are both nearby.**
Finish: **Westferry Station (Docklands Light Rail).**
Length: **3¼ miles (5.2 kilometres).**
Time: **2½ hours.**
Refreshments: **Apart from places like the Dickens Inn in St Katharine's Dock at the beginning, almost the only places to stop on this walk are a handful of historic riverside pubs strung out along the route and all mentioned in the text.**

Come out of Tower Hill station and go down the steps into the subway with a section of the old City wall on your left and the Tower of London ahead. When you get to the ruins of the old postern gate in the City wall, turn left along the side of the Tower moat, following the signs to St Katharine's Dock. Go under the next road and then branch right across the small bridge into the water garden. Turn left by the World Trade Centre into Commodity Quay, which faces one of the three basins in St Katharine's Dock. A hospital, a medieval church and over one thousand houses were demolished to make room for this dock, which opened in 1828. Tea, rubber, wool, marble, sugar, tallow, and ivory were all unloaded at the quays and stored in the dock's multi-storey warehouses supported on their thick iron columns.

Commercial commodities

At the end of Commodity Quay, turn right along the flagged terrace in front of the new shops in the ground floor of the warehouse. Go through the archway into the entrance basin connecting with the river. Turn right here and then cross the bridge by the new glass-walled chapel marking the approximate position of old St Katharine's Church.

Go to the left under the Tower Hotel and then left again over the red bridge across the entrance to the dock. The entrance's relatively small size was one reason why St Katharine's was never a great commercial success. It survived, however, along with London's other wet docks until competition from the new container ports further downstream forced them all to close in the 1960s.

Keep to the left along the dockside and then turn right round the end of the Dickens Inn. Turn left behind the row of houses facing the basin. Go left again at the

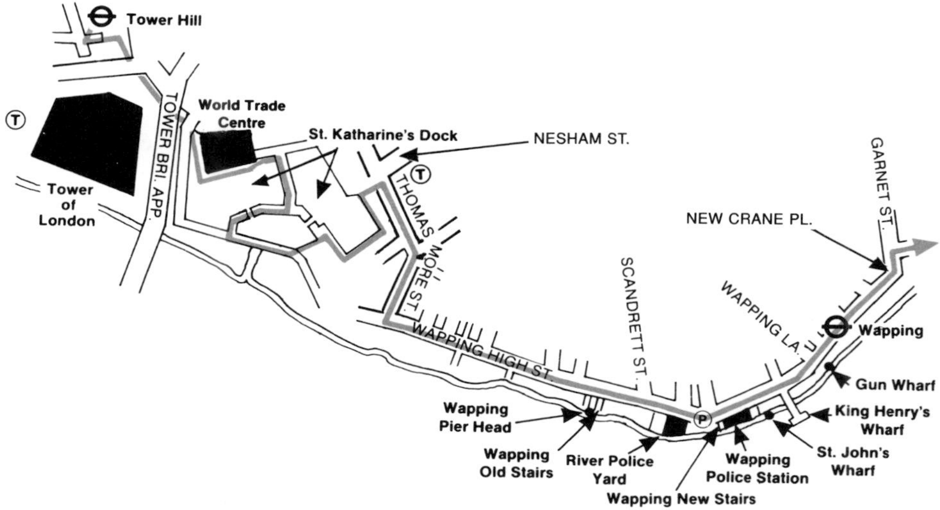

end and then right to the gate leading into Thomas More Street Ⓣ, bordered by dock walls. Turn right here, right again at the first junction and then left at the second junction into Wapping High Street, a long street that follows the course of the river almost as far as Limehouse. The road was built around 1570 to link the legal quays in the City - the only quays at which ships could lawfully unload their cargo - to new storage warehouses downstream at New Crane Wharf. Inevitably, people settled along the road and it was later described by John Stow, a 16th-century historian of London, as a 'filthy strait passage, with alleys of small tenements or cottages...inhabited by sailors' victuallers'. So began the maritime community of the East End.

On the left you pass new housing developments built over the London Docks. Opened in 1805, the year of Nelson's victory at Trafalgar, London Docks were about three times larger than St Katharine's Dock and, with their monopoly on the import of tobacco, rice, wine and brandy, were commercially very successful. So prosperous were they, in fact, that in 1864 they took over St Katharine's. Apart from the two entrance basins, most of the docks have now been filled in, the 20-acre (8-hectare) western dock being buried beneath the new headquarters of Rupert Murdoch's News International, publishers of *The Sun* and *The Times*.

After a while you come to Wapping Pier Head, a double row of Georgian houses facing each other across railed gardens. The houses were built for officials of

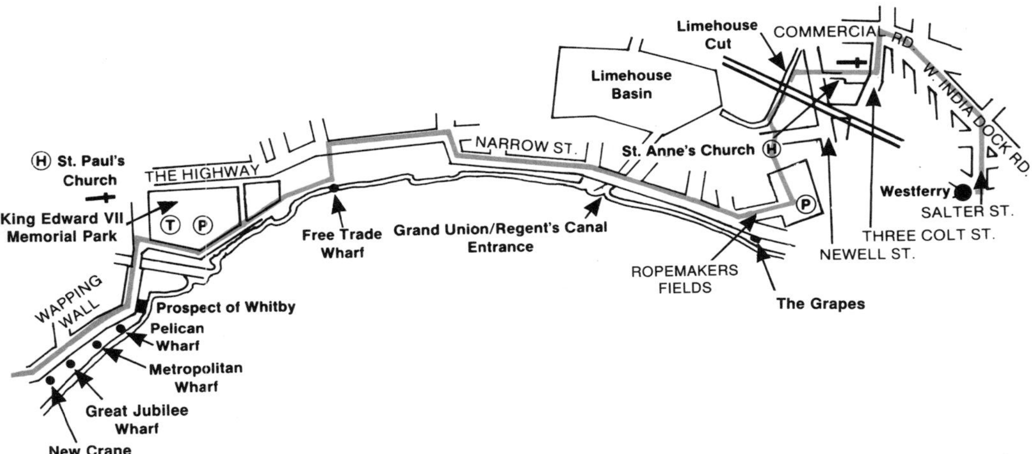

the dock company and the central gardens cover the original entrance to the docks. Cobblestones set in the garden on the left describe the arc of the dock entrance gates. The entrance basins mentioned above were built later to accommodate larger ships.

Convicts' quay

Continue through the Pier Head houses. On the right the Town of Ramsgate pub marks the entrance to a narrow alleyway leading to Wapping Old Stairs. At low tide you can go down these stairs onto the rocky riverside and get a good view of both Butler's Wharf on the Surrey bank, and of Tower Bridge. During the bloodless revolution of 1688 it is said that the bloodthirsty Judge Jeffreys was captured here as he tried to flee the country in a collier bound for Hamburg. Later, convicts were chained up in the pub's cellars before being transported to Australia. More recently the warehouses here were used for oranges and spices. An old lady I met who had lived in Wapping all her life told me how the dockers used to break open a crate of oranges each morning and throw the fruit to the children as they passed by on their way to school. On the left in Scandrett Street are Wapping's former 18th-century charity school and the remains of its church, bombed during the war.

Further along, the white building covered in abstract concrete shapes is the boatyard of the river police. Set up in 1798 to deal with endemic pilfering from the thousands of merchant ships moored in the river (a contemporary estimate put the value of goods stolen at £½ million per year), they were the first properly organized police force in the country. They are now part of the Metropolitan Police and patrol the Thames in a fleet of 33 boats.

Next to the boatyard is a riverside garden Ⓟ from which there is a fine view of the lonely Angel pub on the south side of the river in Bermondsey. Beyond the next warehouses are Wapping New Stairs and the station of the river police. After the

Captain Kidd pub and Swan Wharf you come to King Henry's Stairs leading to a riverboat pier from which there is a good view of Rotherhithe and the former Surrey Docks. In the 16th century there was a cannon foundry here making guns for Henry VIII's navy, hence the local names of King Henry's Wharf and Gun Wharf. Later the spot became the traditional place of execution for convicted pirates. Captain Kidd – the naval officer who, having been sent on an anti-pirate mission to Madagascar, turned pirate himself – was hanged here in 1701. For maximum deterrent effect the sentence was usually carried out at low tide and three high tides were allowed to wash over the corpse before it was cut down and buried. The last hanging at Execution Dock took place in 1830.

The High Street now curves to the left beside Gun Wharf and then passes Wapping Station. The Underground line runs under the river through the world's first underwater tunnel. Engineered by the Brunels, it was completed in 1843 after 20 years of tunnelling. Follow the road round to the left into New Crane Place and then turn right into Wapping Wall. The original road was laid out on top of a sea wall, constructed between St Katharine's and Shadwell after the old medieval flood defences had been washed away by heavy tides in the 1560s.

New wharf development

Now you pass New Crane Wharf and Great Jubilee Wharf, and then Metropolitan Wharf, an old pepper warehouse converted into offices and studios. Next is Pelican Wharf, and beyond that on the corner is the Prospect of Whitby pub, named after a ship from the Yorkshire port that once berthed here regularly. Like the Angel at Bermondsey, this is another pub of great antiquity, though its claim to be the oldest riverside inn in London should be taken with a substantial bucket of salt.

Follow the road round to the left past the old London Hydraulic Power Company's pumping station. Between 1893 and 1977 this supplied hydraulic power for cranes and lifts not only to the wharves here in Docklands but also to theatres and office buildings as far away as Earl's Court in west London. You now cross the bridge over the entrance to Shadwell Basin. Once the eastern entrance to London Docks, this basin is now used for swimming and canoeing, and new houses have been built on the quays. To the right of the basin you can see the spire of St Paul Shadwell Church Ⓗ, traditionally known as the church of the sea captains. Captain Cook, the discoverer of Australia, was a regular worshipper in the church and in 1763 James, his eldest son, was baptized here. Like his father, James also served in the navy but was drowned in 1794.

Intrepid explorers

Immediately after the bridge turn right into a path besides the sports ground leading to the King Edward VII Memorial Park Ⓟ Ⓣ. Opened in 1922, the park covers the site of the old Shadwell fish market which lay between Shadwell High Street (now The Highway) and the river. On the right adjoining the Rotherhithe Tunnel ventilation shaft is a coloured tablet commemorating the Elizabethan navigators who sailed from the Thames here to find a north-east passage round Russia to China. The expedition set sail in 1563 but had not gone far before all the ships were separated in a gale. Sir Hugh Willoughby and his crew froze to death in the Arctic winter but the others returned safely, one of them via the court of Ivan the Terrible in Russia. Sir Francis Drake found a way to China 25 years later, using the southerly route around Cape Horn. The Ratcliff Cross mentioned on the tablet stood on the riverside marking the position of Ratcliff Stairs, the most important station for Thames watermen east of the Tower. The walk passes the site of the stairs shortly.

Now walk along the riverside, from which there is a good view of Canary Wharf on the Isle of Dogs. Go through the gate and continue in front of the new flats on what was Free Trade Wharf. Beyond the flats turn left between two rows of the original Free Trade warehouses and walk up to the main road, The Highway. Turn right here and walk to the traffic lights. Away to your left the old house with the plaque on it is the present base of the Royal Foundation of St Katharine's, the organisation displaced to make way for the eponymous dock in 1828.

Now turn right into Narrow Street, the old link between Shadwell and Limehouse. Where the road bends left is the site of Ratcliff Stairs. After a while the road crosses the entrance to Limehouse Basin, itself the entrance to the Regent's Canal and thus to the whole of the national canal network. A short canal called the Limehouse Cut also runs from Limehouse Basin, linking up with the River Lee navigation to the east.

Sailors' leisure

Further along this street you come to the Grapes, the third of the old riverside pubs on the north bank. Once there were dozens of pubs along the river - 36 in Wapping High Street alone - where originally sailors and then dockers slaked their thirst. Fork left here into Ropemakers Fields. When you get to the pub continue on into the park Ⓟ and turn left. Just before the path enters the circular railed enclosure sloping up to the footbridge, go right, round the outside of the railings and onto the towpath of the Limehouse Cut. Here turn right. Just beyond the railway bridge turn right up some steps and then left along a path that brings you out on Newell Street, a rare survivor of Georgian Limehouse. The bow-fronted house on the corner of Newell Street ahead was often visited by the London novelist Charles Dickens, whose godfather, Christopher Huffam, lived here. Cross Newell Street and approach the famous parish church of Limehouse - St Anne's Ⓗ - built by Nicholas Hawksmoor in the early 18th century (see the sign on the left-hand gate pier for more about the church' s history).

Go to the right of the church and leave the churchyard by the gate at the opposite end. Turn left into Three Colt Street and then right onto the main road (Commercial Road). Fork right into West India Dock Road (on the left, notice the old ship chandlers' and sail makers' building). Opposite the petrol station turn right into cobbled Salter Street. Westferry Station, where the walk ends, is straight ahead.

Windsor and Eton

Summary: Being only 20 miles (32 kilometres) west of London, the country towns of Windsor and Eton with their royal and aristocratic associations are often included in a visit to the capital. Joined together by a bridge across the Thames, both towns are dominated by the vast, picturesque bulk of Windsor Castle, the Queen's weekend and holiday home and the oldest inhabited castle in Europe. Eton is home to Eton College, England's top public school. Other features of the walk include Windsor town centre and Windsor Park, and Eton's high street and riverside meadows.

***Start and finish:* Windsor and Eton Riverside Station (trains from Waterloo). Windsor Central Station (trains from Paddington, change at Slough) is close by.**
***Length:* 3¾ miles (5.2 kilometres).**
***Time:* 2½ hours.**
***Refreshments:* Take your pick of places in either Windsor or Eton.**

Leave Windsor and Eton Riverside Station and walk along Datchet Road towards the town, with the castle high up on your left. At the road junction with Thames Street is a Lutyens-designed memorial to George V (1910-36). It was he who, during World War I when everything German was vilified, prudently changed the royal family's name from Saxe-Coburg to Windsor. Near the memorial is a plaque recording the execution in 1543 of Windsor's three Protestant martyrs - Robert Testwood, Henry Filmer and Anthony Pierson - all burnt at the stake beneath the castle walls. Turn left here into Thames Street. On the left beyond Old Bank House is yet another memorial, this one representing a grandson of Queen Victoria who succumbed to pneumonia in 1900 while serving with the British Army in South Africa.

Library Terrace

Follow the road round to the right and up the hill under the huge walls and towers of Windsor Castle. Looking up at the castle from the junction of River Street, you can see the 'Lookout' viewpoint on the Library Terrace. On the right is the Library of the Dean and Canons of the castle chapel of St George's; on the left are the homes of various chapel officials such as the Organist and Master of the Choristers.

Continue on up the hill. Originally there used to be shops on the left side of the road as well as the right, but after a serious fire a century ago they were all cleared away to improve the view of the truly monumental castle walls. On the right beneath the oriel window of the Olde King and Castle there is a bust of Edward

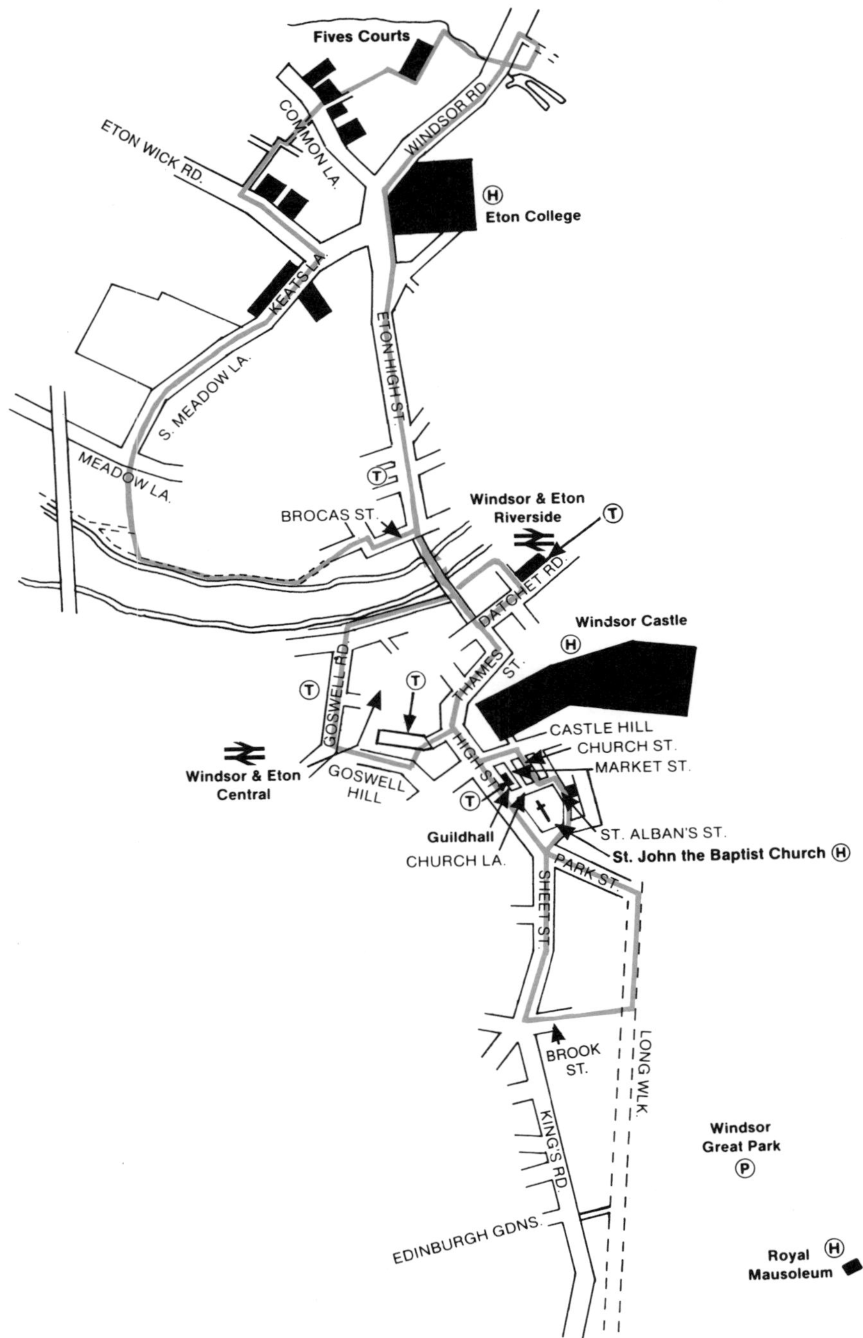
Fives Courts
ETON WICK RD.
COMMON LA.
WINDSOR RD.
Eton College
KEATS LA.
S. MEADOW LA.
ETON HIGH ST.
MEADOW LA.
BROCAS ST.
Windsor & Eton
Riverside
DATCHET RD.
Windsor Castle
THAMES ST.
GOSWELL RD.
Windsor & Eton
Central
GOSWELL
HILL
HIGH ST.
CASTLE HILL
CHURCH ST.
MARKET ST.
Guildhall
CHURCH LA.
ST. ALBAN'S ST.
St. John the Baptist Church
PARK ST.
SHEET ST.
BROOK
ST.
LONG WLK.
KING'S RD.
Windsor
Great Park
EDINBURGH GDNS.
Royal
Mausoleum

VII (reigned 1901-10). Inside the archway beneath is a large picture of Windsor Castle made out of tiles and based on a 17th-century engraving.

At the top of the hill you come to a crossroads. The old market cross of Windsor stood here until 1887 when it was replaced by the statue of Queen Victoria to mark her Jubilee. Go straight on past the statue into the High Street, keeping to the left hand side. Queen Charlotte Street on the left, one of a grid of quaint streets where Windsor market used to be held, is said to be the shortest street in the country. At just 51 feet 10 inches (15.75 metres) one can well believe it. On the opposite side of the High Street are the information centre and Town and Crown Exhibition Ⓜ.

Architectural bravado

Straight ahead Ⓣ is the old Windsor Guildhall, built in 1687 with a corn exchange underneath. Notice how the Guildhall chamber (now used for wedding receptions and similar functions) is supported only by the outer pillars: those near the centre stop slightly short of the roof. Sir Christopher Wren, who lived at Windsor as a boy when his father became dean of the castle chapel, was apparently responsible for this piece of architectural bravado. Having been commissioned by the town council to design the Guildhall, he was convinced that the outer pillars would be sufficient to support the weight of the upper floor. The council disagreed and ordered him to build more pillars in the centre. Wren obeyed, but to prove his point left a tiny gap at the top. Time seems to have proved him rather than the council right.

Continue along High Street past Windsor's parish church of St John's Ⓗ, rebuilt in 1822 with many of the old monuments from the previous church preserved in it. When you get to the junction with Park Street, follow the road round to the right into Sheet Street. Hadleigh House on the left (opposite the entrance to Victoria Street) is named after an 18th-century court physician. Troops from the Victoria Barracks on the right provide the various guards for Windsor Castle. At the far end of the barracks turn left into Brook Street (almost opposite the entrance to Frances Street). This brings you into Windsor Park Ⓟ. Diagonally to your right through the trees you can see the green copper dome of the Royal Mausoleum Ⓗ where Queen Victoria and Prince Albert are buried (they died in 1901 and 1861 respectively). To your right at the end of the three-mile Long Walk the great Copper Horse (an equestrian statue of George III) stands out clearly on the horizon. Turn left into the Long Walk and walk towards the impressive south front of the castle. All around stretch the 4800 acres (1944 hectares) of Windsor Park. Much of it (the Great Park) is open to the public, but the part round the castle (the Home Park) is reserved for the private use of the Queen, who spends most weekends here.

First airmail

When you get to the castle gates, turn left into the funnel-shaped Park Street, part of the old road from Windsor to London before the section through the park was closed. At the end turn right past the old well and the blue pillar box commemorating Britain's first aerial post (flown from Hendon to Windsor in 1911 to mark the coronation of George V) into St Alban's Street. Walk up the hill past the Royal Mews. Beyond the back of the church turn left into Church Lane, one of the grid of market streets just outside the castle gates. On the left-hand corner is the old parish charity school dating from 1705. It is now a masonic hall.

Take the first turning on the right into Church Street, where Charles II's mistress Nell Gwyn supposedly had a house (half-way along on the right). You come out in front of the Henry VIII Gate of the Castle Ⓗ. To your right, where the public entrance is, you can see the Round Tower. Perched on a vast mound of earth and surrounded by a deep ditch, this is the oldest part of the Castle, which was originally built by William the Conqueror following the victory of the Normans at the Battle of Hastings in 1066. Through Henry VIII's Gate you can just make out the west end of St George's Chapel, built in 1475 for the knights of the Order of the Garter, England's leading order of chivalry. Henry VIII himself is buried here, next to wife number three Jane Seymour

Turn left now and walk down towards the Victoria statue. On the left, No. 2 Castle Hill bears a plaque to author and publisher Charles Knight (1791-1873). Knight's father was Mayor of Windsor and a bookseller in the town on this site. George III frequently popped out of the castle for a browse in the shop and was once observed eagerly scanning a copy of Tom Paine's revolutionary *Rights of Man*. Knight junior was also in the book trade, but on the publishing side. He made strenuous but ultimately vain attempts to bring history and other 'serious' subjects to a wider audience.

Cross Thames Street to Ye Harte and Garter (the entrance to the Dungeons of Windsor Ⓜ is left of the hotel entrance) and then turn right and left into Windsor and Eton Central Station. Built in 1897, with a special royal waiting room, to mark Queen Victoria's Diamond Jubilee, the station has now been much reduced in size and turned into a shopping and café area. Beyond the first arcade of shops turn left down the steps and then right at the bottom into Goswell Hill. Walk down the hill past the shops built in the viaduct arches until you come to the main road (Goswell Road). Turn right under the viaduct here and walk along past Alexandra Gardens on the left Ⓣ to the Thames-side walk. Turn right along the river bank opposite the Eton College boathouses.

When you get to the bridge cross over into Eton High Street. Pubs, restaurants and antique shops line both sides, reflecting the place's popularity with tourists. At Nos. 47-49 on the right is the half timbered 15th-century Cockpit restaurant with the town stocks outside. At No. 29 further on on the right is the old Eton parish school, founded in 1812 under the will of Mark Porney, a former College French master. The next part of the High Street is less touristy and more tradional country townish. A particular feature is the gents outfitters and tailors, catering to the conservative but demanding sartorial tastes of the generally wealthy schoolboys. The last one on the right – Tom Brown's – has been here for over 200 years.

As you cross Barnes Pool Bridge over the dried-up watercourse you leave the town and enter the main school area. Ahead on the right the 15th-century chapel - big enough as it is but originally intended to be the size of a cathedral - rises up above the surrounding buildings. This and the courtyard adjoining (visible through the entrance archway underneath the flagpole) are the original parts of Eton College Ⓗ, founded by Henry VI in 1440 for 70 poor scholars. In the 17th century upper-class children began coming here and in the 18th century it became the most exclusive boarding school in the land, a reputation it has never lost since. There are now 1200 fee-paying pupils, or 'oppidans' (boys who live in boarding houses in the town) as well as the 70 scholarship boys or 'collegers' (boys who live in the College). In term time the boys are commonly seen around town in their black tailcoats.

As you pass the school entrance on the right, you also pass on the left the school hall and the domed library. Follow the main road (leading to Slough) round to the right. On the left you come to a playing field area called The Timbralls. Behind the old wall on the right (built in 1717) is another playing field, scene of the Eton wall game, one of the oldest (and oddest) forms of football in existence. Played only at Eton, it dates from the 18th century and involves this wall, a door, an old elm tree and a lot of scrummaging in the mud by its two 10-a-side teams. As a spectator sport it is said to be remarkably dull. The main game of the season is the St Andrew's Day match on the Saturday nearest to 30th November. Boys watch from the top of the wall by climbing up the metal footholds in the central section.

Cross the bridge over the Colenorton Brook and turn right through the gate towards the pavilion. Go back down behind the pavilion, cross the footbridge and turn right under the bridge. Follow the track beside the stream. When the vehicle track turns right over the bridge keep going straight on along the footpath. When you reach the buildings turn left. The next section of the walk takes you through more modern parts of the school, including boarding houses, classrooms and faculty buildings. On the right are the school fives courts. Eton schoolboys invented the game of 'fives' - which has spread to other public schools - by hand-hitting a ball against a section of the chapel wall in the old school yard while waiting for roll call. All Eton fives courts now reproduce the features of the original court, including the ledge and buttress in the chapel wall and the low step in the old quadrangle floor.

Half way along the courts, turn right through the arch and go diagonally left (the Drawing School is on your right). When you reach the road, go left and right into the roadway to the left of the entrance into Warre House. Carry straight on here as far as you can (the roadway becomes a footpath after a while). When you come to another road turn left and then by the phone box right into unsigned Keats Lane. At the end of the buildings the road becomes South Meadow Lane. Continue along the road (or if you prefer take the path just inside the playing field) until you come to a junction. Go straight over here and follow the track slightly left towards the river. This is Brocas Meadow where there is a fun fair every August. The view of the castle from here is particularly fine.

When you reach the river turn left and follow it back to town. You re-enter Eton with the Watermans Arms just ahead. Go right of the pub back onto the High Street. Turn right over the bridge and then left onto the riverside walk. Take the first right. Windsor and Eton Riverside Station, where the walk ends, is ahead on the left.

Hampton Court

Summary: The great Tudor palace of Hampton Court sits on the Thames in south-west London, surrounded by beautifully kept gardens and 1100 acres (445 hectares) of rough deer park (Hampton Court Park and Bushy Park). The walk begins in the palace grounds. Next comes Bushy Park, with the path following the Chestnut Avenue to begin with, and then meandering through the glades in the secluded Waterhouse Woodland Garden in the centre of the park. The last leg of the walk is set in the riverside village of Hampton, the main features of which are the 18th-century Garrick's Villa and Shakespeare Temple. The village also has a fine church, riverside gardens, an excellent antiquarian bookshop and several pubs.

Start: **Hampton Court Station (trains from Waterloo; riverboats from Westminster Pier).**
Finish: **Hampton Station (trains from Waterloo but different line from above).**
Length: **3½ miles (5.6 kilometres).**
Time: **2 hours.**
Refreshments: **Various pubs and restaurants around the entrance and exit to the palace grounds, plus more pubs and takeaways in Hampton village at the end of the walk, some near the station. There is a restaurant within the grounds of Hampton Court and the Waterhouse Garden in Bushy Park at the half-way point is a fine site for a picnic.**

From Hampton Court Station go straight over the bridge across the River Thames towards the palace Ⓗ, its fantastic roofscape a forest of bulbous, twisting Tudor chimneys with the pitched roof of Henry VIII's great hall rising up in the middle. Henry's Lord Chancellor, Cardinal Wolsey, began the palace as his own residence after buying the estate in 1514. Then, when his credit with the king began to sink, Wolsey handed the palace over to Henry in a desperate attempt to retain royal favour. It failed and in 1530 Wolsey died in disgrace. Nearly 200 years later, William III and Queen Mary commissioned Sir Christopher Wren to demolish the Tudor state and royal apartments and replace them with a completely new building grafted on to the stock of the old. George II (reigned 1727-60) was the last monarch to actually reside in the palace, though it is still owned by the sovereign.

Tudor palace

When you draw abreast of the Mitre hotel on the left, turn right through the palace's main gate into the drive leading to the great gatehouse. Left of the gate-

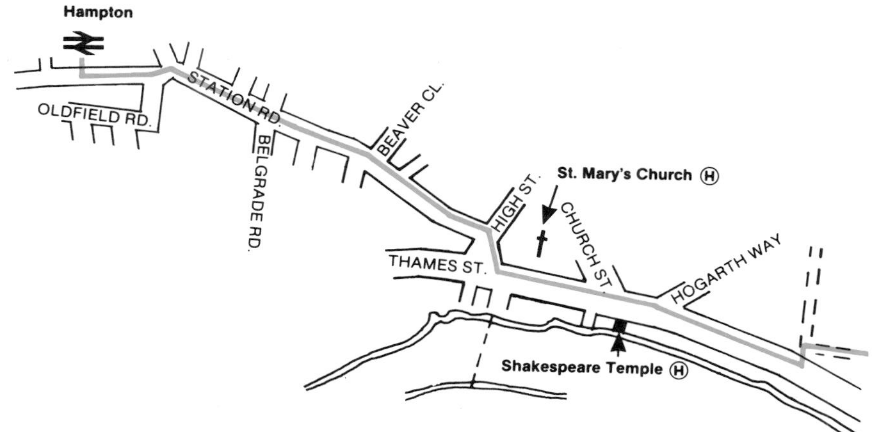

house, a lower and wider gateway leads to the enormous kitchens, cellars and other domestic offices on the north side of the palace. The long low building immediately on your left was once the palace stableblock.

In front of the gatehouse turn left and go through the ivy-covered archway into the Tiltyard Garden. Before you get to the Tiltyard Tearooms, turn right through the gate and go straight on into the Wilderness garden area Ⓣ with the palace on your right. When you reach the far side go through the gate and turn right along the gravelled path through the palace's immaculate flower gardens. On the right the balconied building is the palace real tennis court where successive monarchs played the ancient game of real (or royal) tennis. The game is still played here by a local club. Then comes the east front of the palace itself. From the mid point three walks radiate left towards Hampton Court Park Ⓟ, the central one following Charles II's Long Water canal towards Kingston-upon-Thames.

At the end of the east front turn right through the gate into the privy garden where the king and queen would have walked in private protected from the public gaze. Go straight along the terrace in front of the palace and through the gate into the Pond Garden. On the right is the Orangery, housing a famous series of paintings by the Renaissance artist Mantegna. On the left are two pond gardens, with the riverside Banqueting House visible between. At the end, the greenhouse houses a massive grapevine whose root system is so extensive that a large area of garden outside has to be left uncultivated so that the vine can be properly treated. The vine was planted in the 18th century when Capability Brown was in charge of the gardens. Grapes from it are sold in season.

Retrace your steps towards the entrance to the Pond Garden, passing on the left in the corner of the wall a lead water-tank. The river water referred to on the sign comes from the Longford River, an 11-mile (18-kilometre) canal cut from a local river to provide gravity-fed water to the palace. Since 1629 the same canal has been supplying water to all the fountains and lakes around the palace, and also to the Waterhouse Garden which you will come to later in the walk.

Go through the gate out of the Pond Garden and turn right up the steps into the long pergola which in 1995 replaced a hornbeam tunnel known as Queen Mary's Bower. At the end go down the steps and walk past the amazing iron gates fashioned by master blacksmith Jean Tijou, one of the many craftsmen employed by Wren on the new palace. Go up the steps on the far side and walk along the raised terrace back towards the palace. To the left you can see clearly how the new palace was

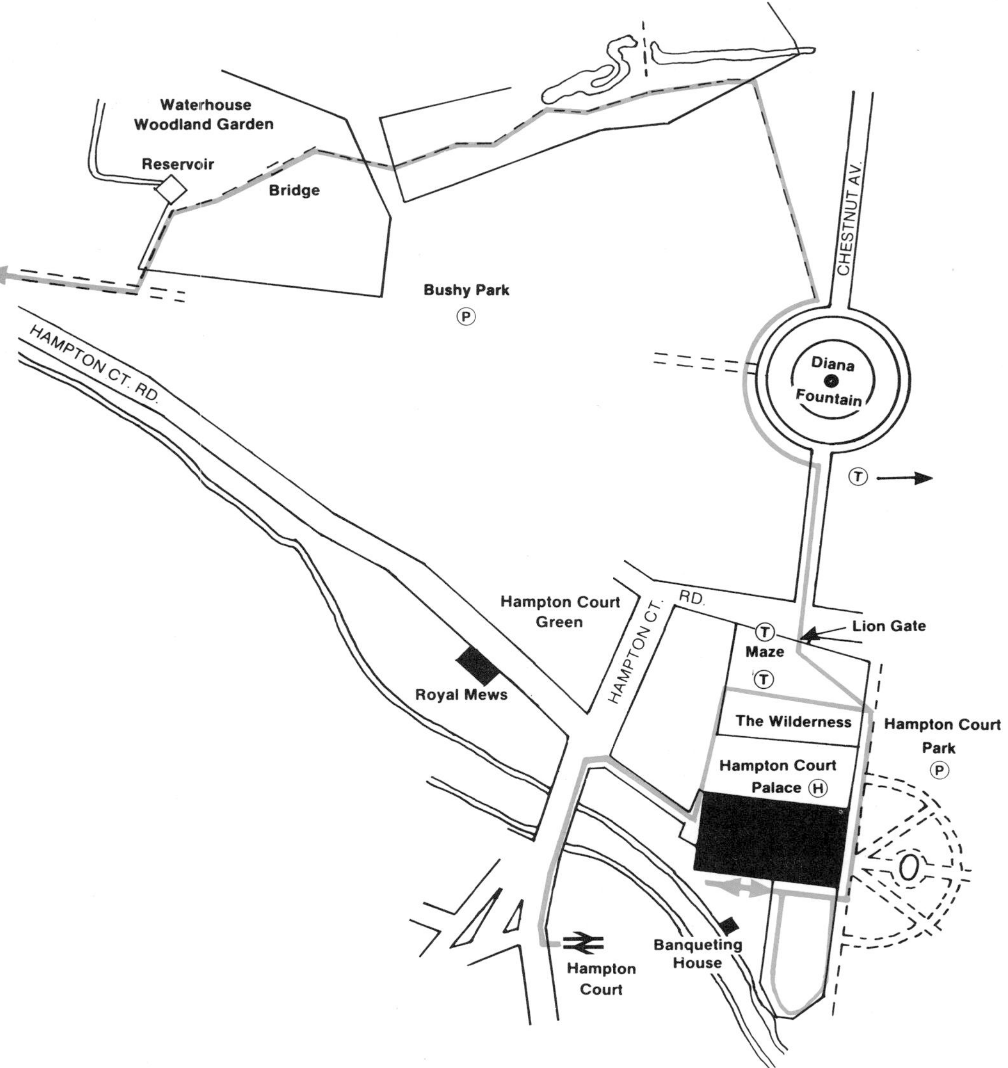

grafted on to the old one. Go down the steps at the end, turn right out of the privy garden and then left. Retrace your steps past the east front and tennis court. Go back through the gate into the Wilderness and then fork right. After a while you come to the palace's famous maze and the Lion Gate (Ⓣ men only), the northern entrance to the palace grounds.

Verdant parks

Go through the Lion Gate, cross the road dividing Hampton Court Park and Bushy Park Ⓟ, and then go through the gate into Bushy Park, keeping to the grass on the left-hand side of the Chestnut Avenue. This straight road runs for a mile (1.6 kilometres) through the park, broken only by the round pond and Diana Fountain visible a short distance ahead. Cardinal Wolsey created Bushy Park out of three older parks in 1514. Wren later added the Chestnut Avenue and Lion Gate to form an impressive approach to his new palace.

When the road divides to skirt the pond, keep to the left-hand side. On the far side of the pond keep the rows of trees bordering the avenue's left hand side on *your* right and follow the grassy track towards the palisade surrounding the Waterhouse Woodland Garden - your next destination. Just before you reach the little bridge over the stream veer left towards the white sign marking the entrance to the woodland garden. Go through the gate and turn left along the zigzag path, keeping the water on your right. Laid out in the 1940s in this remote location, the woodland garden remains little known despite its obvious charms and is often completely deserted.

Follow the path as it winds through the trees, passing a bridge and a gardener's house *en route*. Go through the gate at the end of the garden, cross the tarmac path and go through the next gate by the police box. Walk about 20 yards (18 metres) and then take the first turning on the left along a narrow path. Follow this path round to the right over a stream, and then to the left, walking straight along the right bank of the stream. Cross over a larger bridge (with handrails) and turn right into a pathless woodland glade. Aim for the opposite right-hand corner and rejoin the path by a tree stump. Follow this path round to the left until you come to a small embanked reservoir. Turn left here so that the reservoir is on your right, and follow the path past the reservoir and water house, and then alongside a stream flowing out of the reservoir.

You will soon come to a gate leading out of the garden back into the deer park. Go through the gate and turn right along the lime avenue leading to the old park-keeper's lodge and the stockyard and park headquarters, site of the medieval Hampton farm. Stay on the avenue or walk on the tarmac path on your left. Near the end, follow the tarmac path as it veers to the left to a gate leading out of the park. Go through the gate and turn right onto the busy riverside Hampton Court Road leading to the village of Hampton. (Turning left here will take you back to Hampton Court.)

Hampton's heritage

After a while you come to the entrance to the stockyard on the right. Opposite is Garrick's House where David Garrick, army officer and nephew of his namesake, David Garrick, the leading actor of the 18th century, lived from 1778 until his death in 1795. Cross Hogarth Way. The large house on the right, converted into flats in the 1920s, was Garrick the actor's country house, bought in 1754 and known as

Garrick's Villa. The following year he built the temple Ⓗ on the left to house a statue of Shakespeare which is now in the British Museum. The temple is connected to the house by a tunnel under the road.

Continue past the house and cross Church Street. Hampton Church Ⓗ on the right was completely rebuilt in 1831, but its ancient monuments were preserved, including one to Sibel Penn, nurse to Henry VIII's only son, Edward VI. Sibel died of small pox in 1562 and her kindly, grey-cloaked ghost is said to haunt this church, Hampton Court where she worked, and also the house now standing on the site of her old home, Penn's Place, marked by a plaque back round the corner in Church Street.

Walk past the church and the Bell Inn. When this book first came out (in 1991) Betty's confectionery and tobacco shop stood on the corner. It was run by an extraordinary woman called Betty Kenton who, under her maiden name of Ambler, had been British champion women's sculler in 1935 and 1938. There was a photograph of her in the shop to prove it. Betty's husband ran the boatyard across the road and operated one of the last remaining foot ferries on the Thames. The grumpy old ferryman, who had been doing the job for 50 years, waited inside the shop for custom. In 1995 the Kenton's lease of the ferry expired and they decided to close the shop and retire. The following year two local couples acquired the lease and they now run the ferry, which is said to be at least 500 years old.

The walk now turns right into Hampton High Street but first take a peep down Thames Street ahead in order to see the local antiquarian bookshop. It has old sofas and armchairs and classical music playing on an ancient radiogram and its huge stock is well worth a leisurely browse.

Now turn right into the High Street and then take the first turning on the left into Station Road for the last part of the walk. On the right beyond Beaver Close the road passes some pretty cottages, and then a terrace of small, plain three-storey Georgian houses, the first with a little stable and loft in the front garden. Beyond the shops and Belgrade Road on the left, new housing covers water filter beds originally built in 1855 by the Southwark and Vauxhall Water Company after central London's private water companies had been forced to move their Thames intakes upstream into the cleaner, non-tidal part of the river. The old pumping houses still stand on the riverside.

Continue to the end of the wall and cross Oldfield Road (the Railway Bell pub is opposite on the right). Hampton Station, where the walk ends, is further along on the right.

Syon Park to Strawberry Hill

Summary: This is a riverside walk in west London, going upstream from Syon Park to Strawberry Hill on the opposite bank to the better-known Kew and Richmond. On the way the walk passes through the old village centres of Isleworth and Twickenham and includes the handful of riverside mansions that remain from the whole string that once lined this stretch of the Thames: Syon House, Marble Hill House, Orleans House, York House and Horace Walpole's Gothic fantasy, Strawberry Hill. One of the more unexpected sights on the walk is the British Legion's poppy factory in Richmond.

Start: **Syon Lane Station (trains from Waterloo).**
Finish: **Strawberry Hill Station (trains from Waterloo).**
Length: **4½ miles (7.2 kilometres).**
Time: **2½ hours.**
Refreshments: **Near the beginning of the walk, try the café-restaurant in Syon Park or the riverside London Apprentice pub in Isleworth a little further on. Places to stop in the middle of the walk are non-existent unless you cross the road bridge into Richmond. In the second half of the walk, there is another café at Marble Hill House and then plenty of places, including riverside pubs, in Twickenham.**

Come out of Syon Lane Station onto the road bridge, turn right and then immediately fork left. Eventually you come out onto London Road opposite a grand but disused entrance into Syon Park, complete with iron brackets ready to receive flaming torches and a stone lion above the central arch. The lion is the heraldic crest of the Percy family, Dukes of Northumberland, who have owned Syon Park since the time of Elizabeth I. Before that it was a monastery. Turn left along London Road past the Park Tavern and then cross at the traffic lights into the lane signposted Thames Path and Syon House Ⓗ.

Syon House tragedies
The first landmark you see is the glass dome of the Great Conservatory. The house itself does not come into view until you have passed the entrance to the restaurant Ⓣ and garden centre and have joined the road leading out of the park. All you actually see from this distance are the castellated façade of the north front and the matching lodges at either end of the ha-ha. To your right is the large expanse of parkland cushioning the house from surrounding suburbia. There is more parkland,

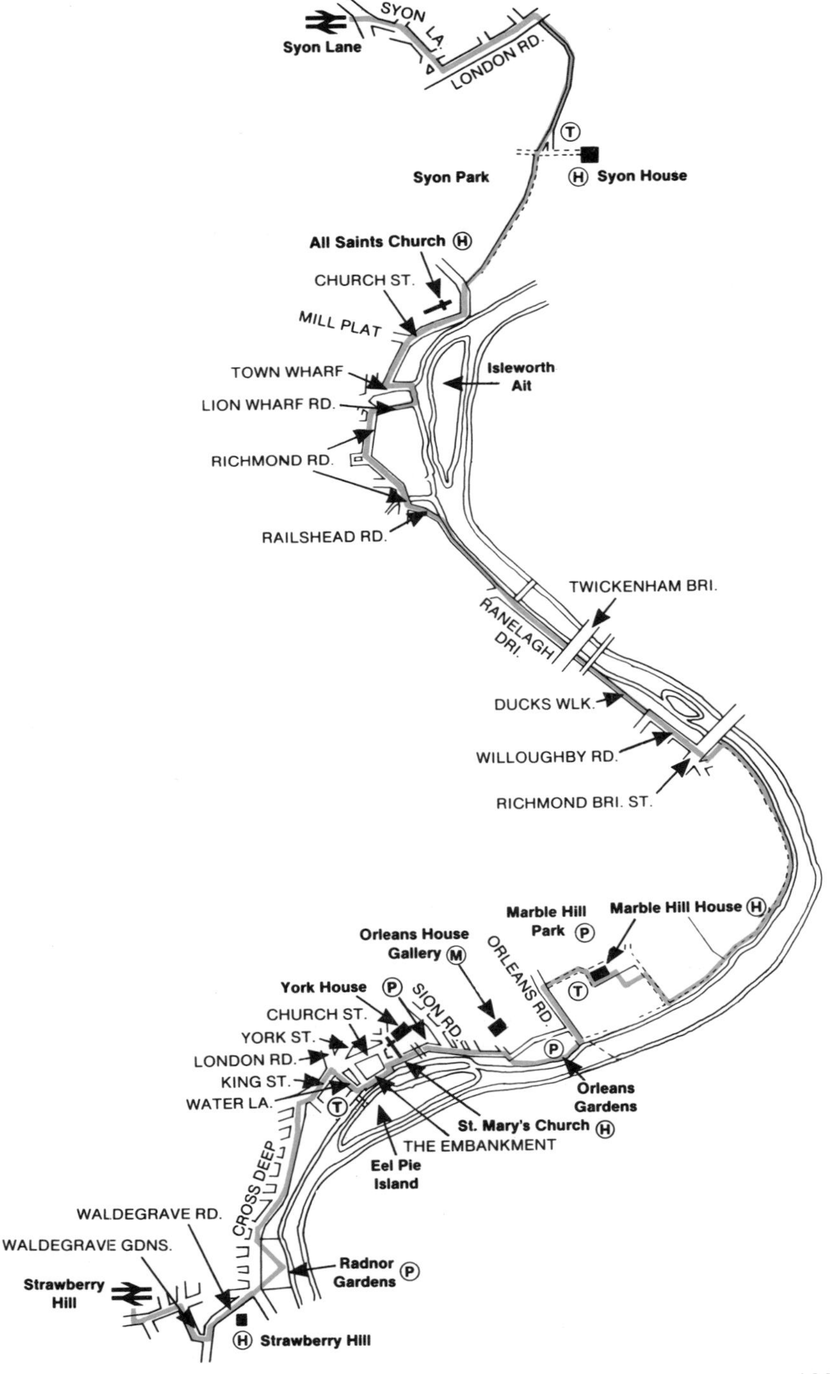

Syon Lane
SYON LA.
LONDON RD.
Syon Park
Syon House
All Saints Church
CHURCH ST.
MILL PLAT
TOWN WHARF
LION WHARF RD.
RICHMOND RD.
Isleworth Ait
RAILSHEAD RD.
TWICKENHAM BRI.
RANELAGH DRI.
DUCKS WLK.
WILLOUGHBY RD.
RICHMOND BRI. ST.
Marble Hill Park
Marble Hill House
Orleans House Gallery
ORLEANS RD.
York House
SION RD.
CHURCH ST.
YORK ST.
LONDON RD.
KING ST.
WATER LA.
Orleans Gardens
St. Mary's Church
THE EMBANKMENT
Eel Pie Island
CROSS DEEP
WALDEGRAVE RD.
WALDEGRAVE GDNS.
Strawberry Hill
Radnor Gardens
Strawberry Hill

including gardens landscaped by Capability Brown, behind the house and between it and the River Thames.

The early history of Syon House has its sad episodes. As a plaque on one of the barns indicates, Richard Reynolds, a senior monk at Syon Abbey, was executed in 1535 for refusing to accept Henry VIII's religious reforms. Soon after, young Katherine Howard, Henry VIII's fifth wife, was imprisoned here before she was beheaded for treason in 1542. A few years later Lady Jane Grey, married to the son of the Earl of Northumberland, was offered the crown at Syon after the death of Edward VI. Her reign lasted for only nine days and within a year she too had gone to the block.

Follow the road to the park gate and turn left along Park Street towards the riverside by Isleworth churchyard. Only the old tower remains of the original village church Ⓗ, most of which was destroyed by fire in 1943. Several stones are set in the corner of the churchyard wall recording various floodwater levels. The earliest is March 1774; the highest is 1928 when 14 people were drowned in central London. The island opposite is Isleworth Ait (sometimes spelt 'Eyot', meaning island). At low tide the river retreats, leaving a land bridge across to the island. The Romans are said to have crossed the Thames here in 54BC.

Continue along Church Street between the 15th-century London Apprentice pub (so-called because City apprentices used to row here on their days off) and the attractive houses by the church. Just before you reach the bridge over the Duke of Northumberland's River, a lane leads off to the right giving access to the tiny Ingram almshouses built in 1664. Called Mill Plat, the name recalls the mill which not long ago stood on the river here. Local people still remember buying bread in the village made from flour ground at the mill.

Go past the lane and straight over the bridge into the new square, in the middle of which stands the former village school, founded 1630. Keep left of the school and just beyond turn left along Town Wharf to the new Town Wharf pub on the riverside. Isleworth's non-unionised dock operated well into the 1960s, accommodating ships bringing wood and coal from as far away as Scandinavia. Some local people also remember barges carrying blocks of ice for local butchers' shops. There is still some commercial boat-building and repairing in the yards on the ait. Looking left, there is a good view of the church and pub on the riverside corner. Turn right along the terrace and then right again - *before* the gardens in front of the new houses - into unsignposted Lion Wharf Road. Turn left along the main road at the top (Richmond Road) past the Nazareth House Convent and home for the elderly, founded in 1892.

Richmond riverside

When you get to the River Crane, turn left into Railshead Road and rejoin the River Thames. On the right Gordon House, residence in the 19th-century of Lord Frederick Gordon, is now the Twickenham campus of Brunel University. On the opposite bank is the Old Deer Park at Richmond, now the Royal Mid-Surrey golf course. Far ahead you can see houses and the Star and Garter home for disabled servicemen on top of Richmond Hill. In the foreground an iron footbridge crosses over Richmond Weir and Lock. This is actually only a half-lock because the weir can be lowered when the water level is sufficiently high. The real barrier between the tidal and non-tidal Thames is upstream at Teddington, just beyond the end of this walk. As you pass the bridge the road rejoins the river on Ranelagh Drive. The next bridge is Twickenham road bridge and immediately beyond that is a small turret-like building which gives access to a large underground water main. Continue under the next bridge, the railway bridge linking Twickenham and Richmond.

Just past the railway bridge the private moorings and houses on Ducks Walk obstruct the view of the river. Ducks Walk leads straight into Willoughby Road. At the end of Willoughby Road cross the main road (Richmond Bridge Road) at the traffic lights and turn left beside (not over) Richmond Bridge to rejoin the river. The walk now follows the river all the way to Twickenham, apart from a brief deviation around Marble Hill House.

As you proceed along the riverside path you draw abreast of the British Legion poppy factory - the long white building with the flagpole - halfway up the hill on the opposite bank. The red paper poppies we wear on Remembrance Day are made here. The river now begins to bend to the right away from Richmond Hill and the Star and Garter Home. On the far bank Petersham House stares at you across Petersham Meadows. Behind the house the red brick campanile of what used to be All Saints' Church at Petersham is also conspicuous. Beyond Glover's Island Petersham's River Lane ends in a public slipway on the opposite bank.

On this side of the river, private gardens give way to the public park surrounding Marble Hill House Ⓗ. Turn right into the park Ⓟ when you come to the gateway in the railings and pass the huge walnut tree, reputedly over 200 years old and probably part of the original 18th-century garden design. Further along the path turn left towards Lady Suffolk's subterranean grotto. Just beyond the grotto turn right round the corner of the wood towards the house. George II's lover the Countess of Suffolk built it in 1729 as a refuge from Court and her husband, both of which she detested.

Orleans exile

Go right or left to the entrance front of the house and head off left past the ice house towards the coach house café Ⓣ. Pass by the left-hand side of the coach house and then turn left back down to the river along (unsignposted) Orleans Road. A gateway in the wall on the right leads to the Orleans House Gallery Ⓜ, a council-owned collection of pictures, including many local views, housed in the remains of another 18th-century riverside mansion. Louis-Philippe, King of France 1830-48, lived here as the emigré Duc d'Orléans from 1815 to 1817. Later his widow lived here, and then his son, the Duc d'Aumale. At the bottom of Orleans Road, Hammerton's Ferry, one of the last full-time Thames foot ferries, carries walkers to and from the National Trust's Ham House Ⓗ on the opposite bank.

At this point turn right into Orleans Gardens Ⓟ and walk along the riverside beside the horse chestnuts, carefully pruned to hang over the water rather than the park. Towards the end of the gardens the remains of Orleans House come into view. The main block, which was demolished in 1926, was on the right of the octagon. Rejoin the road (Riverside) and turn left towards Twickenham.

Beyond the pub, Sion Road on the right is an attractive 18th-century terrace with an unusual Egyptian-style decoration under the eaves, picked out in black.

Notice the street sign high up on the right bearing the date 1721. Sion Road leads up to the council offices in York House, a 300-year-old mansion set in fine gardens, including a sunken garden, a water garden and a balustraded riverside terrace reached by a bridge over the road. The Yorke (sic) family originally owned the estate, hence the name, but in the 19th-century the exiled French royal family used it in addition to Orleans House and seven other houses in the vicinity. Have a look around York House gardens Ⓟ if time and energy permit.

Continue along Riverside, under the York House gardens bridge and on to Twickenham Embankment by St Mary's Church Ⓗ, where poet and local resident Alexander Pope was buried in 1744. Opposite is car-less Eel Pie Island, named after a famous hotel which in the 19th century was the island's only building. In the early 1960s the old hotel ballroom was a jazz club where several famous groups like the Rolling Stones cut their teeth. The island's former boatyard now provides workspace for a community of artists and craftspeople.

Turn right by the Eel Pie Island bridge into Water Lane Ⓣ. At the end of the lane paved Church Street on the right leads back down to the church (halfway along on the right is a shop selling products from the Eel Pie Island studios). Ahead London Road will take you towards Twickenham rugby stadium, Harlequins' club ground and venue for England internationals. The walk, however, goes to the left, along King Street, before turning left at the traffic lights into Cross Deep, a road running parallel to a stretch of the Thames called Cross Deep.

Beyond Cross Deep House and St James's School turn left opposite the Pope's Grotto pub into riverside Radnor Gardens Ⓟ, once the site of a house belonging to the Earl of Radnor. The local council bought it in 1902 which explains why the remarkable Twickenham war memorial is here. Alexander Pope's villa, one of the best known riverside houses in the 18th century, stood on the downstream side of the gardens with a tunnel-grotto linking it to its 5-acre (2-hectare) gardens on the other side of Cross Deep road. By all accounts Pope's Villa was a remarkable place, but that didn't stop a later owner, fed up with the number of pilgrims coming to see where the great poet lived, from knocking it down.

Gothic humour

Leave the gardens by the gate at the end and cross the road into the left of the two roads which lead off on the far side (Waldegrave Road). The road passes the entrance to Strawberry Hill Ⓗ, probably the most famous of all the old riverside mansions in south-west London. At a time when the classical style of ancient Greece and Rome was fashionable, Horace Walpole, author of the Gothic novel *The Castle of Otranto* and son of the prime minister Sir Robert Walpole, built this mansion in a medieval Gothic style with turrets, battlements and pointed windows. Although it was intended as a joke (he actually called it his 'little plaything . . . the prettiest bauble you ever saw'), it had a great influence on the next generation of architects. The house is now part of Surrey University.

Walk round the corner, turn right into Waldegrave Gardens and then turn left into Tower Road. Walk along to the level crossing and Strawberry Hill Station where the walk ends.

Richmond

Summary: Richmond, Ham and Petersham are all by the River Thames in south-west London. This circular walk starts on Richmond Green where part of an old royal palace and many fine Court houses still stand. It then joins the Thames towpath before climbing Richmond Hill. The panoramic view from the top is one of the best on the river. The walk passes through Richmond Park before descending the western slope of the hill into Petersham (burial place of the discoverer of Vancouver Island) and Ham. Old mansions abound. The walk loops round Ham House and then returns to Richmond along the towpath through Petersham meadows.

Start and finish: **Richmond Station (District Underground line, Silverlink Metro and trains from Waterloo; riverboats from Westminster Pier).**
Length: **4½ miles (7.2 kilometres).**
Time: **3 hours.**
Refreshments: **Variety of pubs, restaurants and take-away places at the beginning and end of the walk in Richmond, plus a pub (Dysarts) at the half-way stage in Petersham. There are also cafés in Pembroke Lodge in Richmond Park (about a third of the way through the walk - recommended for its spectacular views) and at Ham House, where the walk turns back along the river to Richmond.**
Route note: The walk passes the grounds of Ham Polo Club. Matches are played on Sunday afternoons, May to September.

Leave Richmond Station Ⓣ, turn left and go over The Quadrant at the zebra crossing. Go through the arch to the right and turn left over the bridge into Little Green. Continue straight ahead into the main Richmond Green. In Tudor times this green served as the jousting field of the royal palace which was situated in the far right corner. Much later, houses, many of which remain, were built along the left and far sides of the green for court attendants and servants. The best of these houses are at the opposite end in Old Palace Terrace and Old Palace Place and further round to the right in Maids of Honour Row. The latter was built in 1724 for the maids of honour attending on the Princess of Wales, Princess Caroline of Anspach. Newer houses occupy the other two sides of the green.

Richmond's royal residence

Walk to the end of the green and then turn right past Old Palace Place and Maids of Honour Row. The next house, set back behind the wall, is part of the old palace. Turn left by the ancient pine tree in the corner of the garden and go through the

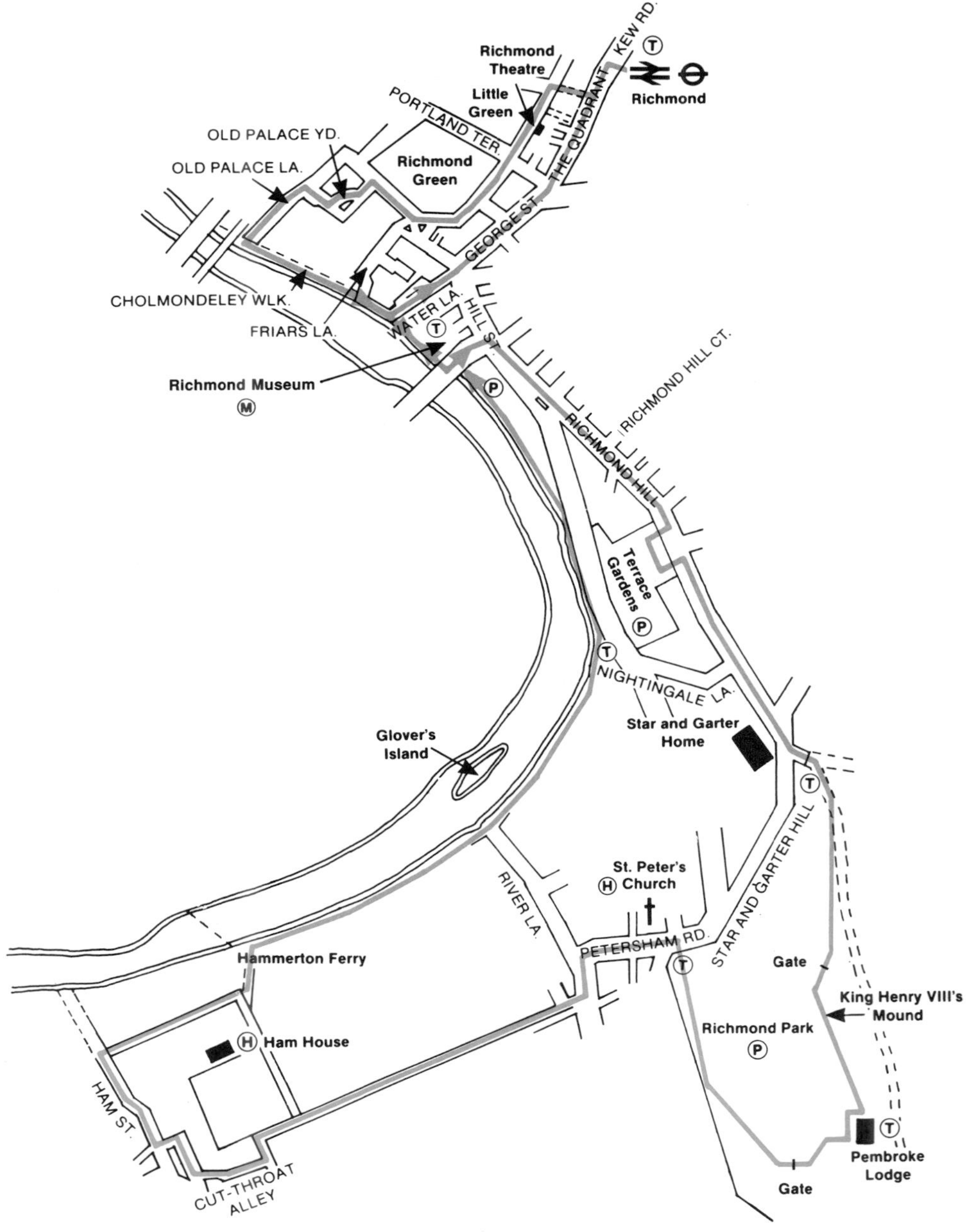

old palace gatehouse with Henry VII's arms above the arch into Old Palace Yard. There had been a royal house at Richmond throughout the medieval period but Henry VII, who preferred this palace to all his others, was the first to make it into a major royal residence. He even changed its name from Shene to Richmond after his earldom of Richmond in Yorkshire. Elizabeth I, the last of Henry's Tudor dynasty, was the last monarch to use the palace. Most of it was demolished after Charles I's execution in 1649.

Leave the Yard via the path marked by two white bollards in the far right corner. Turn left into Old Palace Lane and walk down towards the river past the White Swan pub. At the end of the lane on the left stands Asgill House, built in 1758 for Sir Charles Asgill, banker and City lord mayor. A stone plaque on the wall records that the royal palace extended to the river here and that Edward III, Henry VII and Elizabeth I all died here (in 1377, 1509 and 1603 respectively).

Walk to the left along the Thames towpath (here called Cholmondeley Walk) past the gardens of Asgill House, with its superb copper beech and gazebo, and then the gardens of Trumpeters' House, the garden front visible at the end of a long lawn framed by trees. Trees are the glory of Richmond.

On the left, Friar's Lane, marking the site of the Franciscan friary of Shene founded by Henry VII in 1501, now joins the riverside. Next on the left is Water Lane by the White Cross Hotel (the friary's badge was a white cross). Beyond Water Lane is a terraced garden with a 1980s' development of neo-Georgian offices on top of the bank. The Victorian building on the left is the old Richmond town hall, now the central library, tourist information office and local museum Ⓜ.

Terrace panorama

When you get to Richmond's Georgian bridge climb the steps on the left and walk to the roundabout. Here turn right into Hill Street and then go across the road using the zebra crossing. Continue up the hill, taking the left fork by the row of three antique shops. When you get to Richmond Hill Court (near the top of the hill on the left) cross over to the path along the top edge of the Terrace Gardens Ⓟ which cover the side of the hill. The second flight of steps carries you up to the top terrace with its views far away to the west over the river. 'Heavens! What a goodly prospect spreads around, of hills and dales, and woods, and lawns and spires and glittering towns and gilded streams', exclaimed poet and Richmond resident James Thomson in 1727. Explanatory panels in the middle of the top terrace pinpoint the main landmarks in the panorama. Directly ahead, the roof of Ham House is visible above the trees to the left of the river; below are Petersham Meadows and the white Petersham Lodge; to the left of the meadows are Petersham House and Petersham Church. The large brick building near left is the Petersham Hotel. Behind you is Downe House, the home of Rolling Stone Mick Jagger.

Cross Nightingale Lane. The Wick on the corner belongs to The Who's Pete Townshend. Beyond, Wick House was built for painter Sir Joshua Reynolds in 1771. It's now a hostel for nurses at the Royal Royal Star and Garter Home on the summit of the hill which you come to shortly. Founded after World War I, the Star and Garter cares for disabled servicemen and takes its name from its predecessor on the site, the Star and Garter Hotel, opened in 1738. Like other hotels and inns on the river, the Star and Garter's heyday came in the 19th century when hordes of visitors travelled out from London on the new railway in search of fun and fresh air.

The novelist Charles Dickens held an annual private dinner at the hotel to celebrate his wedding anniversary. Fire put an end to the hotel in 1870.

Cross the busy road (Star and Garter Hill) to the right of the roundabout and go through the gate into Richmond Park Ⓟ Ⓣ. Created for deer hunting in 1637 by Charles I, Richmond Park, unlike the Old Deer Park on the other side of Richmond, still has deer in it: about 600 is the normal stock level. Of course, the park is no longer used for hunting, but many people still ride through the woodland or on the rough open ground. There is also plenty of space for two golf courses, several cricket fields and over 20 football pitches, plus lakes for fishing.

Henry's lookout

Take the hard path to the right along the edge of the hill, not the rough path going *down* the hill. After a few hundred yards, go through a big gate into Pembroke Lodge Gardens and then along the terrace, past flower beds and seats on the left and the ugly memorial to poet James Thomson on the right. Continue through the John Beer Laburnum Walk. Then turn left and climb to the top of King Henry VIII's Mound, the highest point in the park. Henry apparently stood here in 1536 waiting to see a rocket fired from the Tower of London to announce that his second wife, Ann Boleyn, had been successfully beheaded. Today, you are supposed to be able to see both St Paul's Cathedral in the City and Windsor Castle from this point. St Paul's is plainly visible through the park's trees and across west London and the view to it is now protected by law. Windsor Castle is not so easy to make out. In fact, I do not think I have ever managed to pinpoint it.

Descend the knoll on the opposite side and continue along the hillside terrace until you come to Pembroke Lodge Ⓣ, a molecatcher's cottage converted for the Countess of Pembroke in 1780. Queen Victoria's Prime Minister and Foreign Secretary Lord John Russell lived here for 30 years. Disliking society in London, he held cabinet meetings and did much of his government work here. Later his grandson, the philosopher and mathematician Bertrand Russell, spent his childhood in the Lodge before going to university. Today the Lodge is a café and restaurant with views from its terrace rivalling if not surpassing those from the Lauderdale House café in Highgate.

Go down the steps in front of the terrace and follow the fence to the left for a few yards until you come to the garden gate. Go through the gate and head off right, down the hill to the broad track you can see running left and right. Ahead is the white gateway leading into Sudbrook Park, now a golf course with a grand 18th century club-house. The red-brick campanile belongs to Petersham's redundant All Saints' Church, now used as a recording studio.

Walk to the right along the broad track and head for the village of Petersham, aiming for the black and white Dysarts pub ahead. Cross Petersham Road here - the road is very busy - and turn left. Along the lane to the right is Petersham's little parish church Ⓗ, with the grave of George Vancouver, discoverer of Vancouver Island, in its churchyard. Described in the 18th century as the most elegant village in England, Petersham still has many fine houses today. Opposite is Montrose House, built for a judge around 1700; the Dowager Duchess of Montrose lived here in the

1840s. Next on this side of the road is Petersham House, built around 1674. Beyond is Rutland Lodge, built in the 1660s, occupied by the Duchess of Rutland in the 1740s and converted into flats after a serious fire in 1967. In River Lane on the right 37-year-old George Vancouver settled in 1795 to write up his voyages for publication. He died three years later.

Follow the road round the sharp left-hand bend and then, just before the Fox and Duck pub on the left, turn right. Go to the right of the gatehouse and then, when you reach the gate into the Deutsche Schüle (built in 1690 as Douglas House and bought by Germany in 1969 for use as a German school), branch left onto the long straight avenue that was once the drive to Ham House. Walk past Ham Polo Club to the end of the avenue by the garden wall of Ham House. The south front is visible through the gates on the right. To the left, Melancholy Walk leads to Ham Common. Follow the wall of Ham House to the left and then right round the corner into Cut-Throat Alley. This brings you out on Ham Street, connecting Ham Common with the river.

Whipping boy

On Ham Street, turn right and follow the wall until you come to the entrance to Ham House Ⓗ. Turn right again and walk along the avenue towards the north front of the house. Now owned by the National Trust and open to the public, this fine Stuart house was the home of the Earls of Dysart until 1948. The first earl was granted the house, along with other property in Ham and Petersham, by Charles I in 1637. The earl had grown up with the king and, some say, had been his whipping boy: whenever the young prince did anything wrong, it was poor Dysart that was punished for it, not the prince.

Orleans House on the opposite bank of the river is just visible through the trees to the left. At the end of the avenue take the path to the left leading to the Thames towpath. Hammerton's foot ferry operates here on a daily basis for most of the year (weekends only November-January). Turn right along the towpath towards Glover's Island and Richmond Hill. The view is nearly as good as the one from the top of the hill, especially if the sun is behind you. On the left, Marble Hill House gradually appears (for this and Orleans House see the Syon Park to Strawberry Hill walk, page 135).

Follow the towpath alongside Petersham Meadows, grazed by cattle from Petersham Farm. After a while the towpath bears right and then left Ⓣ into riverside Buccleugh Gardens Ⓟ, once the grounds of Buccleugh House. Nothing remains of the house except the brick shelter on the right and, just beyond, the tunnel that led from the house to more gardens on the other side of Petersham Road. Here, now a public park called Terrace Gardens Ⓟ, there is still a fine river god statue which the then occupant of Buccleugh House bought from the Coade factory at Lambeth in 1781 (see the Lambeth and South Bank walk, page 84).

Continue along the riverside path under the bridge and back along the new terrace. By the White Cross Hotel turn right into Water Lane. Walk up to the main road (George Street) and follow it along to the left until you come to Richmond Station where the walk ends.

Kew to Hammersmith

Summary: Kew and Hammersmith, with Chiswick in between, are all on the River Thames in west London. Apart from the first section of the walk around Kew Green and a short-cut through the landscaped grounds of Chiswick House, the walk follows the river throughout, first along Strand-on-the-Green and then along Chiswick Mall and Hammersmith's Upper and Lower Malls. These are all one-sided streets, separated from the river by a path or quiet road, and lined with fine 18th-century houses interspersed with old pubs such as the City Barge or the Dove. The most famous of the riverside houses is Kelmscott House where William Morris spent the last two decades of his productive life.

Start: **Kew Gardens Station (District Underground line; Silverlink Metro trains; riverboats from Westminster Pier).**
Finish: **Hammersmith Station (District, Metropolitan and Piccadilly Underground lines).**
Length: **4½ miles (7.2 kilometres).**
Time: **2½ hours.**
Refreshments: **Pubs and tea rooms in and around Kew and Kew Green (particularly the outstanding Newens' tea rooms in Kew Road near the start of the walk) and later on several historic riverside pubs: the City Barge at Strand-on-the-Green (a third of the way along the route) and the Ship and the Dove on the Upper Mall at Hammersmith (three-quarters of the way along the route). There is also a good café in the grounds of Chiswick House at the half-way point.**

Standing at the main exit from Kew Gardens Station Ⓣ, take the right fork of the road and then turn right onto Kew Gardens Road. Follow it round to Kew Road where you will see the wall of the Royal Botanic Gardens on the far side. Turn right past Newens' tea rooms, resisting, if you can, the temptation to sample their deservedly famous Maids of Honour tarts. When you reach the traffic lights some way ahead on this busy stretch of road, cross the road to your left, turn right briefly, and then go left again into Kew Green, walking along the south side with Kew's 18th-century church Ⓗ on your right.

Before the Botanic Gardens

The old village green, with its pond in one corner and cricket pitch behind the church, is overlooked by elegant Georgian houses. Most of these houses were built in the 18th century for the courtiers and officials attached to the royal court during its summer residence in Kew. What are now the Royal Botanic Gardens Ⓗ was once the site of the royal palaces, of which only Kew Palace, bought by George III in 1770 and now a museum, survives. George III's mother, Princess Augusta, founded the botanic gardens in 1759, and Queen Victoria handed them over to the nation in 1841. In the beginning the gardens were only 9 acres (3.6 hectares), but they now cover over 300 acres (121 hectares).

Continue along the south side of the green past St Anne's Church, burial place of two famous painters: Johann Zoffany (died 1810) and Thomas Gainsborough (died 1788). The latter's grave is the flat slab surrounded by black railings on the south side. Both had houses nearby. Further along on your left, No. 47 is now the administrative offices of the gardens. Its gates were the gardens' original entrance. Today the main entrance is through the massive black and gilt gates ahead at the western corner of the green. Follow the road round past the entrance and along the north side of the green, passing on the left the Herbarium (where dried specimens of all the world's plants are stored) and then Ferry Lane, which once led to the now-defunct Brentford Ferry. When you reach the main road again, go over the road at the zebra crossing and then turn left over Kew Bridge towards Brentford. The island on the left is Brentford Ait and the graceful tower to its right is part of the former Grand Junction Water Works, now the Kew Bridge Steam Museum Ⓜ.

Along the Strand

On the other side of the bridge turn sharp right down by the shops and follow the road round to the left along the river. When the road diverges from the river, bear right along the footpath between the river and Strand-on-the-Green. The Strand was just a small fishing community until the great Court era of Kew from the mid 18th-century onwards. Zoffany lived in one of the biggest of the new houses built at that time (No. 65) and used the local fishermen as models for a painting of the Last Supper he executed for a local church.

Further along the Strand you come to the old City Barge pub, which claims to date from 1484 and was originally called the Navigator's Arms. The name was changed after a boathouse was built nearby to store the lord mayor of London's state barge. Beyond the bridge are the 17th-century Bull's Head pub and some tiny almshouses, built in 1724. The squat, modern building on the opposite side of the river is the Public Record Office, where national archives stretching back to the time of William the Conqueror are stored.

When the path comes to an end continue straight on into Grove Park Road, bearing left when Grove Park Road branches off the main thoroughfare. The Grove Park Estate was built in the grounds of Grove House, an 18th-century mansion which was still standing in 1928. At the end of the road (on the right is St Paul's Church) turn left and then left again over Grove Park Bridge. When you are half-way over the bridge, turn right down the steps and walk up to Chiswick Station. Turn left into Park Road, then right into Staveley Road and left by the public telephone box into the grounds of Chiswick House Ⓟ Ⓣ. At the toilets near the entrance turn right and walk straight on.

Chiswick House Ⓗ was built in the 1720s by the amateur architect Lord Burlington, essentially as a place where he could display his art collection and entertain his friends. It was one of the earliest Palladian houses in England and is, therefore, an important architectural monument. The gardens are significant too, because they were the first to break away from the formal Dutch style and experiment with a more natural approach. Both house and garden owe much to the 18th century's reverence for classical antiquity so you will find numerous temples, columns and urns.

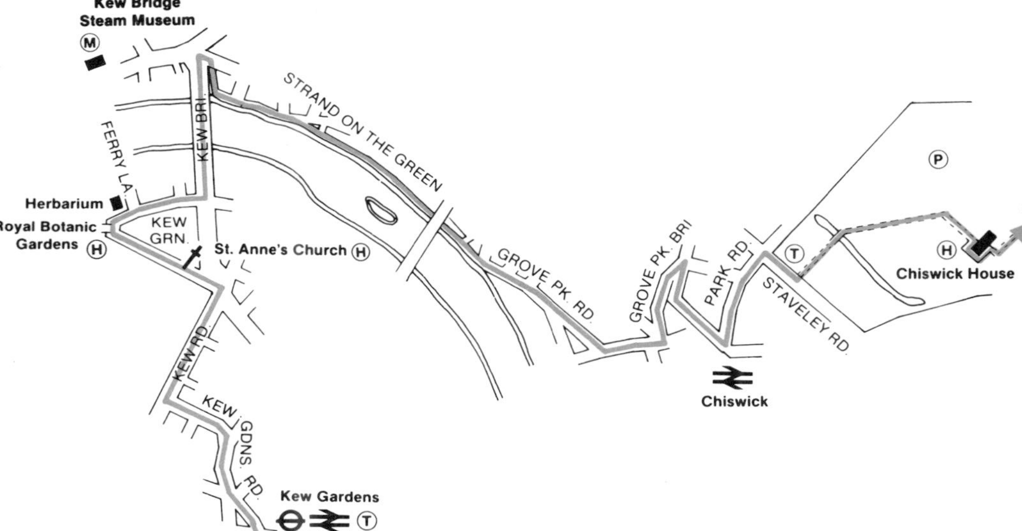

When you get to the bridge, go straight over and right up the bank. Pass the sunken pond with the central obelisk and then walk down the avenue of urns to the house. Go round the house to the right, between the gate pillars, and then turn immediately left along a path which leads past the café Ⓣ and eventually to a small lodge. Leave the park by the gate to the right of the lodge.

Artists and actors

Turn left along Burlington Lane towards Paxton Road, crossing the lane at the traffic lights. Beyond St Mary's Convent turn right into Powell's Walk. This ancient right of way takes you to Chiswick Old Burying Ground and St Nicholas's Church Ⓗ, the nucleus of the old riverside village of Chiswick. Modern Chiswick's centre of gravity has since shifted north to Chiswick High Road, leaving old Chiswick a quiet backwater, cut off from the rest of London by the Great West Road, driven through the suburban streets between old and new Chiswick in the 1950s.

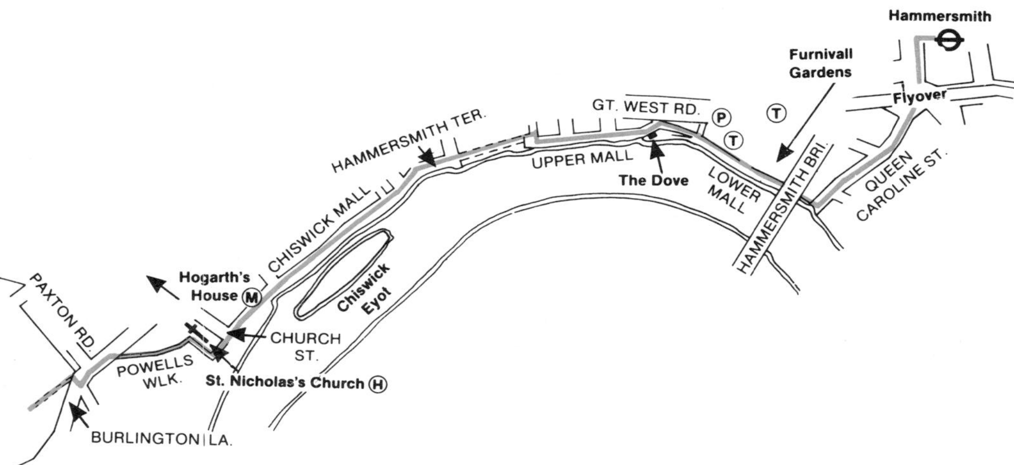

Go round to the right of St Nicholas's 15th-century tower and through the south porch into the little churchyard. Several well-known people are buried at St Nicholas's, including Lord Burlington of Chiswick House and his landscape designer William Kent. The most prominent grave in this part of the graveyard (on the right, surrounded by railings) belongs to 18th-century artist William Hogarth and his wife and mother-in-law. They all lived together in Hogarth's little country house at Chiswick, now a Hogarth museum Ⓗ.

Go straight past Hogarth's tomb and out of the churchyard into Chiswick Mall (Hogarth's house is to the left: along Church Street, under the roundabout, and into Hogarth Lane). Handsome houses face south across the river. The first is the local parsonage. Bedford House was the home of the acting family, the Redgraves. The finest is Walpole House, the one with the railings and gate in front, nearly opposite the far end of the island (Chiswick Eyot). Relations of Sir Robert Walpole, England's first Prime Minister, lived here in the 18th century. Later it was used as a school. William Thackeray boarded there for a while and probably used it as the model for Miss Pinkerton's Academy in *Vanity Fair*. One of the first occupants of Walpole House was Charles II's mistress, the Duchess of Cleveland, 'fairest and lewdest of the royal concubines'.

Private printing presses

At the end of Chiswick Mall the small cottages of Durham Wharf interpose between the river and the road so that the river is temporarily lost to view. The cottages are followed by the more substantial houses in Hammersmith Terrace, built in the 1750s with gardens right on the river. No. 7 bears a plaque to Sir Emery Walker (1851–1933), an expert on printing types and a partner in two local printing presses, the Kelmscott Press and the Doves Press. No. 3 was the home of calligrapher Edward Johnston (1872-1944), teacher of graphic designer and artist Eric Gill, and a collaborator on the Doves Press. A P Herbert, a colourful MP who wrote many books about the Thames before his death in 1971, lived for more than 50 years at Nos. 12-13.

At the end of the terrace the walk returns to the riverside in a public garden laid out on the site of the old West Middlesex Water Company pumping station, part of which remains as a brick arcade. Ahead, there is a fine view of Hammersmith Mall as it curves round to Hammersmith Bridge. Continue past the 18th-century Old Ship pub, through the tunnel created by the overhang of a modern apartment block, and then past Linden House, for over a century the headquarters of the London Corinthian Sailing Club, founded in 1894. Races are started from the box on the right. The long low building on the opposite bank is St Paul's School, founded in the shadow of St Paul's Cathedral in the City in 1512, moved to Hammersmith in 1884 and to this site in 1968.

This stretch of the river (Hammersmith Reach) offers the best sailing on the tidal part of the Thames. But it is probably used as much by rowers as by sailors (and it is roughly the half-way stage of the Oxford and Cambridge boat race course). You can see the first boathouses in Hammersmith Upper Mall soon after the road rejoins the riverside a few steps ahead. The five-bay Georgian house at the end of the Mall, with its own front garden behind walls and railings, is Kelmscott House, designer William Morris's London home from 1877 until his death in 1896. Morris named the house after his country home in Kelmscott, Oxfordshire. This was also on the Thames and more than once Morris rowed with family and friends the whole way upriver from one house to the other. An earlier occupant was Sir Francis Ronalds (1788-1873), who developed the world's first electric telegraph in the garden. He was forced to abandon it after the government, blind to its revolutionary importance, said it could not see a use for it!

Fine book-making

Thomas Cobden-Sanderson, a friend of Morris, lived next door at No. 22. Sanderson gave up being a barrister while in his 40s and started the Doves book-bindery, where he carried out a lot of work for William Morris's Kelmscott Press. Later, after Morris had died and the Kelmscott Press had folded, Cobden-Sanderson and Emery Walker from Hammersmith Terrace founded the Doves Press alongside the bindery. During the 19th century the craft of good book-making had sunk to a low ebb in Britain. These three men - Walker, Cobden-Sanderson and Morris - were largely responsible for reviving it and starting the private press movement which is still flourishing today. Cobden-Sanderson also invented the term 'arts and crafts' for the movement which Morris inspired.

The Doves Press and Bindery occupied a small house just beyond the 18th-century Dove pub on the right. It was here, in the 18th century when the Dove was a coffee-house, that poet James Thomson wrote part of his famous poem *The Seasons*, and also the words of *Rule Britannia*.

Walk on into Furnivall Gardens Ⓟ Ⓣ, laid out over Hammersmith's wharf area following World War II bombing, and then along the Lower Mall past more boat-houses, pubs and houses. Continue under colourful Hammersmith Bridge, dating from 1887, to the end of the riverside walk. Turn left into Queen Caroline Street and walk to the flyover. There is a subway further on which will take you to Hammersmith Station and the bus station in the traffic island on the right, where the walk ends.

Barnes to Fulham

Summary: Barnes and Fulham, with Putney in between, straddle the River Thames in west London. The central section of the walk follows the river, first along the towpath and then on Putney Embankment, a great rowing centre. Otherwise, apart from its first stage in the old village of Barnes (still with its green, duckpond, pub and church), the walk goes mainly through parks and gardens, including the public grounds of 16th-century Fulham Palace, the former summer retreat of the Bishops of London. The palace's gardens are among the loveliest and least known in London. Other features of the walk include Putney and Fulham churches with their Civil War associations, and the remains of the 300-year-old Fulham Pottery.

Start: **Barnes Bridge Station (trains from Waterloo).**
Finish: **Putney Bridge Station (District Underground line).**
Length: **3½ miles (5.6 kilometres).**
Time: **2 hours.**
Refreshments: **Plenty of places in Barnes at the start of the walk (including the Sun Inn on the village green) and in Putney High Street by Putney Bridge, a little over half-way into the walk. Near the end there is a good café in Fulham's Bishop's Park.**

Come out of Barnes Bridge Station, cross the road and turn right along a breezy, open stretch of the River Thames. This is the last stage of the 4½-mile (7-kilometre) Oxford and Cambridge University Boat Race, which ends upstream of the bridge at Mortlake. On the right, the red-brick house on the corner of Cleveland Gardens was home to *Planets* composer Gustav Holst while he was teaching music at nearby St Paul's School.

Suburban village

Follow the road round to the right into Barnes High Street. Although it is a suburb firmly entrenched in the London conurbation, Barnes still retains much of its old village character. Round the corner at the end of the High Street you will find the village green with a duckpond in the middle and a central island where swans breed. On the right of the pond, Milbourne House - the oldest house in Barnes - was home briefly to the 18th-century novelist Henry Fielding, author of *Tom Jones*. As you turn left along Church Road you pass the village pub overlooking the green and the pond. Further on along Church Road you come to Barnes' church, St Mary's Ⓗ, looking every bit the rustic country church with its lychgate, yews and well-tended graveyard.

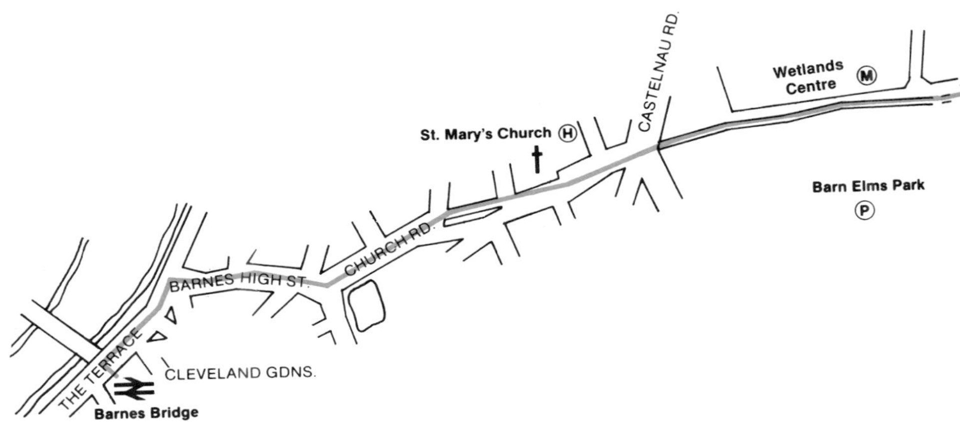

When you come to the traffic lights at the junction with Castelnau Road, go straight across into the lane which runs alongside Barn Elms Park Ⓟ. Barn Elms House, demolished after a fire in 1954, was the manor house of Barnes and the modern park its grounds. The only relic today is a section of the old lake. Previous residents include Queen Elizabeth's minister and spymaster, Sir Francis Walsingham, and the 18th-century banker and Lord Mayor of London, Sir Richard Hoare, who is buried in St Mary's Church. From 1894 until 1939 the old house was an upper-class country club. On the left the Wetland Centre Ⓜ stands on what was until the early 1990s a vast reservoir as big as the park itself.

When the road enters the sports centre, keep to the pavement and go through the gate into Queen Elizabeth Walk. This will bring you out onto one of the quietest and most rural stretches of the Thames towpath in London. Opposite you can see Fulham football ground, and to the right of the ground, Bishop's Park, your eventual destination. Turn right and walk along to a small dock where the Beverley Brook joins the Thames. Here the towpath turns into Putney Embankment Ⓣ, a great rowing centre and start point of the Oxford and Cambridge boat race since it was first held over the full Putney to Mortlake course in 1845. There are lots of boathouses here and boats are constantly being carried in and out, so watch out as you walk along.

Follow the Embankment along to Putney Bridge. Putney Church Ⓗ, on the other side of Putney High Street, is dwarfed by the office blocks behind. In this church in 1647, England's anti-royalist New Model Army held a two-week conference known to history as the Putney Debates. Ostensibly the debates were about whether the army should be disbanded without back-pay or indemnity for damage done during the war against the king. In practice, they ranged over a whole spectrum of political ideas embodied in the 'Agreement of the People', including the then revolutionary concept of 'one man, one vote'. The army radicals lost the argument and Oliver Cromwell finally crushed them after a mutiny two years later.

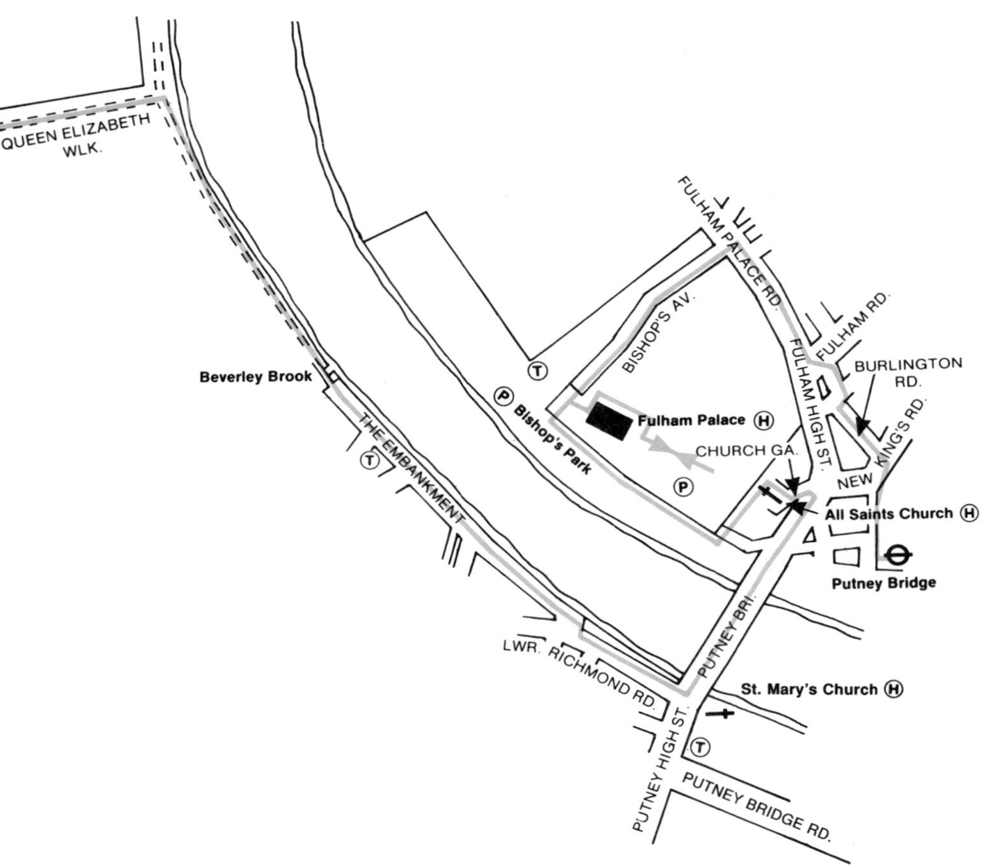

Fulham and its palace

At this point, turn left over the bridge towards Fulham and its parish church of All Saints on the opposite side. When you come to the junction with New King's Road (which branches right) turn left into Church Gate. On the right at the end is a fine range of almshouses, still used by local people. These were built in 1869, having been endowed in 1680 by Hereford MP and local landowner Sir William Powell. (The original Powell almshouses were in nearby Burlington Road which you come to in a minute.) Go through the gate into the churchyard. As well as being Fulham's parish church, All Saints Ⓗ also has close connections with the Bishops of London because it was the closest church to their summer home, Fulham Palace, and at least ten bishops are buried in the churchyard. Inside there are many fine monuments, including two from the Civil War. One commemorates William Rumbold, a royal official who was both Surveyor-General of the Customs and Comptroller of the Great Wardrobe. In his latter capacity, he carried off the royal standard to Charles I at

Nottingham when the Civil War broke out. Rumbold died in 1667 at nearby Parson's Green. The other monument, dated 1665, commemorates 25-year-old Thomas Carlos, whose father, Colonel William Carlos, hid in the oak tree at Boscobel with the future Charles II, after the defeat of the royalists at Worcester in 1651.

Go to the right round the west end of the church, and turn right into Bishop's Park Ⓟ. The park was originally part of the grounds of Bishop's Palace, which you will come to shortly. Walk through the park, either along the riverside or through the centre, and when you come to the crossroads next to the open-air performance area turn right out of the park between on the left, the café Ⓣ and aviary and on the right, the entrance lodge of Fulham Palace Ⓗ. Immediately turn right into the grounds of the palace and walk straight through to the gateway leading into the central courtyard. It was only in 1973 that the Bishops of London gave up Fulham Palace, having used it - mainly as a summer home - for a thousand years. In its present form, the building is only about 500 years old, being essentially a Tudor mansion of the 16th-century ranged round a cobbled courtyard. The garden front was added much later in 1814.

Secret garden

To gain access to the gardens, go back out of the courtyard gateway, turn right, go through the gate and then turn right again. The palace gardens are among the most attractive and secluded in London, particularly the walled garden, which is reached through a low Tudor archway in the old brick wall on the opposite side of the gracious lawns. Here in this old kitchen garden, which, with its dilapidated greenhouses, feels like some kind of secret garden, you could be a million miles from central London.

Retrace your steps to the original entrance to the palace grounds near the exit from the park and turn right along Bishop's Avenue, with bowling green and tennis courts on your left and the Warren allotment gardens on your right. Beyond the school, Moat Garden on the right has been created out of the remains of the huge moat system which once surrounded Fulham Palace. Archaeologists say this defensive system is at least as old as the time of the Danish occupation (800s to 1000s) and could even date from Roman times several hundred years before that.

On the main road (Fulham Palace Road) cross over at the lights left, and turn right. At the roundabout junction with Fulham Road, go over the zebra crossing to the left and into Burlington Road – where the almshouses used to be. At the end of this road there is a disused 19th-century pottery kiln, part of the old Fulham Pottery which was based here until lack of space forced it to move to Battersea in the 1980s. The move severed a 300 year-old link with the past for the pottery had been here since 1672. Ex-lawyer John Dwight established it after learning how to produce a much sought-after type of pottery called salt-glazed stoneware, until then only obtainable in Germany. Dwight also tried to manufacture porcelain in England for the first time – without success.

At the end of Burlington Road, turn right onto New King's Road, cross the road using the traffic island, and go along the path by the bus stop which leads to Putney Bridge Station and the end of the walk.

Dulwich

Summary: Set in woods, parks and playing fields, semi-rural Dulwich in south London has been carefully preserved by the major landowner in the area, the Dulwich College Estate. On the walk you will see old Dulwich College (17th-century almshouses and chapel) and new Dulwich College (Victorian public school), the Dulwich Picture Gallery (England's oldest public art gallery), 18th-century cottages, shops and mansions, Dulwich tollgate, Dulwich Park and the Sydenham Hill Woods nature reserve, one of the closest wildlife reserves to central London.

***Start:* West Dulwich Station (trains from Victoria).**
***Finish:* North Dulwich Station (trains from London Bridge).**
***Length:* 3½ miles (5.6 kilometres).**
***Time:* 2 hours.**
***Refreshments:* Nowhere to stop until you get to the Wood House pub on Sydenham Hill, about halfway round and at the end of a fairly steep climb. Further on there is another pub at the bottom of the hill, a café in Dulwich Park and more pubs in Dulwich Village towards the end of the walk.**

Come out of West Dulwich Station onto Thurlow Park Road and turn right, away from the traffic lights. Walk past the entrances to Gallery Road on the left and Alleyn Park on the right into Dulwich Common. This road used to run across the common ground of Dulwich Manor until in the 19th century the common was enclosed and divided up. In 1870, 40 acres (16 hectares) were used for the new buildings and playing fields of Dulwich College, which you can see on your right. Dulwich College was originally founded in 1619 as a school and almshouse by Dulwich's childless lord of the manor, a wealthy actor and friend of Shakespeare called Edward Alleyn (pronounced Allane). The initial educational provision was for 12 poor boys, but in the 19th century the school expanded into a leading public school. The original College buildings still stand in the centre of Dulwich and you see them later in the walk.

Bears, bulls and mastiff dogs

The left-hand side of Dulwich Common is lined with old houses. The fifth house along, Old Blew House, is supposed to be the oldest house in Dulwich, though it was obviously refaced in the 18th century. Alleyn, who owned most of the land in Dulwich having bought the estate in 1605 with the proceeds of his acting, his successful business ventures and the fees from his lucrative post of Master of the Royal

Game of Bears, Bulls and Mastiff Dogs, owned the house and donated it to his native parish, St Botolph Bishopsgate in the City, for the benefit of its poor.

When you get to the crossroads turn right into College Road and cross over by the pond. Continue along College Road until you come to Pond Cottages, a row of 18th-century cottages once lived in by farmworkers and mill-hands. The central

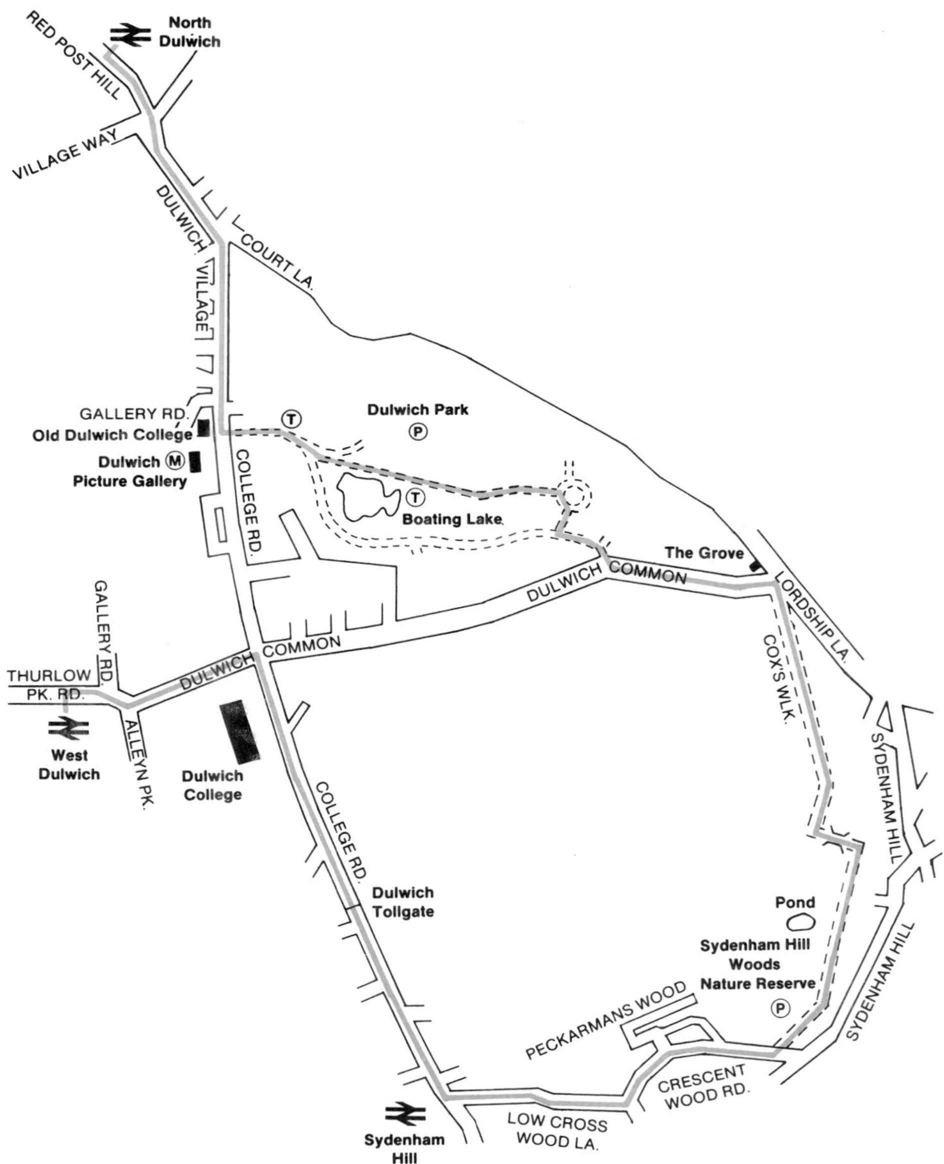

pair are covered in black weatherboard, once a common style of building in Dulwich. The school physical education centre is at the end of the lane.

Continue along College Road past the school buildings and more playing fields and tennis courts. After a while you come to the Dulwich tollgate: the money collected from motorists is used to pay for the upkeep of College Road, which is privately owned by the College Estate. Tollgates (or turnpikes, as they were called) were once a common sight in England, but most of them disappeared in the 1860s when local councils took over road maintenance from the turnpike owners. Dulwich tollgate is the only one left in London and raises some £17,000 a year.

Go past the gate and continue along College Road up the hill. After a while the white posts by the roadside start again and you come to Sydenham Hill Station. Directly opposite, turn left through the wicket gate into Low Cross Wood Lane. A steep climb brings you to the summit of the hill and the Dulwich Wood House pub. Turn left here along Crescent Wood Road. When you get to the last of the modern houses on the left (No. 65), turn into Peckarmans Wood leading round behind them for a panorama over central London, 5 miles (8 kilometres) away. In summer, much of it is obscured by trees, but on a clear day you can still make out St Paul's Cathedral and the International Financial Centre in the City, and the Canary Wharf Tower in Docklands.

Ancient woodland

Retrace your steps back to the road and walk along to the gate in the fence on the left, just before the pillar box. Go through the gate and into Sydenham Hill Woods nature reserve Ⓟ. Managed by the London Wildlife Trust, the reserve is based on an ancient wood and incorporates a disused railway cutting, last used in 1954, and the ruins of several 19th-century houses, demolished in the 1960s. Take the right fork at the noticeboard (the walk is aiming for point 7 on the map - the noticeboard is at point 1). Point 2 is in the middle of the site of an old tennis court. Point 3 is marked by a Lebanese cedar. The ruin at point 4 has actually been designed to look like the remains of a Gothic abbey. Take the right fork just after the contrived ruin (go left if you want to go down to the pond - in which case go right round and rejoin the path). Pass point 8 and on the left now you can see the railway cutting. Walk straight ahead, go down the bank, cross the footbridge over the cutting where Impressionist Camille Pissarro once set up his easel and turn right into Cox's Walk. Over to the left of you is Dulwich and Sydenham Hill golf course.

Cox's Walk brings you to the junction of Dulwich Common and Lordship Lane. The Grove pub is on the corner. There has been a pub here for nearly 300 years. In 1704 it was called the Green Man and the innkeeper was John Cox. Under his son's management, water from a well in the garden, which was found to have medicinal properties, was developed into a fashionable local spa called Dulwich Wells. Later the inn was converted by Dr Glennie into a school for young gentlemen. The doctor's most famous pupil was the poet Lord Byron, who spent two years here while a London specialist treated his club foot. Byron left the school in 1801 to go to Harrow.

Polish national gallery

Cross over to the other side of Dulwich Common and turn left. Walk along beside the modern flats and just beyond the end turn right through Rosebery Gate into Dulwich Park Ⓟ. Follow the road round to the left and then take the first path on the right into the inner ring. Turn left (there should be a small pavilion to the right) and then left again into the main path going through the middle of the park towards the children's playground and bowling green. In this part of the park there is also a café Ⓣ, an aviary and a boating lake.

Continue past the café along the right-hand side of the lake and then go straight on along the car road Ⓣ to Old College Gate with the old college ahead of you. To the left is the Dulwich Picture Gallery Ⓜ, set back from the road in its own grounds. When Alleyn died in 1626 he left the college some pictures, but not enough to warrant a purpose-built gallery. In 1811, at the suggestion of one of the college fellows, the landscape painter Sir Francis Bourgeois left the college another 370 pictures, including many first-class works collected for an unrealized national gallery in Poland. Architect John Soane was commissioned to design a gallery for the pictures, which became the first public picture gallery in England.

Return to Old College Gate and walk to the right towards Dulwich Village along the right-hand side of the road. The old college on the left is grouped around three sides of a square, the fourth being open towards the fountain which marks the junction of three roads: College Road, Gallery Road, and ahead, Dulwich Village. If you look back into the courtyard of the college, the end wing is the chapel, the right-hand side the offices of the College Estate, and the left-hand side the present-day almshouse providing 16 homes, four more than Alleyn initially provided for. At the beginning of Gallery Road is the 19th-century schoolhouse designed by Charles Barry, architect of the Houses of Parliament.

Georgian suburb

Next to the fountain is a triangular milestone, dated 1772, giving distances to both the Treasury in Whitehall and to the Standard in Cornhill - five miles (eight kilometres) in each case. This was useful information for the kind of people (civil servants, lawyers, City merchants and bankers) who were the first occupants of the fine Georgian houses which continue in a virtually unbroken line along the right-hand side of the village street from this point. The other side of the street was (and still is) reserved for the village shopkeepers and tradesmen.

Walk straight along Dulwich Village as far as the old burial ground in the triangle which is formed by the junction of Court Lane and Dulwich Village. Alleyn gave it to the village in 1616, when the village had no church or graveyard of its own, and it was used until 1858. Dulwich's 35 victims of the 1665 Great Plague are buried here.

Continue along Dulwich Village past a row of modern shops and then the parish hall. At the junction with Village Way, with Lyndenhurst (1757) on the corner and Pond House (1739) to the left of it, cross over into Red Post Hill. The walk ends at North Dulwich Station on the right.

Highgate to Hampstead

Summary: This is a long, hilly walk across London's Northern Heights. There are fine views from many places, especially from Parliament Hill (319 feet/97 metres) on Hampstead Heath. The walk starts in Highgate, crosses Hampstead Heath via the grounds of 18th-century Kenwood House, and finishes in Hampstead, one-time spa resort and favoured retreat for generations of artists and writers. The homes of poets Coleridge and Keats and artists Constable and Romney, amongst others, are passed on the walk. Other features include Highgate Cemetery, where Karl Marx is buried, and the National Trust's Fenton House.

Start: **Archway Station (Northern Underground line).**
Finish: **Hampstead Station (Northern Underground line).**
Length: **6 miles (9.6 kilometres).**
Time: **4½ hours.**
Refreshments: **Kenwood is the ideal place to stop because it is exactly at the half-way point. In Highgate, try the terrace café in Waterlow Park (wonderful views) or the Prince of Wales and Flask pubs in Highgate village. In Hampstead, the Wells Tavern, Holly Bush pub on Holly Hill and the café in Burgh House are all recommended. All places are mentioned in the text.**
Route note: **Give yourself a day for this walk, breaking for lunch at Kenwood.**

Leave Archway Station by the 'Highgate Hill' exit, turn left and walk up Highgate Hill as far as the Whittington Stone pub. In front is the Whittington stone where legend has it Dick Whittington heard Bow Bells calling him back to become Lord Mayor of London. Turn left into Magdala Avenue and, at the end, turn left then right into Raydon Street. Carry on into Chester Road and continue along to the junction with Swain's Lane. The horror film-Gothic enclave on the left is called Holly Village, and was built in 1865 by the philanthropist and local landowner Baroness Burdett-Coutts for her estate workers.

Shrine of communism

Turn right up the hill until you come to the twin entrances to Highgate Cemetery Ⓗ, opened in 1839 and now covering 37 acres (15 hectares) on both sides of the road. The western cemetery to the left is the earliest and most interesting from the point of view of its landscape and graves, but the right hosts the cemetery's most famous incumbent, Karl Marx.

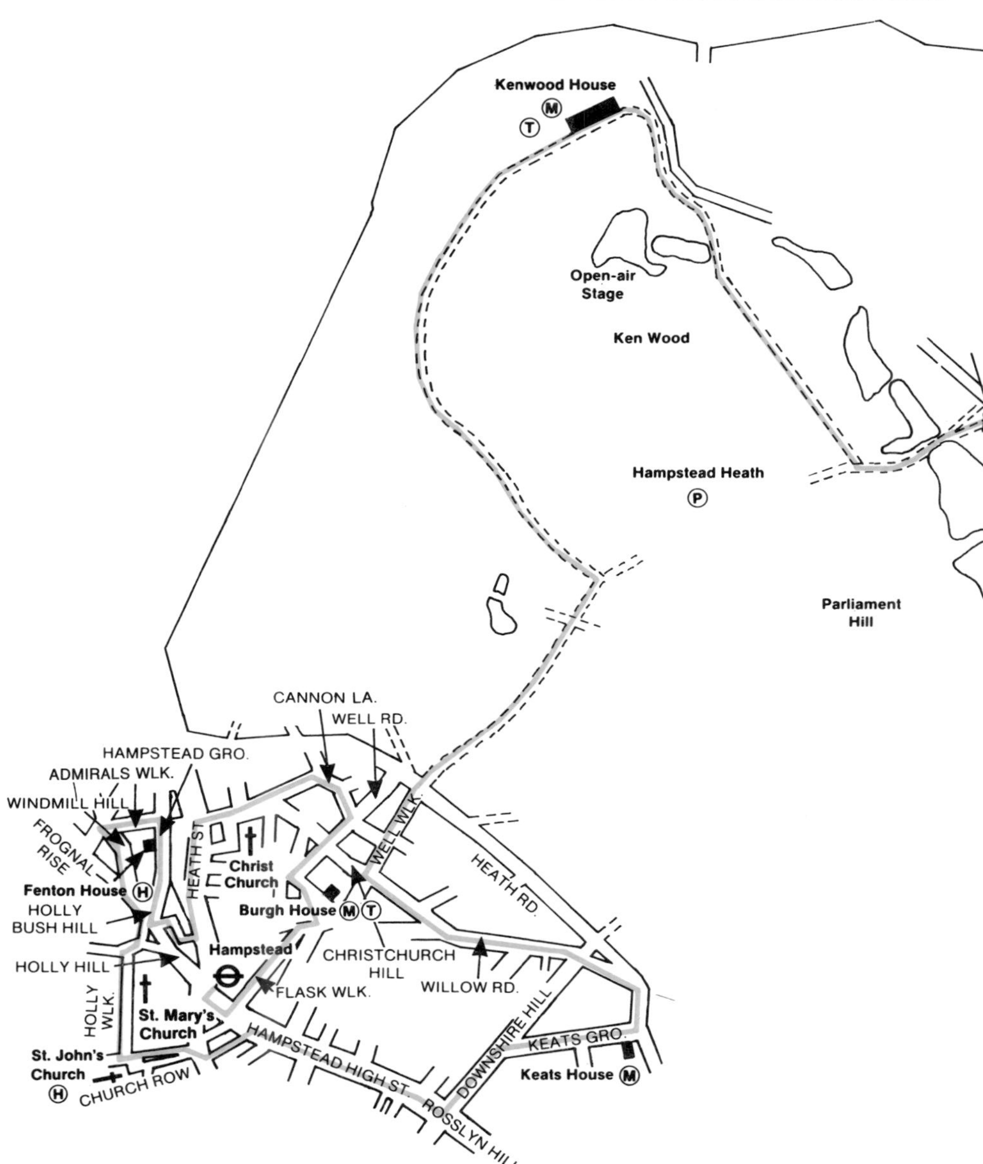

Just beyond the cemetery turn right into Waterlow Park Ⓟ. Take the left-hand fork and then bear right through the line of trees. Cross the bridge over the terrace of pools linking the upper and lower lakes and then fork left (*not* sharp left along the lakeside). At the top of the bank turn left so that the brick wall is on your right, go to the end and then ascend onto the terrace of Lauderdale House. This 17th-century mansion was once the home of the Earl of Lauderdale and the summer retreat

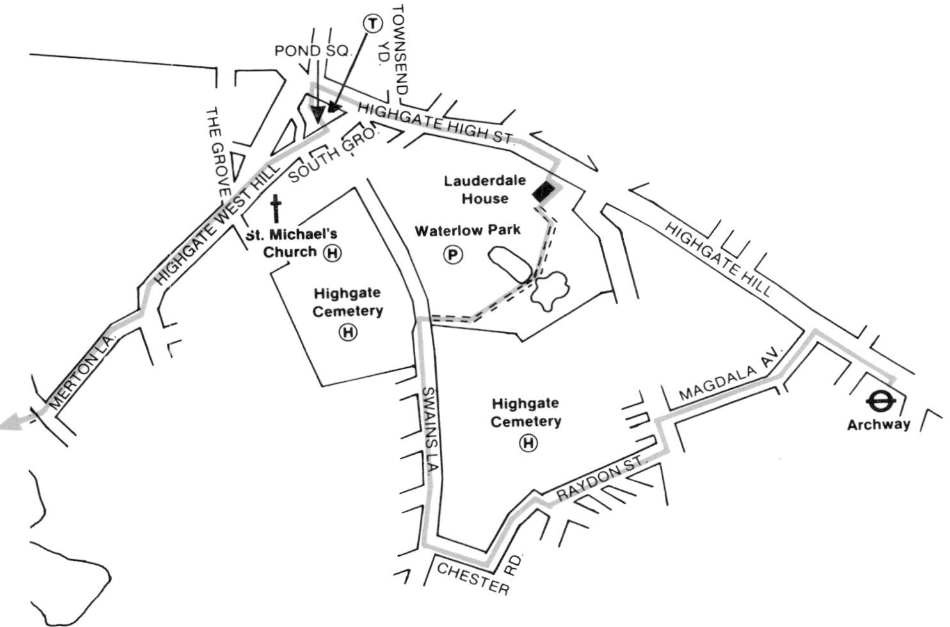

of Charles II's mistress, Nell Gwyn. It is now a centre for exhibitions, concerts and various other events. There is a café at the front (with Ⓣ) and tables outside, with views to the west over the park.

Go round to the back of the house and through the gate onto Highgate Hill. Cross the road and turn left up the Bank, a short terrace of handsome old houses standing well above street level. Turning round, there is a fine view down the hill and away over the City to the south. Continuing up the hill into the High Street of old Highgate village, archways lead off each side into yards, those on the right, particularly Townsend Yard, providing more panoramic views but this time to the east over Hornsey.

At the top of the High Street is the Old Gatehouse pub. The Bishop of London once owned a park up here and the pub stands on the site of one of the three gates that led into the park. The church on the right is the chapel of Highgate School, founded in 1565, which lies directly behind it. Cross the High Street here (the Prince of Wales pub is to the left) and go down a narrow passage just before No. 67 into Pond Square, once Highgate's village green. Turn left and cross the square to South Grove Ⓣ. No. 10a opposite is the Highgate Society which organizes events for the local community. Next door, the Highgate Literary and Scientific Institution is a members-only club with private library, reading room and meeting hall, founded in 1839 to promote 'useful and scientific knowledge'.

Poetical legends

Turn right along South Grove and walk along to the junction with Highgate West Hill. Behind and to the right is the Flask pub, named after the flasks of Hampstead mineral water which could be bought here in the heyday of the Hampstead wells during the 18th century. Across West Hill is The Grove, Highgate's finest street. The nearest houses are the most attractive and also the oldest (they date from the 1680s). No. 3, the house to the right of the one with the blue shutters, was the home for nine years of the poet Samuel Taylor Coleridge, author of *The Rime of the Ancient Mariner* (1798) and the opium-inspired *Kubla Khan* (1816). To the left of these houses there is a double gatehouse leading into the forecourt of Witanhurst, an enormous Edwardian mansion built by a soap magnate, billed as London's largest private house. On your left, the Old Hall and the parish church of St Michael's Ⓗ occupy a marvellous site where a great mansion called Arundel House once stood. The lawyer and philosopher Francis Bacon caught a fatal chill and died here in 1626 after making an early experiment in refrigeration by stuffing a chicken with snow.

Continue on down the hill. Round the corner turn right into Merton Lane. At the bottom of the lane continue straight into the park ahead Ⓟ Ⓣ. This is Hampstead Heath, 800 hilly acres (324 hectares) of mown grass, scrub and rough woodland, crisscrossed by muddy tracks and gravel and tarmac paths. Walk between the two ponds, bear right and, after 100 yards or so, take the right-hand fork. As you climb the hill on the far side of the stream you can see the main front of Witanhurst next to the church. Now you enter the woods and grounds of Kenwood House. The house itself, iced with brilliantly-painted stucco like an enormous cake, soon comes into view through the trees. A private house until as late as 1927, Kenwood Ⓜ is now a public museum with fine 18th-century Adam interiors and a notable collection of pictures bequeathed by its last owner, the Earl of Iveagh, head of the Guinness brewing family. There is a café at the house Ⓣ.

Follow the broad tarmac path along the terrace in front of the house, with the lawn sloping away to the lake on your left. At the end of the terrace, turn right through the gate back into Hampstead Heath and follow the path as it swings to the left. After quite a distance you will come to a gate in some railings. Go through the gate and bear left. Continue straight on for some way until you emerge from the trees and reach a gravel path crossing at right angles. There should be a clear view of Highgate to the left.

The walk turns right here towards Hampstead, but if you have the energy you could make a 15-minute diversion to Parliament Hill for one of the best panoramic views of London. To get there, go straight on through the trees for some way. The viewpoint is easily identified by the benches standing out on the skyline.

Hampstead's health farm

To continue to Hampstead, stand on the gravel path with Highgate to your left, turn right down the hill, and then go up the other side to the main road (Heath Road). This is the western edge of Hampstead. Cross the road into Well Walk. Half-way along on the right a drinking fountain marks the site of the chalybeate spring which gave Well Walk its name and made Hampstead a popular spa resort in the early 1700s. After about a century the craze for drinking the waters died out and Hampstead was left to the artists, writers and intellectuals who had already begun to settle there in search of peace, solitude and fresh air. On the left, No. 40

Well Walk was the family home of the painter John Constable from 1827 until his death ten years later.

At the Wells Tavern turn left down Christchurch Hill. Continue into Willow Road, cross Downshire Hill and go round the corner of Heath Road (the modern Royal Free Hospital is ahead) into Keats Grove on the right. John Keats, the Romantic poet lived in the white house an the left Ⓜ, and wrote some of his best work here, including his famous *Ode to a Nightingale.*

Continue along Keats Grove into Downshire Hill, which some say is Hampstead's grandest street. At the top of the street turn right into Rosslyn Hill, leading into Hampstead High Street. Beyond the King William IV pub on the left take the second turning on the left off the High Street under an archway into Perrins Court. At the end turn right and then left into Church Row, certainly Hampstead's most historic street. It was built in the early 1700s, just as the spa was becoming popular and not long after William of Orange became king, hence the Dutch style of the houses - tall and narrow with an abundance of glass, very similar to houses in the older parts of Amsterdam.

Authors and artists

As the street widens, it frames Hampstead's parish church of St John's Ⓗ (1745) at the end. John Constable the painter is buried in the churchyard (tomb location signposted). Keep to the right here and then turn right up Holly Walk, with the 1811 churchyard extension on your right. Further along on the right is St Mary's Catholic Church with a statue of the Virgin Mary in the blue niche above the door. Opened in 1816 for the use of French emigrés, it was tucked away in this remote spot because Catholics did not enjoy full freedom of worship at this time. At the top of Holly Walk turn right by a house where Robert Louis Stevenson, author of *Treasure Island*, once stayed, into Mount Vernon and follow the lane down to the left to the green on Holly Bush Hill. Go straight across into Windmill Hill (*not* down the slope of Frognal Rise to the left) and follow the road as it winds round to Lower Terrace. On the opposite side of the green, the terraced cottage with the blue door (No. 2) was another of John Constable's homes in Hampstead. He lived here in the 1820s making endless studies of clouds and atmospheric effects in the big Hampstead skies.

Just before the green, turn right into Admiral's Walk. Round the corner is Grove Lodge, where John Galsworthy wrote most of *The Forsyte Saga* (1922). Next to Grove Lodge is Admiral's House. This house was never actually lived in by an admiral, but it does have a 'quarter-deck' from which - in the 18th century - an enthusiastic naval tenant used to fire cannons to celebrate naval victories. The prolific 19th-century architect Sir George Gilbert Scott later lived here.

Admiral's Walk joins Hampstead Grove, running left and right. Up to the left the Whitestone Pond and Jack Straw's Castle (a pub) crown the highest point in London - 440 feet (134 metres) above sea level. The walk, however, turns to the right and passes on the left the house of George du Maurier, author of *Trilby* (1894), and on the right the National Trust's Fenton House Ⓗ, built by a City merchant in 1693, as it descends the hill to Holly Hill green once more. On the left, just beyond the painter George Romney's house, turn left into Holly Mount, a quiet hill-top backwater with a good pub, the Holly Bush, and more good views of the City and west London from the look-out point at the end of the street.

West Country tales

From the viewpoint, descend the steps leading to Heath Street and turn left, going over the road on the zebra crossing. Continue up the hill and turn right by the Friends' Meeting House at the junction with Hampstead Square. Continue on into Cannon Place. Sir Flinders Petrie, the first scientific excavator of ancient Egypt, lived at No. 5 on the left. At the end of the street on the right, Cannon Hall was the home of the actor-manager Sir Gerald du Maurier, son of George, mentioned previously, and father of the late Daphne du Maurier, author of *Rebecca* and other famous West Country tales, who grew up here. Long before, Cannon Hall was a magistrate's house with its own gaol built into the garden wall. You pass the entrance to it after turning right beyond the hall into Cannon Lane, leading down to Well Road.

Turn right into Well Road, cross Christchurch Hill and turn left into New End Square. Further down on the left, Burgh House Ⓜ Ⓣ plays a central part in both Hampstead's history and its contemporary life. Built in 1703, it was the home of Dr William Gibbons, the first man to draw attention to the medicinal qualities of Hampstead's spa water. Today it is Hampstead's community centre and local history museum.

Past Burgh House, turn right into Flask Walk, named after the old Flask Tavern where spa water was bottled for sale in London. Funnily enough, the street is shaped rather like a bottle, wide at the bottom and narrow at the neck where it joins Hampstead High Street. Turn right out of Flask Walk onto Hampstead High Street. The walk ends at Hampstead Station round the corner to the right.

Greenwich

Summary: This is a circular walk around the Georgian riverside town of Greenwich in east London. Greenwich is famous for the old royal palace and park, the former Royal Observatory and the Greenwich meridian, as well as the concentration of maritime history in the shape of the National Maritime Museum and the *Cutty Sark* and *Gypsy Moth IV*. From a steep hill behind the town there are panoramic views of Greenwich, the Isle of Dogs, the River Thames, and the Millennium Dome.

Start and finish: **Island Gardens Station (Docklands Light Rail). Greenwich Pier (riverboats from Westminster, Charing Cross and Tower Piers) and Greenwich Station (trains from Charing Cross) are possible alternative approaches.**
Length: **3½ miles (5.6 kilometres).**
Time: **2½ hours.**
Refreshments: **Plenty of pubs and restaurants (especially fish restaurants) in Greenwich itself. Otherwise try the riverside pubs (particularly the Cutty Sark on Ballast Quay which you pass towards the end of the walk) or the café half-way round the walk in Greenwich Park. There is also a basic open-air café across the river from Greenwich in Island Gardens where the walk starts and finishes.**

Walk away from Island Gardens Station Ⓣ and the railway line into Island Gardens itself Ⓟ. From here there is a classic view of Greenwich on the opposite side of the river. From left to right the riverside features visible are: the four-chimneyed electricity generating station for London's Underground system; Trinity Hospital (all white); the Trafalgar Tavern (light brown); the Royal Naval College with the Queen's House in the middle and the park beyond; the masts and rigging of the *Cutty Sark*; the dome of the Greenwich foot tunnel (to match the one to your right); the diminutive form of the round-the-world-yacht *Gypsy Moth IV*; and finally the waterfront at Deptford, where Henry VIII established the first royal dockyard.

The Royal Naval College and the Queen's House were originally part of a huge new royal palace begun by the Stuarts in the 1600s to replace the rambling old Tudor palace dating from the 1400s. The Queen's House was built first. Then came the riverside section, divided into blocks to preserve the view from the Queen's House. During building, which spanned a century, royal plans for Greenwich changed and the palace-to-be became a royal hospital for wounded seamen equivalent to the soldiers' hospital at Chelsea. The 19th century saw the hospital build-

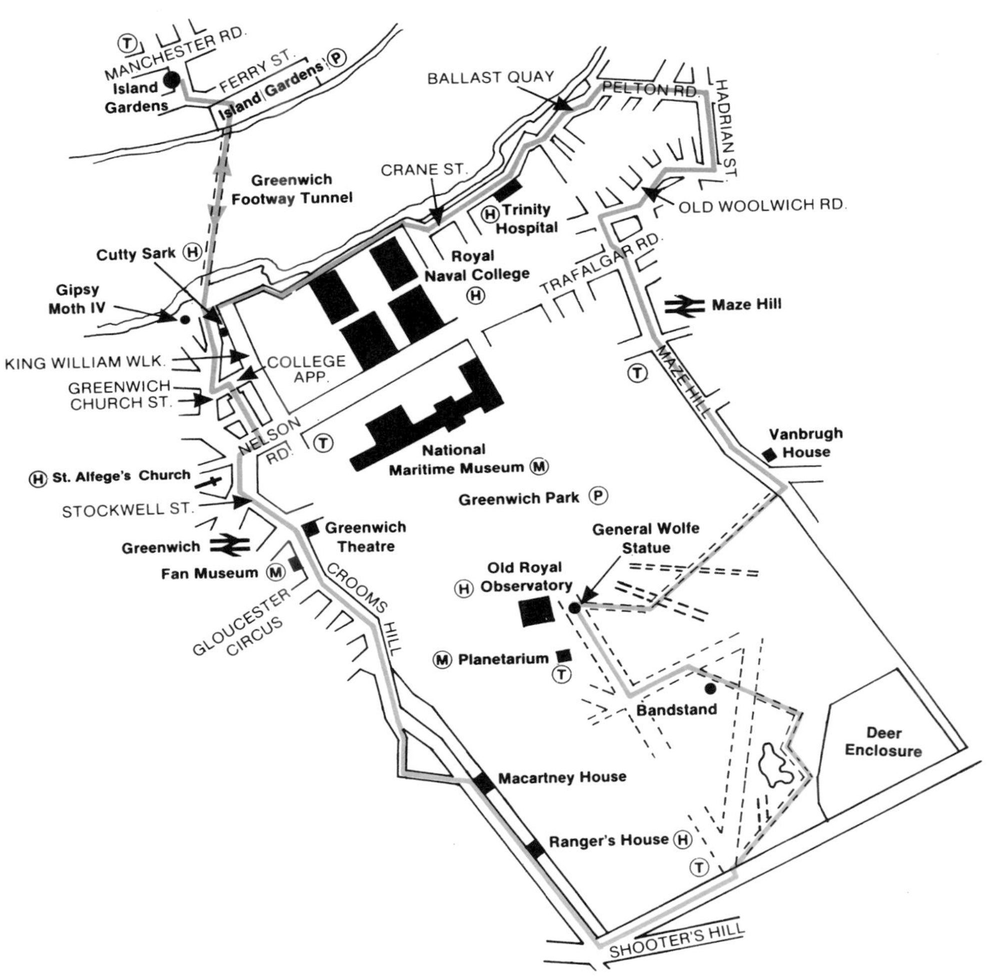

ings taken over by the Royal Naval College and the Queen's House by a school for sailors' orphans. The Queen's House, with colonnades and wings added, now belongs to the National Maritime Museum, while the former College buildings are divided between the museum and Greenwich University.

Maritime history

Enter the dome to your right and use the foot tunnel to cross the river to Greenwich. The tunnel was opened in 1902 for dockers employed in the West India Docks on the Isle of Dogs behind you. You emerge from the tunnel on a riverside plaza with the *Cutty Sark* Ⓗ straight ahead and *Gypsy Moth IV* to your right. The *Cutty Sark* was built in 1869 for the China tea-trade but really made her name freighting wool from Australia. She was the fastest clipper of them all and on a good day could cover over 350 miles (563 kilometres) The *Gypsy Moth IV* was the yacht in which 65-year-old Sir Francis Chichester completed the fastest solo circumnavigation of the world in 1966-67.

The old town centre of Greenwich and St Alfege's Church Ⓗ are straight ahead of the tunnel entrance. Aim for the church. When you get to the main road (heavy commercial traffic is the bane of Greenwich) turn left and then cross over (using the traffic lights at the end of the road if necessary) to get into Greenwich market. As you go through the arch into the covered courtyard, built in 1831, look up and behind you to see the admonition to the market traders: 'A false balance is abomination to the Lord but a just weight is his delight.' The old food market no longer functions but there is an arts and crafts market here at weekends.

Leave the market through the corresponding arch at the far end and turn right on Nelson Road. Turn left in front of St Alfege's Church into Well Street. Alfege was an 11th-century Archbishop of Canterbury who was brought to Greenwich by Danish invaders and murdered on the site of the church in 1012. King Henry VIII was baptized in the old church. The present church was the first to be built under a new church building act of 1712.

Beyond the church, turn left into Stockwell Street. On the corner of Nevada Street opposite Ye Olde Rose and Crown pub there is a fine example of an old coaching inn in something like its original state. To the left of the yard, on the restaurant, there is a painted sign which gives you some information about the old inn, and also the Stock Well.

Civil rights for children

Continue on into Crooms Hill. On the left is the old Greenwich Theatre. Then follow a terrace of houses built in 1702 with a bequest from a local benefactor, John Roan, Yeoman of His Majesty's Harriers (died 1644). The idea was that the houses would generate an income to educate 'poor town-borne children of East Greenwich . . . until the age of fifteen years'. The owners of the houses, although freeholders, still pay their annual £1.34 (or thereabouts) to the John Roan Secondary School in Maze Hill. Opposite this terrace there is another one composed of rather grander Georgian houses. The two at the top house the Fan Museum Ⓜ.

Further along on the right, on the corner of the entrance to Gloucester Circus, there is a plaque to Benjamin Waugh, ex-congregationalist minister and founder, in 1888, of the National Society for the Prevention of Cruelty to Children. Almost singlehandedly, Waugh conceived the idea of civil rights for children and in 1889 got an act of Parliament passed which meant that children who were maltreated by their parents could be taken into protective custody.

From this point Crooms Hill runs up the steep hill alongside Greenwich Park. Elsewhere, a high brick wall surrounds the park, but here the wall has been replaced by railings so that the houses have a view into the park. Sir William Hooker's gazebo on the right was obviously built while the wall was still *in situ* so that he could see over it into the park. Just inside the park here is an old conduit house, part of the original water supply for Greenwich Palace.

Beyond the Catholic church, branch right up the cobbled path on the other side of the green. St Ursula's Convent School is on the right now and the beginnings of Blackheath lie ahead. Turn left along the gravel road leading away from the school entrance. When you get to the tarmac road look back at the view across south London. In the centre, about 6 miles (9 kilometres) away, you can see disused Battersea Power Station, with its four distinctive chimneys. Cross over to the large house with the bricked-up windows and the postbox by the front door. This is Macartney House, where General Wolfe lived in the 18th century. Aged only 32, Wolfe captured Quebec by leading his army up steep cliffs above the St Lawrence River and then launching a surprise attack on the French garrison. He was killed in the attack and later buried in St Alfege's Church.

Turn right along the lime avenue planted to commemorate the Queen's Silver Jubilee in 1977. After a while you come to Ranger's House Ⓗ, formerly the official residence of the Ranger of Greenwich Park. In the distance, opposite the house, you can see the aerial of the Crystal Palace television transmitter, about 5 miles (8 kilometres) away. Further round to the right the view is of the tower blocks of south London.

London panorama

Continue along the avenue and turn left round the corner of the park wall. You can now see the full extent of Blackheath, a windy plateau crossed by the main road from London to Canterbury and Dover. Blackheath village is on the far side. Follow the park wall past the pond on the right (relic of gravel digging) to the gate in the middle and turn left into the central avenue Ⓣ Ⓟ. Turn right through the small gate in the railings and go into the park's flower garden. On the right is a huge sweet chestnut, planted as long ago as the 1660s. Follow the path round between the lake on the left and the deer enclosure on the right. Just before the path dips into a hollow, turn right and then left along the side of the main lawn area, which is dotted with flower beds and trees. Go through the gate at the end of the path and cross over to the bandstand. Turn left along the roadway and then at the crossroads turn right along the central avenue, past the Planetarium Ⓜ Ⓣ. Aim for the statue of General Wolfe silhouetted against the sky at the far end.

The view from the statue is stupendous. Away to the left are the tower blocks of the City. St Paul's Cathedral is plainly visible, but the tallest building is the International Financial Centre. The squat structure to the left of the tower is the new Lloyd's building. Ahead are the cranes and new buildings in the old docklands on the Isle of Dogs, dominated by Canary Wharf Tower, at 800 feet (244 metres) Britain's tallest building. Over 100 feet (30 metres) below is the Queen's House and the National Maritime Museum Ⓜ and, on the riverside, the former Royal Naval College. To the right is the Millennium Dome.

On the left is the Old Royal Observatory Ⓗ. Charles II commissioned it in 1675 for 'the finding out of the longitude of places for perfecting navigation and astronomy'. The royal astronomers started by fixing the meridian here, where they were

***Plate 25:** The Tudor part of Hampton Court (see the Hampton Court walk, page 127).*

Plate 26: *The house of the eighteenth-century actor, David Garrick, at Hampton (see the Hampton Court walk, page 130).*

Plate 27: *Deer roaming in Richmond Park (see the Richmond walk, page 140).*

Plate 28: *Kew Palace in the Royal Botanic Gardens (see the Kew to Hammersmith walk, page 142).*

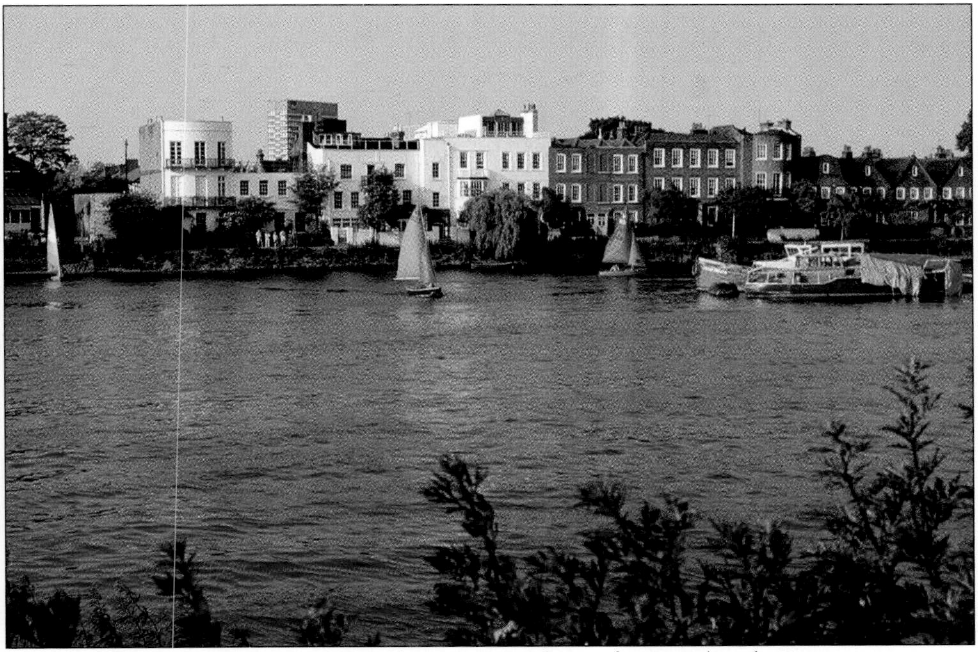

Plate 29: *Strand-on-the-Green across the river from Kew (see the Kew to Hammersmith walk, page 143).*

Plate 30: *Riverside view of the former Royal Naval College and the Queen's House* (see *the Greenwich walk, page 161).*

Plate 31: *The Cutty Sark on Greenwich riverside at dusk* (see *the Greenwich Walk, page 163).*

working. Denoted by a brass strip set in the ground, you can see it running through the cobbled courtyard and down the wall outside. Although the Royal Observatory did not succeed in its main longitude quest, over the next couple of centuries the majority of the world's navigation charts came to be based on the Greenwich Meridian, and Greenwich Mean Time was accepted as the international standard in 1884. The Royal Observatory's telescopes are now stationed in the Canaries.

Take the path behind you leading away from the observatory and Wolfe's statue. After passing the 800-year-old Queen Elizabeth's Oak, a casualty to the gales of recent years, you eventually come to the gate on the east side of the park. Just outside the park on the edge of Maze Hill is Vanbrugh House, an extraordinary building complete with turrets and towers and castle-type battlements. The house was designed by and for Sir John Vanbrugh around 1720 when he was appointed architect to Greenwich Hospital and is now divided into flats.

Turn left past the house and go down to the bottom of Maze Hill, passing the entrance to Maze Hill Station. Cross the main road (Trafalgar Road) into Hoskins Street. Walk straight down to Old Woolwich Road and turn right. Follow this for some way until you get to Hadrian Street and turn left. At the end turn left again into Pelton Road and walk down to the end to join the riverside walk extending left and right in both directions. To the right, the Thames Path leads along a still-working section of the river to the Thames Barrier.

Turn left past the old Harbour Master's office and walk along Ballast Quay. Round the corner is the Cutty Sark pub with fine views of the river, especially of Blackwall Reach and the Millennium Dome to the right. At the end of the quay continue straight on where the path narrows. Round the corner the path broadens out again on the quay in front of the electricity generating station. Once again you are standing on the meridian line.

Greenwich reclaimed

Beyond the power station is Trinity Hospital Ⓗ, an almshouse for retired Greenwich men, which was founded under the will of Henry Howard, Earl of Northampton, who died in 1614. Northampton had been brought up at Greenwich and after Queen Elizabeth's death in 1603 had bought the manor and Greenwich Castle. He was bitterly disappointed when James I reclaimed Greenwich as a royal possession, settling it on his queen, Anne of Denmark, for whom Inigo Jones then built the Queen's House. Compared with its giant neighbour Trinity Hospital is tiny, but it has an enormous garden which stretches right back to Old Woolwich Road. Stones in the wall opposite the entrance record exceptionally high tides on the Thames.

From the hospital, continue on into narrow Crane Street behind the Trafalgar Tavern, opened in 1837. Turn right round the corner of the pub and then left along the terrace in front of the former Royal Naval College Ⓗ. Further along the path rejoins the pier. If you want to see the College's Painted Hall and Chapel turn left between the College and the *Cutty Sark* (the entrance is further along on the left). Otherwise, go into the foot tunnel once more and make your way back to Island Gardens Station and the end of the walk.

Opening times

Opening times are listed by walk and the order places come in the walk. They often change so always ring in advance to avoid disappointment. Be aware that last admissions are sometimes as much as an hour and a half before advertized closing times. Church phone numbers are for rectory/vicarage unless otherwise indicated. Church offices are usually staffed mornings only.

KENSINGTON

Kensington Roof Gardens 99 Kensington High Street, W8. 0171 937 7994. Mon-Sun 9-5 provided club is not in use.

Leighton House Museum and Art Gallery 12 Holland Park Road, W14. 0171 602 3316. Mon-Sat 11-5.30.

St Mary Abbots Church Kensington Church Street, W8. 0171 937 2419 (office). Mon-Sun 7-7.

CHELSEA

Royal Hospital Royal Hospital Road, SW3. 0171 730 0161. *Hall, chapel and museum* Mon-Sat 10-12, 2-4, Sun 2-4. *Gardens* Mon-Sun 10-4.

National Army Museum Royal Hospital Road, SW3. 0171 730 0717. Mon-Sun 10-5.30.

Chelsea Physic Garden Royal Hospital Road, SW3. 0171 352 5646. Easter-Oct Wed 2-5, Sun 2-6.

Carlyle's House 24 Cheyne Road, SW3. 0171 352 7087. Apr-Oct Wed-Sun and Bank Hols 11-5.

Chelsea Old Church Old Church Street, SW3. 0171 352 7978. Days vary 10-1, 2-5 (4 in winter).

Moravian Church Exhibition Centre 381 Kings Road, SW10. 0181 874 0268. Mar-Nov 2-4 or by appointment.

St Luke's Church Sydney Street, SW3. 0171 351 7365 (office). Mon-Sat 12-2.

BAYSWATER TO BELGRAVIA

Kensington Palace – see Central Parks listing below.

Science Museum Exhibition Road, SW7. 0171 938 8000. Mon-Sun 10-6.

Natural History Museum Cromwell Road, SW7. 0171 938 9123. Mon-Sat 10-5.50, Sun 11-5.50.

Victoria and Albert Museum Cromwell Road, SW7. 0171 938 8500. Tue-Sat 10-5.45, Sun 12-5.45.

Brompton Oratory Brompton Road, SW3. 0171 589 4811. Mon-Sun 6.30-8.

CENTRAL PARKS

Cabinet War Rooms Clive Steps, King Charles Street, SW1. 0171 930 6961. Mon-Sun 9.30-6 (opens 10 Oct-Mar).

St James's Park and Green Park Park Office, The Storeyard, Horseguards Approach, SW1. 0171 930 1793.

Wellington Museum Apsley House, 149 Piccadilly, W1. 0171 499 5676. Tue-Sun 11-5.

Hyde Park Park Manager, Ranger's Lodge, Hyde Park, W2. 0171 298 2100.

Kensington Gardens Park Manager, The Magazine, Kensington Gardens, W2. 0171 298 2100.

Serpentine Gallery Kensington Gardens, W2. 0171 402 6075. Open during exhibitions – ring for details.

Kensington Palace (State Apartments and Royal Ceremonial Dress Collection) Kensington Gardens, W8. 0171 937 9561. May-Oct Mon-Sun 10-6, Nov-Apr Wed-Sun 10-4.
St Mary Abbots Church – see Kensington listing above.

REGENT'S CANAL
British Waterways The Toll House, Delamere Terrace, W2. 0171 286 6101.
London Zoo – see Regent's Park listing below.
London Canal Museum 12-13 New Wharf Road, N1. 0171 713 0836. Tue-Sun and Bank Hols 10-4.30.

REGENT'S PARK
Regent's Park Park Manager The Storeyard, Inner Circle, Regent's Park, NW1. 0171 935 1259.
London Zoo Regent's Park, NW1. 0171 722 3333. Mon-Sun 10-5 (closes 4 Nov-Feb).

MARYLEBONE
Heinz Gallery 21 Portman Square, W1. 0171 580 5533. During exhibitions Mon-Fri 11-5, Sat 11-2.
Wallace Collection Hertford House, Manchester Square, W1. 0171 935 0687. Mon-Sat 10-5, Sun 2-5.
St Peter's Church Vere Street, W1. 0171 629 3615. Mon-Fri 9-5.
St Marylebone Parish Church Marylebone Road, NW1. 0171 935 7315. Mon-Fri 12.30-1.30.
Madame Tussaud's Waxworks Marylebone Road, NW1. 0171 935 6861. June-mid Sep Mon-Sun 9-5.30, Oct-May Mon-Fri 10-5.30, Sat and Sun 9.30-5.30.
London Planetarium Marylebone Road, NW1. 0171 935 6861. Mon-Sun 9.30-5 (in school terms opens 11.30 Mon-Fri).

MAYFAIR
St James's Church 197 Piccadilly, W1. 0171 734 4511 (office). Mon-Sun 8.30-6.
Piccadilly Market St James's Forecourt, 197 Piccadilly, W1. Tue-Sat 10-6 (opens 8 on Wed).
Royal Academy of Arts Burlington House, Piccadilly, W1. 0171 439 7438. Mon-Sun 10-6.
Faraday Museum Royal Institution of Great Britain, 21 Albemarle Street, W1. 0171 409 2992. Mon-Fri 10-4.
Farm Street Church 114 Mount Street, W1. 0171 493 7811. Mon-Sun 7-7.
Grosvenor Chapel South Audley Street, W1. 0171 499 1684. Mon-Fri 8-6.
St George's Church Hanover Square, W1. 0171 629 0874. Mon-Fri 8-4.

WESTMINSTER AND ST JAMES'S
St Margaret's Church Westminster, SW1. 0171 222 6382. Mon-Sat 9.30-4.30, Sun 2-4.30.
Banqueting House Whitehall, SW1. 0171 930 4179. Mon-Sat 10-5.
Horse Guards Whitehall, SW1. Changing the Guard Mon-Sat 11, Sun 10. Details on 0891 505 452 (recorded information line).
Buckingham Palace SW1. *State apartments, Queen's Gallery and Royal Mews* ring 0171 799 2331 (recorded information line) for opening times. *Changing the Guard* 11.30, daily in summer, alternate days Sep-Mar. Details in daily press or on 0891 505 452 (recorded information line).

Guards Chapel Birdcage Walk, SW1. 0171 414 3228. Mon-Thur 10-4.
Guards Museum Wellington Barracks, Birdcage Walk, SW1. 0171 930 4466. Sat-Thur 10-4.
Westminster Abbey Broad Sanctuary, SW1. 0171 222 5152. *Abbey* Mon-Fri 9-4.45, Sat 9-2.45. *Cloisters, Chapter House, Pyx Chamber and Museum* Mon-Sun, at least 10.30-4. *College Garden* Tue and Thur, at least 10-4. *Chapter Library* May-Sept Wed 11-3.
Jewel Tower Old Palace Yard, Abingdon Street, SW1. 0171 222 2219. Mon-Sun 10-1, 2-6 (closes dusk Oct and 4 Nov-Mar).
Houses of Parliament SW1. 0171 219 3000. Ring for details of debates and select committees. Visits bookable through MPs.

BLOOMSBURY
British Museum Great Russell Street, WC1. 0171 636 1555. Mon-Sat 10-5, Sun 2.30-6.
Thomas Coram Foundation 40 Brunswick Street, WC1. 0171 278 2424. Usually Mon-Fri 10-4 but times under review so ring to confirm.
Dickens House Museum 48 Doughty Street, WC1. 0171 405 2127. Mon-Sat 10-5.

SOHO TO TRAFALGAR SQUARE
Pollock's Toy Museum 1 Scala Street, W1. 0171 636 3452. Mon-Sat 10-5.
National Gallery Trafalgar Square, WC2. 0171 747 2885. Mon-Sat 10-6 (closes 8 on Wed), Sun 12-6.

COVENT GARDEN
St Martin-in-the-Fields Church Trafalgar Square, WC2. 0171 930 0089. Mon-Sun 9-5.
Royal Society of Arts 8 John Adam Street, WC2. 0171 930 5115. Visits by appointment.
Queen's Chapel of the Savoy Savoy Hill, WC2. 0171 836 7221. Tue-Fri 11.30-3.30 (may be closed Aug-Sep).
Theatre Museum Russell Street, WC2. 0171 836 7891. Tue-Sun 11-7.
London Transport Museum Covent Garden, WC2. 0171 836 8557. Sat-Thur 10-6, Fri 11-6.
St Paul's Church Bedford Street, WC2. 0171 836 5221. Mon-Fri 9-4.

LAMBETH AND THE SOUTH BANK
Museum of Garden History St Mary-at-Lambeth Church, Lambeth Road, SE1. 0171 401 8865. Mon-Fri 10.30-4, Sun 10.30-5.
Lambeth Palace Lambeth Road, SE1. 0171 928 8282. Visits by appointment.
Florence Nightingale Museum Stangate House, Lambeth Palace Road, SE1. 0171 620 0374. Tue-Sun 10-4.
London Aquarium County Hall, Westminster Bridge Road, SE1. 0171 967 8000. Mon-Sun 10-6.
Hayward Gallery Belvedere Road, SE1. 0171 928 3144. During exhibitions Mon-Sun 10-6 (closes 8 Tue and Wed).
Museum of the Moving Image South Bank, SE1. 0171 928 3535. Mon-Sun 10-6.
National Theatre Upper Ground, SE1. 0171 633 0880. Guided tours Mon-Sat 10.15-5.30.
Courtauld Institute Gallery Somerset House, Strand, WC2. 0171 873 2526. Mon-Sat 10-6, Sun 2-6.
St Mary-le-Strand Church Strand, WC2. 0171 836 3205 (office). Mon-Fri and Sun 11-4.
'Roman' Bath 5 Strand Lane, WC2. 0171 641 5264. Visible through window at all times; group visits by appointment.

INNS OF COURT

St Clement Danes Church Strand, WC2. 0171 242 8282. Mon-Sun 8-5.

Royal Courts of Justice Strand, WC2. 0171 936 6000. *Hall* Mon-Fri 9.30-4.30. *Courts* 10.30-4 with lunch adjournment 1-2; closed Easter and Whitsun vacations and Aug-Sep.

The Old Curiosity Shop 13 Portsmouth Street, WC2. 0171 405 9891. Mon-Sun 9.30-5.30.

Sir John Soane's Museum 13 Lincoln's Inn Fields, WC2. 0171 405 2107. Tue-Sat 10-5.

London Silver Vaults Chancery House, Chancery Lane, WC2. 0171 242 3844. Mon-Fri 9-5.30, Sat 9-12.30.

Lincoln's Inn Chapel Lincoln's Inn, WC2. 0171 405 6360. Mon-Fri 12-2.30.

Temple Church Inner Temple, WC2. 0171 353 1736. Wed-Fri 10-4.

ISLINGTON

Camden Passage Market. 0171 359 0190.

CLERKENWELL

House of Detention Clerkenwell Close, EC1. 0171 253 9494. Mon-Sun 10-6.

St James's Church St James's Walk, EC1. 0171 251 1190. Mon-Fri 12-2.

Clerks' Well Farringdon Lane, EC1. Visits by appointment with Finsbury Library (0171 689 7994). Library closed on Wed, Fri after 1 and Sun.

St John's Gate Museum St John's Lane, EC1. 0171 253 6644. *Museum* Mon-Fri 10-5, Sat 10-4. *Tours of gate, priory church and 12th century crypt* Tue, Fri and Sat 11 and 2.30.

Museum of St Bartholomew's Hospital West Smithfield, EC1. 0171 601 8033/8152. Tue-Fri 10-4. *Guided tours of historic rooms* Fri 2 (book on 0171 837 0546).

St Bartholomew-the-Less Church St Bartholomew's Hospital, West Smithfield, EC1. 0171 601 8888. Mon-Sun 8-6.

St Bartholomew-the-Great Church West Smithfield, EC1. 0171 606 5171. Mon-Fri 8.30-4, Sat 10.30-1.30, Sun 8-8

Charterhouse Sutton's Hospital Charterhouse Square, EC1. 0171 253 9503. Guided tours Apr-Jul Wed 2.15.

Museum of London London Wall, EC2. 0171 600 0807. Tue-Sat 10-5.50, Sun 2-5.50.

FLEET STREET AND ST PAUL'S

City Information Centre St Paul's Churchyard (south side), EC4. 0171 332 1456/3456. Mon-Sun 9.30-5 (closed Sat pm and Sun Nov-Mar).

St Paul's Cathedral St Paul's Churchyard, EC4. 0171 236 4128. Mon-Sat 8.30-4.

St Martin-within-Ludgate Church Ludgate Hill, EC4. 0171 248 6054. Mon-Fri 10-5.

Central Criminal Court Old Bailey, EC4. 0171 248 3277. Courts Mon-Fri 10-1, 2-5 approx.

St Sepulchre's Church Holborn Viaduct, EC1. 0171 248 1660. Wed 12-2.

Dr Johnson's House 17 Gough Square, EC4. 0171 353 3745. Mon-Sat 11-5.30 (closes 5 Oct-Apr).

St Bride's Church Fleet Street, EC4. 0171 353 1301. Mon-Fri 8-4.45, Sat 9-4.45.

St Bride Printing Library Bride Lane, EC4. 0171 353 4660. Mon-Fri 9.30-5.30 (appointments required for exhibition room).

Apothecaries' Hall Black Friars Lane, EC4 – see Skinners' Hall in The City (East) listing below.

St Andrew-by-the-Wardrobe Church Queen Victoria Street, EC4. 0171 248 7546. Mon-Fri 8-6.

College of Arms Queen Victoria Street, EC4. 0171 248 2762. Earl Marshal's Court Mon-Fri 10-4.

BANKSIDE AND SOUTHWARK

Bankside Gallery 48 Hopton Street, SE1. 0171 928 7521. During exhibitions Tue 10-8, Wed-Fri 10-5, Sat and Sun 1-5.
Tate Gallery of Modern Art Bankside, SE1. Opening May 2000. Phone 0171 401 7271 for update.
Shakespeare's Globe Exhibition New Globe Walk, SE1. 0171 902 1500. Mon-Sun May-Sep (performance season) 9-12.15, Oct-Apr 10-5.
Clink Museum Clink Wharf, Clink Street, SE1. 0171 378 1558. Mon-Sun 10-6.
Golden Hinde St Mary Overy Dock, Cathedral Street, SE1. 0171 403 0123. Mon-Sun 10-5.
Southwark Cathedral London Bridge, SE1. 0171 407 2939. Mon-Sun 8-6.
The Old Operating Theatre, Museum and Herb Garret 9a St Thomas's Street, SE1. 0171 955 4791. Tue-Sun 10-4 (closed mid Dec-mid Jan).
London Dungeon 28 Tooley Street, SE1. 0171 403 0606. Mon-Sun 10-4.30.
Winston Churchill's Britain at War Experience 64-66 Tooley Street, SE1. 0171 403 3171. Mon-Sun Apr-Sep 10-5.30, Oct-Mar 10-4.30.
HMS Belfast Morgans Lane, Tooley Street, SE1. 0171 407 6434. Mon-Sun Mar-Oct 10-6, Nov-Feb 10-5.
Tower Bridge Experience Tower Bridge, SE1. 0171 403 3761. Mon-Sun Apr-Oct 10-6.30, Nov-Mar 9.30-6.
Tower of London – see The City (East) listing below.

THE CITY (EAST)

St Olave's Church Hart Street, EC3. 0171 488 4318. Mon-Fri 9-5.
St Michael's Church Cornhill, EC3. 0171 626 8841. Mon-Fri 8-5, Sun 10-1.30.
Mansion House Walbrook, EC4. 0171 626 2500. Visits by appointment.
Bank of England Museum Threadneedle Street, EC2. 0171 601 5545. Mon-Fri 10-5.
Guildhall Guildhall Yard, EC2. 0171 606 3030. *Guildhall* Mon-Sun 10-5 (closed Sun Oct-Apr). *Guildhall Clock Museum* Mon-Fri 9.30-4.45. *Guildhall Art Gallery* in progress - phone for update.
St Lawrence Jewry Church Guildhall Yard, EC2. 0171 600 9478. Mon-Fri 7.30-5.
St Mary-le-Bow Church Cheapside, EC2. 0171 248 5139. Mon-Fri 6.30-6 (closes 4 in Aug). *Bell tower* Mon-Fri by appointment.
St Mary Aldermary Church Bow Lane, EC4. 0171 248 5139. Thur and Fri 11-3.
St Michael Paternoster Church College Hill, EC4. 0171 248 7546. Mon-Fri 9-5.
Skinners' Hall 8 Dowgate Hill, EC4. A selection of City livery halls are open for guided tours a few days each year. Tickets must be obtained in advance through the City Information Office (see the Fleet Street and St Paul's listing above for address and phone number).
Monument Monument Street, EC3. 0171 626 2717. Apr-Sep Mon-Fri 9-6, Sat and Sun 2-6, Oct-Mar Mon-Sat 10-5.
St Mary-At-Hill Church St Mary-At-Hill, EC3. 0171 626 4184 (office). Mon-Fri 10-3.
Tower of London Tower Hill, EC3. 0171 709 0765. Mar-Oct Mon-Sat 9-5, Sun 10-5, Nov-Feb Tue-Sat 9-4, Sun and Mon 10-4.

WAPPING TO LIMEHOUSE

St Paul's Church 340 The Highway, E1. 0171 488 4633. Services only but keys can be obtained from rectory or from caretaker nearby at 298a The Highway.
St Anne's Church Newell Street, E14. 0171 987 1502 (office). Mon-Fri 2.30-4.30, Sat and Sun 2-5.

WINDSOR AND ETON

Royal Windsor Information Centre 24 High Street, Windsor, Berks. 01753 852010. Mon-Fri 10-4, Sat and Sun 10-5.

Town and Crown Exhibition – address and times as Information Centre above.

St John the Baptist Church High Street, Windsor, Berks. 01753 858114. Tue-Thur 10-12.

Royal Mausoleum Windsor Great Park, Windsor, Berks. 01753 868286. A few days in May and Aug – ring for dates.

Windsor Castle Castle Hill, Windsor, Berks. 01753 868286 (switchboard), 01753 831118 (recorded information line). Mon-Sun 10-5.30 (closes 4 Nov-Feb). *St George's Chapel* closed to visitors on Sun. *Changing of the Guard* Mon-Sat, daily in summer, alternate days in winter.

The Dungeons of Windsor 30a High Street, Windsor. 01753 865555. Mon-Sun 10-5.30.

Eton College and **Museum of Eton Life** High Street, Eton, Windsor, Berks. 01753 671000 (switchboard), 01753 671177 (visits manager). Mar-Oct Mon-Sun 10.30-4.30 during hols, 2.30-4.30 during term.

HAMPTON COURT

Thames Passenger Boat Services. 0171 930 4097/4721.

Hampton Court Palace East Molesley, Surrey. 0181 781 9500. Mon 10.15-6, Tue-Sun 9.30-6 (closes 4.30 Nov-Mar).

Bushy Park Park Manager, The Stockyard, Bushy Park, Hampton Hill, Middlesex. 0181 979 1586.

Shakespeare Temple Hampton Court Road, Hampton, Middlesex. Visits by appointment through Orleans House Gallery, Twickenham (see Syon Park to Strawberry Hill listing below for gallery address and phone number).

St Mary's Church Church Street, Hampton, Middlesex. 0181 979 3071. Mon-Sun 9-5 (St Luke's Chapel only but monuments visible through glass doors).

SYON PARK TO STRAWBERRY HILL

Syon House Syon Park, Brentford, Middlesex. 0181 560 0881. Apr-Sep Wed-Sun and Bank Hols 11-5; Oct-mid Dec Sun 11-5. *Gardens* Mon-Sun 10-6 or dusk whichever is earlier.

All Saints Church Church Street, Isleworth, Middlesex. 0181 568 4645. Ruins of old church visible through door.

Marble Hill House Richmond Road, Twickenham, Middlesex. 0181 892 5115. Apr-Oct Mon-Sun 10-6 (closes 4 Oct), Nov-Mar Wed-Sun 10-4.

Orleans House Gallery Riverside, Twickenham, Middlesex. 0181 892 0221. Tue-Sat 1-5.30, Sun 2-5.30 (closes 4.30 Oct-Mar).

Ham House - see under Richmond listing below

St Mary's Church Riverside, Twickenham, Middlesex. 0181 744 2693 (office). Weekday mornings.

Strawberry Hill St Mary's University College, Waldegrave Road, Twickenham, Middlesex. 0181 240 4114. Easter-mid Oct Sun guided tours every half hour starting 2.

RICHMOND

Thames Passenger Boat Services. 0171 930 4097/4721.

Museum of Richmond Whittaker Avenue, Richmond, Surrey. 0181 332 1141. May-Oct Tue-Thur 11-5, Fri-Sun 1-4, Nov-Apr Tue-Thur 11-5.

Richmond Park Park Manager, Holly Lodge, Richmond Park, Surrey. 0181 948 3209.

St Peter's Church Petersham, Surrey. 0181 940 9897. Usually locked – keys available from locations shown on door.
Ham House Ham Street, Petersham, Surrey. 0181 940 1950. Easter Sat-Oct Mon-Wed 1-5, Sat and Sun 12-5.

KEW TO HAMMERSMITH
Thames Passenger Boat Services. 0171 930 4097/4721.
St Anne's Church Kew Green, Kew, Surrey. 0181 940 4616. Sat 10-12 and most weekend afternoons in summer.
Royal Botanic Gardens Kew Green, Kew, Surrey. 0181 940 1171. Mon-Sun 9.30-6.30 (4.30 in winter).
Kew Bridge Steam Museum Green Dragon Lane, Brentford, Middlesex. 0181 568 4757. Mon-Sun 11-5 (engines in steam weekends only).
Chiswick House Burlington Lane, W4. 0181 995 0508. Mon-Sun 10-6 (4 in winter).
St Nicholas's Church Church Street, W4. 0181 995 4717. Sun 2.30-5.
Hogarth's House Hogarth Lane, Great West Road, W4. 0181 994 6757. Feb-Dec Tue-Fri 1-5 (closes 4 Oct-Mar), Sat and Sun 1-6 (closes 5 Oct-Mar)

BARNES TO FULHAM
St Mary's Church Church Road, Barnes, SW13. 0181 741 5422 (office). Mon-Sat 10.30-12.30.
The Wetland Centre Queen Elizabeth Walk, Barnes, SW13. Phone 0181 876 8995 for opening details.
St Mary's Church High Street, Putney, SW15. 0181 788 4414 (office). Visits by appointment.
All Saints Church Church Gate, Fulham, SW6. 0181 736 6301. Wed-Fri 12-3.
Fulham Palace Bishop's Avenue, Fulham, SW6. 0171 736 6301. *Museum* Mar-Oct Wed-Sun 2-5, Nov-Feb Thur-Sun 1-4. *Grounds* Mon-Sun public park hours.

DULWICH
Dulwich Picture Gallery College Road, Dulwich, SE21. 0181 693 5254. Tue-Fri 10-5, Sat 11-5, Sun 2-5.

HIGHGATE TO HAMPSTEAD
Highgate Cemetery Swains Lane, Highgate, N6. 0181 340 1834. *East Cemetery* Mon-Sun 10-5 (opens 11 Sat and Sun and closes 4 Nov-Mar). *West Cemetery* guided tours at fixed times (Sat and Sun only Dec-Feb) – ring for details.
St Michael's Church South Grove, Highgate, N6. 0181 340 7279. Sat 10-12.
Kenwood House and Iveagh Bequest Hampstead Lane, Hampstead, NW3. 0181 348 1286. Mon-Sun 10-6 (closes dusk Oct and 4 Nov-Mar).
Keats House Keats Grove, Hampstead, NW3. 0171 435 2062. Mon-Fri 2-6 (Nov-Mar 1-5), Sat 10-1, 2-5, Sun 2-5.
St John's Church Church Row, Hampstead, NW3. 0171 794 5808 (office). Mon-Fri, Sun and most Sats 9-5.
Fenton House Windmill Hill, Hampstead, NW3. 0171 435 3471. Mar Sat and Sun 2-5, Apr-Oct Wed-Fri 2-5, Sat and Sun 11-5.
Burgh House New End Square, Hampstead, NW3. 0171 431 0144. Wed-Sun 12-5.

GREENWICH
Catamaran Cruisers. 0171 987 1185.
Thames Passenger Boat Services. 0171 930 4097/4721.
Tourist Information Centre 46 Greenwich Church Street, Greenwich, SE10. 0181 858 6376. Mon-Thurs 11-4, Fri-Sun 10.15-4.45 (closes for lunch).
Cutty Sark King William Walk, Greenwich, SE10. 0181 858 3445. Mon-Sat 10-6, Sun 12-6 (closes 5 Oct-Mar).
St Alfege's Church Greenwich High Road, Greenwich, SE10. 0181 853 0687. Mon-Sun 12-5 (closes 4 Nov-Mar).
Fan Museum 12 Crooms Hill, Greenwich, SE10. 0181 858 7879/0181 305 1441. Tue-Sat 11-4.30, Sun 12-4.30.
Ranger's House Chesterfield Walk, Blackheath, SE10. 0181 853 0035. Apr-Oct Mon-Sun 10-6 (dusk in Oct), Nov-Mar Wed-Sun 10-4. Closes 1-2 every day.
Greenwich Park Park Office, Blackheath Gate, Greenwich Park, SE10. 0181 858 2608.
Old Royal Observatory, Planetarium, National Maritime Museum, Queen's House, Greenwich Park, SE10. 0181 858 4422. Mon-Sun 10-5.
Trinity Hospital High Bridge, Greenwich, SE10. Visits by appointment with the Warden (0181 858 1310) or through the Tourist Information Centre (see above for phone number).

Some books on London

Enough books have been written about London to fill a fairly large library. Listed here are just some of those I have found most useful in researching this book. Since its first publication in 1983, the *London Encyclopaedia* has become a classic and must be the starting point for anybody with either a passing or a serious interest in the origins and development of modern London.

Felix Barker and Peter Jackson, *London, 2000 Years of a City and its People*, Macmillan, 1983
Clive Berridge, *The Almshouses of London*, Ashford Press Publishing, 1987
Mervyn Blatch, *A Guide to London's Churches*, Constable, 1978
David Brazil, *Naked City. 150 Faces of Hidden London*, Macdonald, 1987
Arthur Byron, *London Statues*, Constable, 1981
Andrew Crowe, *The Parks and Woodlands of London*, Fourth Estate, 1987
Madge Darby, *Waeppa's People*, Connor and Butler, 1988
Suzanne Ebel and Doreen Impey, *A Guide to London's Riverside. Hampton Court to Greenwich*, Constable, 1985
Michael Essex-Lopresti, *Exploring the Regent's Canal*, KAF Brewin Books, 1987
Sheila Fairfield, *The Streets of London*, Macmillan, 1983
Alec Forshaw and Theo Bergström, *The Open Spaces of London*, Allison and Busby, 1986
Peter Gibson *The New Capital Companion*, Webb and Bower, 1988
Florence Gladstone and Ashley Barker, *Notting Hill in Bygone Days*, Anne Bingley, 1969
Brian Green, *Dulwich Village*, Village Books, 1983
Roy Hawkins, *Green London*, Sidgwick and Jackson, 1987
Christopher Hibbert, *London. The Biography of a City*, Penguin, 1980

Sean Jennett, *Official Guide to the Royal Parks of London,* HMSO, 1979
Andrew Lawson, *Discover Unexpected London,* Phaidon, 1979
The London Encyclopaedia, edited by Ben Weinreb and Christopher Hibbert, Papermac, 1993
Ian McAuley, *Guide to Ethnic London,* Michael Haag, 1987
Hugh Meller, *London Cemeteries,* Gregg International, 1985
Ian Norrie, *Hampstead, Highgate Village and Kenwood,* High Hill Press, 1983
Kevin Perlmutter, *London Street Markets,* Wildwood House, 1983
Sir Nikolaus Pevsner, *London: The Cities of London and Westminster: South: North West: North and North East* (4 volumes in the *Buildings of England* series), Penguin, various editions
Adrian Prokter, *A Guide to the River Thames from Battersea to Woolwich,* London Reference Books, 1983
Steen Eiler Rasmussen, *London the Unique City*, MIT Press, 1982
Barbara Rosen and Wolfgang Zuckerman, *The Mews of London,* Webb and Bower, 1982
Royal London, edited by Christopher Hibbert, Macmillan, 1987
Ann Saunders, *The Art and Architecture of London*, Phaidon, 1984
Ann Saunders, *Regent's Park*, Bedford College, 1981
Survey of London, Institute of Historical Research, 1900–
Christopher Simon Sykes, *Private Palaces, Life in the Great London Houses,* Chatto and Windus, 1985
Richard Trench and Ellis Hillman, *London Under London,* John Murray, 1985
Twickenham 1600–1900, People and Places, Twickenham Local History Society, 1981
Christopher Wade, *The Streets of Hampstead*, High Hill Press, 1984

Index

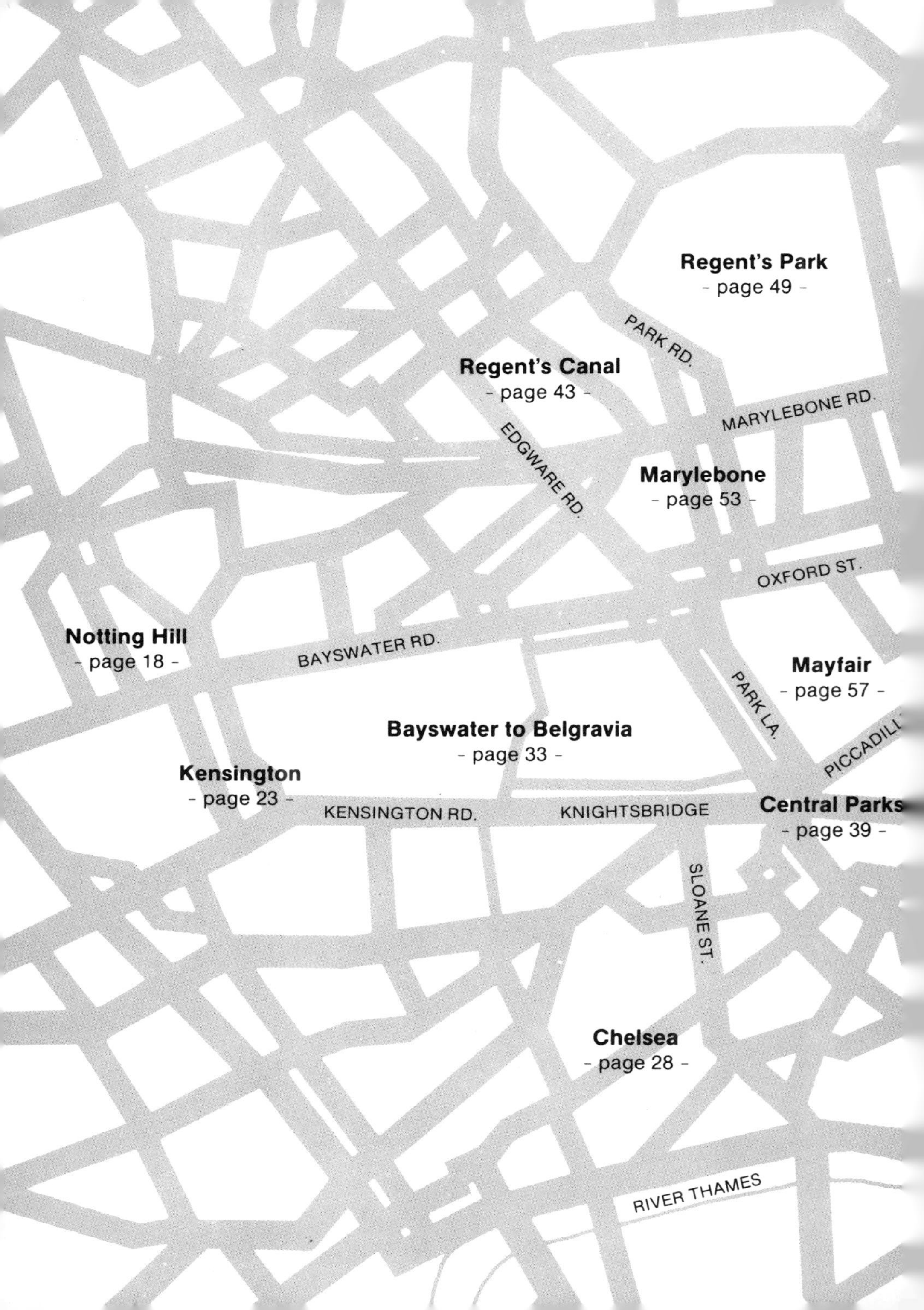

Regent's Park
- page 49 -

PARK RD.

Regent's Canal
- page 43 -

MARYLEBONE RD.

EDGWARE RD.

Marylebone
- page 53 -

OXFORD ST.

Notting Hill
- page 18 -

BAYSWATER RD.

PARK LA.

Mayfair
- page 57 -

Bayswater to Belgravia
- page 33 -

PICCADILL

Kensington
- page 23 -

KENSINGTON RD.

KNIGHTSBRIDGE

Central Parks
- page 39 -

SLOANE ST.

Chelsea
- page 28 -

RIVER THAMES

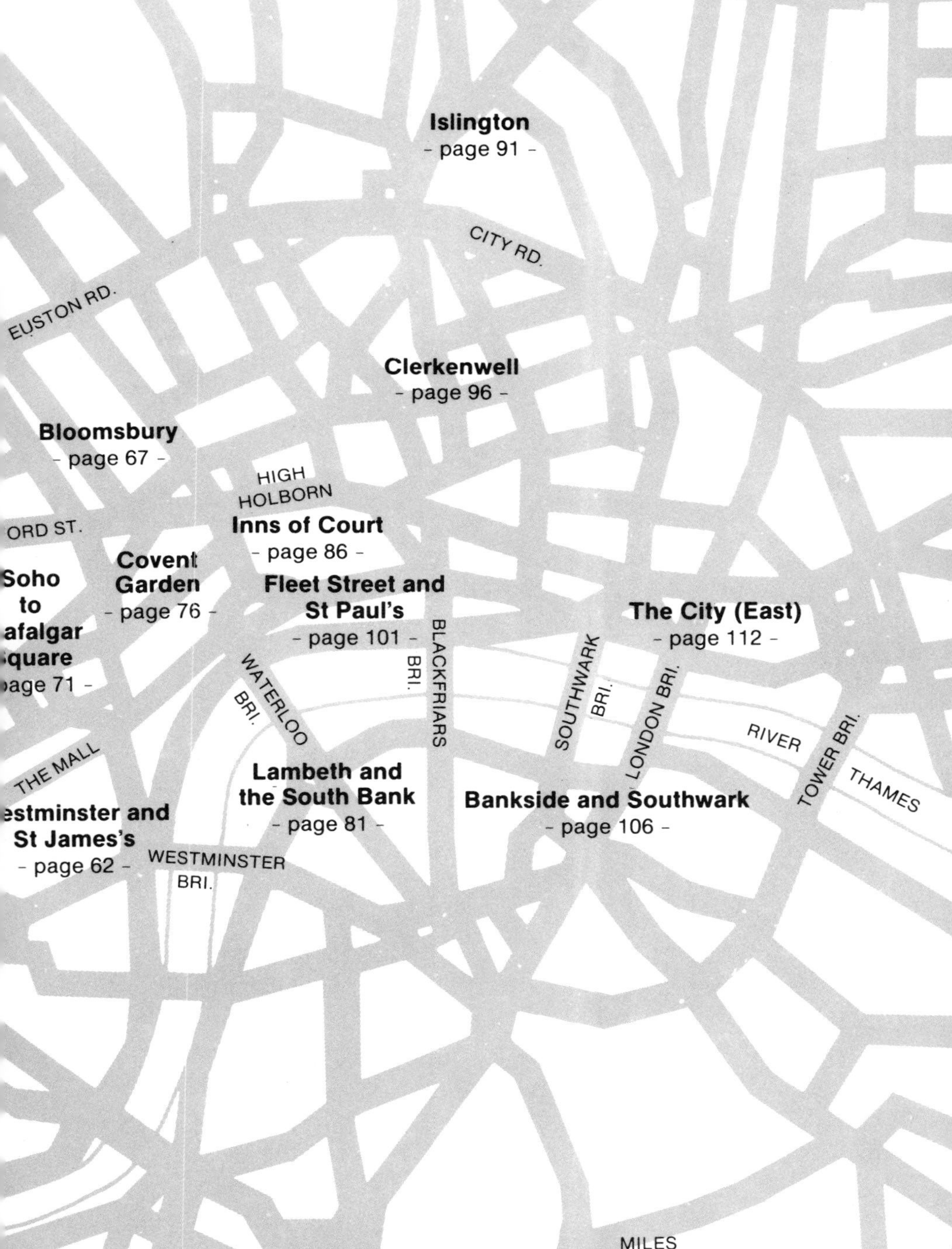

Islington
- page 91 -
CITY RD.
EUSTON RD.
Clerkenwell
- page 96 -
Bloomsbury
- page 67 -
HIGH
HOLBORN
ORD ST.
Inns of Court
- page 86 -
Covent
Garden
- page 76 -
Soho
to
afalgar
quare
age 71 -
Fleet Street and
St Paul's
- page 101 -
BLACKFRIARS
BRI.
The City (East)
- page 112 -
WATERLOO
BRI.
SOUTHWARK
BRI.
LONDON BRI.
RIVER
TOWER BRI.
THAMES
THE MALL
Lambeth and
the South Bank
- page 81 -
Bankside and Southwark
- page 106 -
estminster and
St James's
- page 62 -
WESTMINSTER
BRI.
MILES
0
1
2

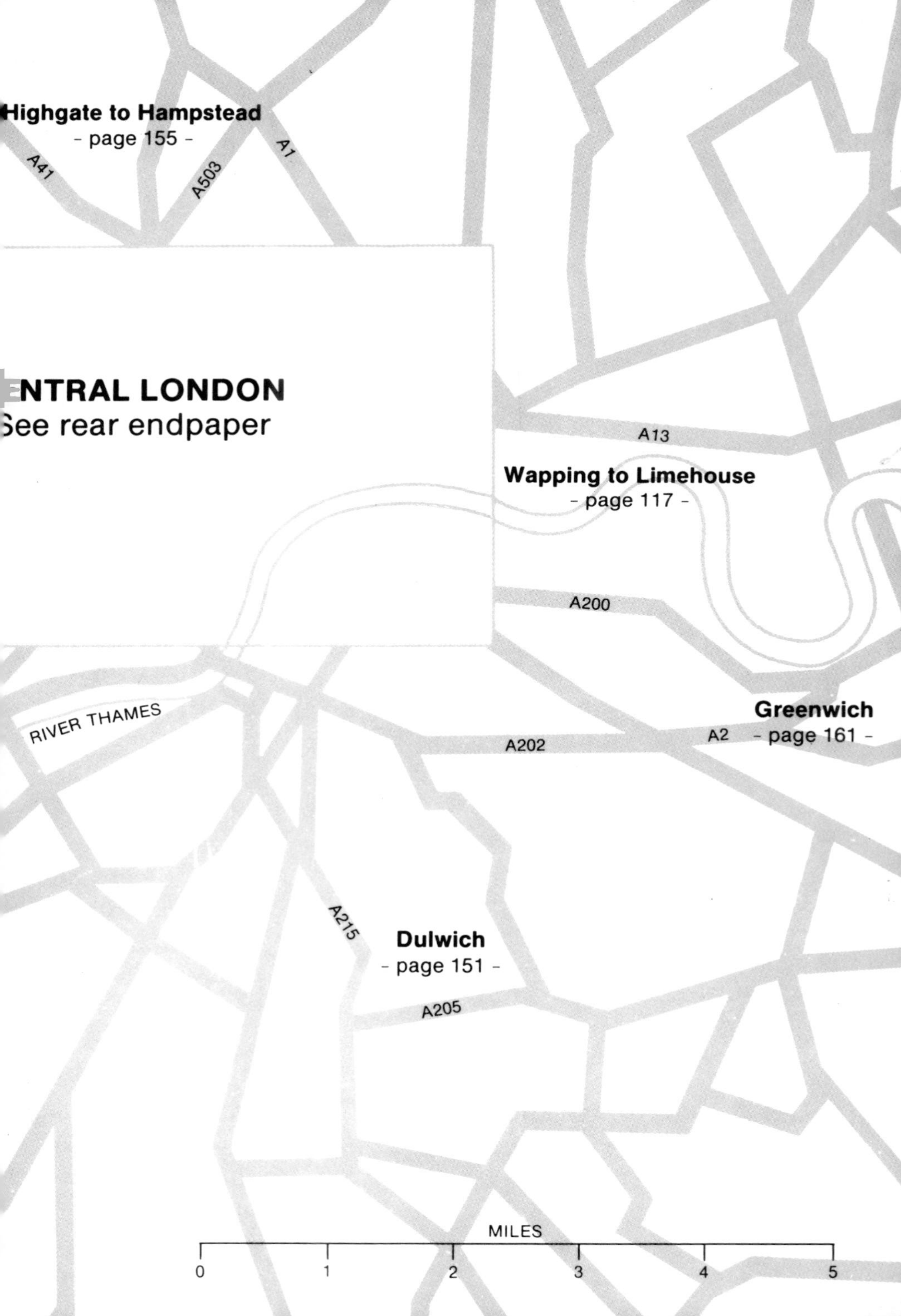
Highgate to Hampstead
- page 155 -
A41
A503
A1
ENTRAL LONDON
See rear endpaper
A13
Wapping to Limehouse
- page 117 -
A200
RIVER THAMES
Greenwich
A2
- page 161 -
A202
A215
Dulwich
- page 151 -
A205
MILES
0
1
2
3
4
5